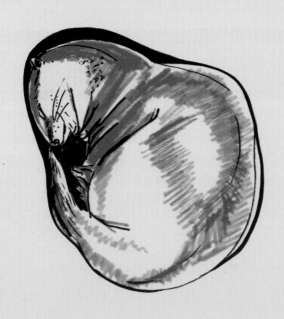

Raven Seek Thy Brother

RAVEN
SEEK THY
BROTHER

Gavin Maxwell

Longmans

LONGMANS, GREEN AND CO LTD
London and Harlow
*Associated companies, branches and representatives
throughout the world*

SBN: 10646 X
© GAVIN MAXWELL 1968
DRAWINGS AND JACKET ILLUSTRATION © ROBIN MCEWEN 1968
FIRST PUBLISHED 1968

Acknowledgments are due to Laurence Pollinger Ltd,
Jonathan Cape Ltd and Holt, Rinehart and Winston Inc.,
for permission to quote from Robert Frost's poem 'Fire and
Ice'; to Faber and Faber Ltd and Oxford University Press
Inc. for quotation from Louis MacNeice's poem 'Postscript
to Iceland, for W. H. Auden'; to the author and Hamish
Hamilton Ltd for quotation from Kathleen Raine's poem
'The Hollow Hill'; and to Rupert Hart-Davis Ltd for quo-
tation from Gavin Maxwell's *Harpoon at a Venture*.

*Printed in Great Britain by
Western Printing Services Ltd, Bristol*

Dedication

For what has died and what remains
  in the small world I can perceive.

For what seems dead and what is living
  and crying still from the wild swans' skeins.

For all I loved and all I grieve.
For all that's endless and forgiving
  of those who've been allowed to enter
  that vast periphery that has no centre.

For fire and rock and rain and storm
  and for the matrix of my home.

For Edal: 1958–1968
Whatever joy you had from her, give back to nature.

Contents

List of Illustrations

Acknowledgments

The end papers and all the drawings in the text are by my friend and colleague, Robin McEwen, who has known Camusfeàrna through its varying fortunes for the past twenty years. I would like too to express my special appreciation to *Time/Life* for their permission to use without charge Mr Terence Spencer's remarkable photographs, of which twelve appear in this book. Finally, my gratitude to Mr George Weston for the great care he has taken in the printing of photographic material.

The photographs on plates 8, 10, 11, 12, 16, 21, 24, 33, 34, 35 and 41 are by Terence Spencer and are reproduced through the courtesy of Time Incorporated. The photograph on plate 9 is by Colin Jones and reproduced by permission of the *Observer*. Plates 3 and 45 are reproduced by permission of Syndication International. Plate 2 and the 1966 photograph of Camusfeàrna are by S. M. Cuddy and plates 7, 14, 23, 36, 37 and 39 are by J. M. Watt. All other photographs are my own.

Foreword

This book is written especially for those who found pleasure in the
first book I wrote about the house I called Camusfeàrna—*Ring of
Bright Water,* and have continued to show an interest in its human
and animal inhabitants. It has been a difficult, sometimes painful,
story to tell in its entirety, but I have done my best to be accurate
both in fact and in date, for I feel that I owe the truth to the many
who have become valued acquaintances, and sometimes friends,
through correspondence. All these have constantly requested news
of Camusfeàrna and of the otters; this book is for them, and in
lieu of letters that I ought to have written and did not; for reasons
that will become obvious to the reader each letter, if it were
factual and honest, would have been of book length. Anyone who
reads this will realize that the immediate sequel to *Ring of Bright
Water, The Rocks Remain,* contained a certain amount of dissimula-
tion which was unavoidable at that time, and which I hope to have
dispelled by this full narrative. This is the history of Camusfeàrna
and its satellite lighthouses during the past five years. It is easier, for
many reasons, to write truthfully about animals than about human
beings (and not only because the animals can't retort that they are
misrepresented) but with the minimal reservations and reticences
that are only decent to the human species, I have done my best to
tell the whole story.

Any narrative that is personal is bound to be eclectic; if it were
not it would not be personal. No doubt, therefore, the humans
concerned would tell a different tale from mine; they would
remember what I have perhaps forgotten and forget what I have
remembered. The end, anyway, would be the same.

To avoid confusion I have retained the name Camusfeàrna
throughout, though with the necessarily precise placing of the two
other lighthouses of Ornsay and Kyleakin it will be obvious to
any interested reader that Camusfeàrna is Sandaig, by Sandaig

Lighthouse, on the mainland of Scotland some five miles south of Glenelg village. The real name of the house on the road a mile and more above my coastal cottage is not Druimfiaclach (which means 'the ridge of the teeth') but Tormor, and the family who used to live there was called MacLeod—John Donald and Mary MacLeod and their children. The MacLeods have gone now and their sons are children no more, married and with families of their own. With the dropping of these aliases there goes, so to speak, the last of the open secrets.

Lastly, I should like to say that, despite apparent and almost uncanny evidence to the contrary, no part of the seventeen chapters of this book was written with hindsight from the events described in the brief epilogue. This actual paragraph, the epilogue itself, the dedication, and the title of Chapter 17, are all that have been added since 20 January 1968.

Kyleakin Lighthouse
July 1968

GAVIN MAXWELL

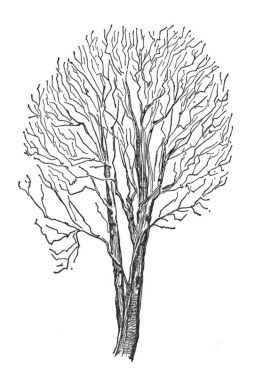

1

The Rowan Tree

On a wild blustery afternoon in the late autumn of 1966 I stood on the steep hillside above the highland seaboard cottage that I had written of in *Ring of Bright Water* as Camusfeàrna, and that had once been my home. The sky, the sea, and the white sand beaches between the islands half uncovered by the ebb tide, I recognized as from long ago, but only visually; they held for me nothing that I wanted to remember. The sharp, penetrating past images that knocked on the door of my conscious mind were almost wholly painful, and I tried hard to ignore them.

The sea was so dark a blue as to be almost black, the wave-crests short, white and vicious. A force nine wind was blowing in from the south-west, hustling great grey clouds that seemed to outrun each other so that they left between them gaps through which a bright white sunlight spotlit here a beach, here a hill, there an island. Across the Sound of Sleat, where a fishing boat was plunging deep with a high white foam about her bows, the foot-hills of Skye were dusted with snow, their summits dead-white against a dark grey sky. Gulls drifted on the wet wind, white too, but the air was too strong for them to pursue a steady course; they slanted, lifted, banked and wheeled, calling raucously to each other as the wind-blasts blew them about. Out in the Sound, foam amid foam, a small school of whales passed—little creatures perhaps thirty feet long. Once I would have been intent, interested to recognize their species, their scientific name. As I looked at them now they seemed no more than a passing disturbance in the water, almost an intrusion.

I was looking down upon Camusfeàrna, and I believed that I was saying goodbye to it after eighteen years. Suddenly there came a sharp flurry of hail, I pulled up the hood of my duffel coat, and crouched back into the steep hillside. It gave no shelter; there was no shelter from any wind, and I knew it, suddenly and completely.

Abruptly a shaft of pallid but finely focused sunlight lit the house and the field below me; the house that I was leaving, as I thought, forever. I tried, with a great effort, to remember it as I had first seen it—a weather-worn cottage within a stone's throw of the sea, standing unfenced upon a green grass field, only the low marram-grown dunes between it and the breaking waves. Untenanted, deserted, waiting. I remembered how I had first come to live there; relying for furniture upon fish boxes and all the extraordinary riches that the sea would throw up after a south-westerly gale. Then, there was no water supply to the house, no telephone, no electricity, no road. I was a mile and a half below my nearest neighbours on the single track road, the family whom I have called MacKinnon, at Druimfiaclach. Like everybody and everything else they had gone; their little house of green corrugated iron stood empty, the once carefully tended flower garden overgrown with weeds and nettles, and now there was no occupied human habitation within five miles of Camusfeàrna.

Many other external things had changed too. This used to be a bare moorland hillside, rough with rock and heather and bracken patches, naked and windswept and virgin; it was so when I first came to live at Camusfeàrna, with nothing but a Primus stove to cook on, nothing but a bucket to draw water from the little river a hundred yards from the house, nothing but the wood thrown up on the beach to fuel the fire in the desolate kitchen. Now there was a dense, dripping ten-year-old growth of sitka and larch at my back as I looked down upon the house, for the landlord had, after various unsuccessful experiments, decided to devote his ground to forestry.

For some unconnected reason, the once green field upon which the house of Camusfeàrna stood was now a jungle of rank rushes reaching almost to the walls of the cottage.

The house had changed too. When I first came to it Camusfeàrna had been a four-roomed cottage, two rooms upstairs and two down. Now, as I looked down upon it, I saw straggling pre-fabricated wings built with the ugliness born of what had seemed necessity and a strict regard for time. On the seaward side of the house stood two broken-down jeeps, whose stamina had not proved equal to the boulders and potholes that composed the two-mile track bulldozed four years before. Between these pieces of defeated machinery and the sea the motor launch *Polar Star* lay high and dry on her massive wheeled cradle, her bronze propellers glinting wetly on the grass below her stern.

Telegraph posts and wires descended the hill from one direction, electric conveyances from another. They converged upon Camusfeàrna, and around the house itself were high wooden palings confining two otters that had once been house-living pets. Each of them, more than three years before, had unpredictably produced reactions as savage as that of an untamed leopard; with dismay and with bitter remorse for wild creatures taken from their natural surroundings, I had recognized that I was the only human at Camusfeàrna who could still trust them, who in daily contact had always found them both friendly and affectionate, and I had constructed for them what I had thought of as being ideal zoo conditions. The massiveness of the damage they had inflicted upon other humans—the hysterical, almost manic, sustained attacks that characterize the mustelline family when the killer instinct is somehow aroused, precluded any possibility of allowing them liberty; the most I could do was occasionally to take them for a walk—separately, for they hated each other—and to employ staff to look after them, for I could not always be at Camusfeàrna.

Now, as I sat huddled into my duffel coat with the hail hitting me and melting so that the ice pellets became chill liquid and found their way through every broken fastening of my clothes, I was surveying what I had done to Camusfeàrna—what I had done to the animals and what I had done to myself.

For the past two years the upkeep of that cottage, centred around the otters, had been much like the maintenance of an Antarctic weather station. It had, in fact, cost more than £7,000 a year, whether I was there or in some distant country.

For the past week it had deluged with rain, it had snowed heavily and then thawed so that the mountain snows came cascading down every crevice of the hillsides, and then it had rained again, so that the Camusfeàrna burn had become a racing, surging white torrent, and flood water lay in wide pools all over the flat ground around the house. These glittered whenever the

3

tearing clouds left the pale autumn sun momentarily uncovered; one in particular caught my attention because of its curious shape, a perfect figure of eight. It was in the otter enclosure at the northern end of the house, the pen occupied by Teko, the male otter who had been at Camusfeàrna for seven years. This was what was called a zoo pattern of behaviour, repetitive, compulsive action born of boredom and frustration; for hour after hour, day after day, he would walk this same track until it had become a pathway beaten bare of vegetation and deep enough to hold water. In time, I thought, it would be grass-grown again, and the fences would be pulled down, for they would have no further use. I had given up at last; Camusfeàrna was to be closed down, and both otters were to go to a zoo. I did not know where I should go to live myself.

A single raven swept by, high on the hustling wind, his deep guttural croaks almost muted by its force. I remembered how Wilfred Thesiger had once told me that when a camel caravan in Southern Arabia would sight a single raven overhead the Bedouin would attempt to annul the evil omen by calling to it, 'Raven, seek thy brother!' It seemed too late now for that invocation.

Between me and the forlorn watery pattern in Teko's enclosure stood the rowan tree, the magic tree that stands beside every old Highland cottage, and round which is centred so much of Gaelic superstition and lore. The rowan is the guardian, the protecting power, the tree of life, infinitely malignant if harmed or dis-respected; capable, too, of carrying within itself the good—or evil—wishes of those who have the power to commune with it. Few highlanders will cut a rowan, even in the course of modern forestry operations, nor bring its bright berries into a dwelling, for they are the blood of the tree and it will curse those who shed its blood.

My rowan had shed its berries now, and the gales had stripped its branches of their scarlet leaves; but it held my attention, because I was seeing it with a new eye, and a strong, sudden, and recent recollection. Sitting there huddled against the gale on the wet hillside above Camusfeàrna my mind went back four months to the summer, to a garden on the shores of the Aegean. The sun was parching, the cicadas screeching in a heavy-laden fig tree, the flowers of Morning Glory that twined a trellised column beside

4

my chair were shut tight against the brilliant butterflies that danced before them.

I sat reading the typescript of an unpublished autobiography, the life story of a poetess. I was reading with perhaps more than ordinary attention, for these pages concerned myself and painful happenings that had taken place many years before. And then suddenly a paragraph seemed to separate itself from the page and to hit up at me with an almost physical impact. Here was my rowan tree.

I cannot recall the words, the sentences, that composed that paragraph; only the shocking image with which they left me. We had quarrelled violently at Camusfeàrna, and as she left the door she had turned and said to me with a venom that utterly belied her words, 'May God forgive you', and I had replied, 'He will.' That short exchange was not on the page before me, but I was reading a sequel unknown to me, for it was years before we had met again, by chance in a London street, after my marriage to someone else.

She had always believed that she possessed great and terrible occult powers, and in that moment of hatred she had not doubted her ability to blight the years ahead of me. She had gone back to Camusfeàrna secretly by night—I pictured it now as a wild night of wind and sleet-storm, roaring surf, and a witch's moon—and she had put her hands upon the trunk of the rowan tree and with all the strength of her spirit she had cursed me, saying, 'Let him suffer here as I am suffering.' Then she had left, up over the bleak hillside.

I put down the manuscript and stared at the coarse dark-green grass of the Greek lawn, thinking how exactly the pattern of the last years had paralleled her blind desire for destruction. A little of this she must have known, for it was public knowledge, and I wondered if she had exulted; but there was much more that she could not know. She could not know, amongst much else, that by now I had already taken the bitter decision to send the otters to a zoo, to find homes for my dogs, and to leave Camusfeàrna. I bore her no ill-will now, whether or not her curse could have influenced events: I just did not understand how such love and hatred could coexist.

Some say the world will end in fire
And some in ice
From what I've tasted of desire
I hold with those who favour fire
But if it had to perish twice
I think I know enough of hate
To say that ice is also great
And would suffice.

As I looked at the grass beyond my feet I saw a pale object about half the size of a match stick moving spasmodically among the leaves. Sometimes it fluttered like a flag, sometimes it moved a few inches to the right or to the left, sometimes it advanced a little, sometimes retired. Leaning forward, I saw that it was a sliver of white, papery foliage being carried by an ant about a quarter of its size. The ant was trying to move it in my direction, but constantly it jammed between the blades of grass as would a tree trunk carried horizontally through a forest. Then the ant would shuffle, sidestep and reverse, manoeuvre one end of its burden between the obstacles, and at length move an inch or two forward. I looked round me in search of its possible destination. Behind me, and to my right, forming the corner of a rectangle, was a rough brick wall perhaps

five feet high, and at the top of the wall was a terrace that led away into parched and uncultivated ground. Perhaps, I thought, the ant's nest was somewhere in the wall, but this at its nearest point was still some twenty feet from the ant, and between the grass and the wall was a yard or so of empty herbaceous border, where the earth had been dug and lay in hard uneven lumps the size of a golf ball; whatever the ant's destination it appeared patently impossible of achievement.

At the end of a quarter of an hour it had reached the manuscript that lay on the grass at my side. There, squarely on the typed words 'rowan tree', it paused to rest, shifting its burden between the mandibles as if to achieve a more balanced grip. I thought of Bruce and the spider; I became wholly and childishly absorbed, and the ant's adventure became mine.

The ant rested for a full minute upon the glaring white paper, its antennae waving slowly as if questing for knowledge of the hazards before it. Then, quite suddenly, as though at the fall of a starter's flag, it shot across the page at tremendous speed and plunged once more into the grass jungle between it and the wall. The same enormous but patient energy animated every movement; the same reversals and backward haulage, the same sidestepping and apparent understanding of mechanical principle, the same firm sense of direction—straight to the wall. When at length it had struggled free of the herbage and into the dry earth-cakes of the border, the enormity of the obstacles ahead seemed to cause no loss of heart; at the foot of each steep earth mountain—each, in ratio to the stature of the ant, several hundred feet high to a human—it would turn carefully, readjust its grip, and reverse up the slope. At the summit it would turn again to face forward and rush down the ensuing slope. The ant never once tried to avoid an obstacle in its path nor to circumvent the next, even when to the human eye this appeared easy; both the purpose and the direction were absolutes.

From the time at which I had first sighted with an abstracted eye the ant and the curious banner-like burden to which it appeared to attach so supreme an importance, almost half an hour had passed before it reached the foot of the wall. The bricks towered above the insect, rough and uneven; some sloped outward with vertiginous overhangs, and in their deep crevasses were dense meshes of whitish cobwebs, layer upon layer of them, like some elaborately contrived barricade.

The ant paused at the foot of the wall, the foremost pair of legs raised and feeling at it as though trying to assess the magnitude of the barrier in front. Then it turned, and began to reverse up the sheer surface at incredible speed, head downward with the prize clenched between its jaws. The first three bricks were easy; then the ant reached a ledge, backed on to it, and set off forwards again.

At three feet from the ground the going became difficult, and a brick above leaned outward with a sharp overhang. The ant tried it forwards very slowly, all six feet testing every possible foothold. The length of its body now leaned outward from the perpendicular. It slipped back half an inch, miraculously recovered its hold, then slipped again. For a moment it hung by its two front feet only. There was a twisting of the body as the other legs reached frantically inward for foothold; then it fell, all the way to the rough baked earth at the foot of the wall. In our terms of relative measurement it was as if a human mountaineer had fallen an unbroken thousand feet.

For a moment the ant lay upon its back, quite motionless, the white papery object, which I now thought of as a message, still firmly held. The legs began to wave slowly, the ant righted itself, faced the wall, and rushed at it again as though in great anger.

The first high fall. I remembered mine; my marriage had been a misery for both partners. I had taken longer to recover than the ant.

At the second attempt the ant avoided, whether by chance or foresight, the brink from which it had fallen; it turned towards the corner of the wall, reached a point some inches higher than before,

and found the spread canopy of cobwebs overhead. The message became enmeshed and, in a desperate scrambling struggle to loose it, the ant fell again. This time he took a little longer to recover, and when he did he was unconcerned with the wall; all that mattered was the search for what he had lost. He ran rapidly in small circles and tangents, pausing only momentarily to test the air with his antennae. At the end of several minutes he had not moved a foot from the spot on to which he had fallen.

The second fall. Marriage finished though not yet dissolved; the otters imprisoned as a public danger, Camusfeàrna mechanized and staffed and under siege by sight-seers, the idyll over and the message lost somewhere in the fall. I had searched as the ant did, but I too had run in circles.

I leaned over, careful not to throw the shadow of my arm over the distraught ant, and dislodged the message from the spider's web. It fluttered down and landed six inches away from him, lying whitely in the pale, hard earth, hidden from him, I realized, by enormous mountain ridges. It was minutes before he found it. There was an almost visible triumph and satisfaction as he adjusted his posture, gripped it anew, and rushed at the wall. He was tired now, and the ascent was slower, more hesitating; he did not even regain his former height; when he fell he lay longer, and when he moved again there was evidence of injury; only five of his six agile legs remained functional. I did not think he would try again, but he did, because he still carried his message.

The third fall. The motor accident, the unrealized injury, hospital and helplessness, pain and dragging convalescence, the feeling of defeat, a slow fighting defection from everything that had made my life what it was, an unwilling return to an unwanting womb. The ant had certainly done better.

· · ·

9

In all the ant fell six times, and each time his recovery took longer, but after the second fall he never lost what he carried.

The seventh time, incredibly, he scaled the wall, the whole five feet of it. It had taken him an hour and twenty minutes; he was injured and exhausted, but he was there. He stood on the brink of the terrace above, on the flat dust-covered path beyond which there was jungle. I stood up and stepped over to watch him. He did not seem to move at all, but having anthropomorphized him— (he must have been neuter, a worker, but my identification with him had made him male)—I thought of him as panting with great breaths, stretching and reassuring tortured muscles, secure in the knowledge of having overcome at last the most terrible part of his journey. He still held the message; sometimes he moved it slightly between his jaws.

He had remained so for perhaps two minutes when the climactic drama took place. From the other side of the yard-wide dust path, out of the uncultivated scrub beyond, came scurrying a smaller ant, redder than he was, appearing to be of a different species. It ran swiftly across the dust, as if orientated to a known destination. It seized the message from my ant's jaws, apparently encountering no resistance, and returned at enormous speed in the direction from which it had come, disappearing quickly into the undergrowth. My ant seemed unconscious of loss; for a moment the whole

action seemed like a relay race in which each individual had fulfilled his role and played a faultless part. So, too, it had seemed to me when I was weak and exhausted; a relay race in which, at the end of my course, I had nothing to do but pass on the baton and trust my successor to carry it home to the laurels. I had nothing to do, I thought, but to rest and recover.

But then, very suddenly, my ant appeared to realize that he was no longer holding anything between his jaws. He behaved as he had at the second fall, when the message had remained entangled in the spiders' webs; he ran violently in circles, with tremendous agitation, two of the six legs held high and no longer touching the ground. After perhaps half a minute he appeared to pick up a scent, and raced after his despoiler. Then he was lost to my sight among the high vegetation.

All this I remembered in a series of vivid visual images while I crouched shivering on the cold wet hillside above Camusfeàrna, looking down at the house that had been my home. The sun was beginning to set now, a cold glary sunset behind the jagged peaks of Skye, the clouds damp and muzzy with the south-westerly gale. I looked down at Camusfeàrna, trying to refocus my eyes which had been too long centred upon the slow heat of that Greek garden in July. There was water in my shoes and cold water running down my spine. The ant, I supposed, was dead now, but he remained a challenge. I was not dead yet.

I watched as a girl came out from the door of Camusfeàrna, carrying fish for the otters. She and her seven-year-old daughter were the only other human occupants of the house. There were more than a dozen dogs around her. Three of them were mine, two deerhounds and their six-months-old puppy. The rest varied in size from Great Danes to miniature poodles; I had no contact with any of these, no contact with Camusfeàrna any more.

I stood up and started to walk down to the house. It was dark now, and only lights showed, the lights of the house, of Isle Ornsay Lighthouse, and of a single fishing boat in the Sound, heading south for Mallaig. I was on a fleeting farewell visit to Camusfeàrna; everything had been arranged. The otters were going to a zoo, the remaining dogs to what good homes they might find. Gus, my favourite dog, the reputedly savage and untamable Pyrenean Mountain Dog, who in reality had been as soft and soppy as a spaniel, had been killed during my absence, hanged by his own choke chain while left out at night.

For the few short weeks of my visit to Camusfeàrna I had tried to avoid seeing the otters. Their end in a zoo was something to which I could never reconcile myself, the institutionalization of unwanted children; but there had seemed no alternative. I could not even earn the money to support them; though already I had received an uncountable number of letters from the public censuring my decision in the most unequivocal terms. What could they know of the impossibilities? Seven thousand pounds a year to keep Camusfeàrna alive but barren—how many of my correspondents could find that money, now or ever, to keep something beautiful even dimly alive in an oxygen mask? And for how long? I had known that it was over, done, finished; but still the unknown faces, unknown voices, had hammered at me to do the impossible, even the ridiculous. Some asked why I did not 'set them free'. As well to ask why one could not set free a dog that one had owned and cherished for seven years; these two otters, Edal and Teko, had been bottle-reared by humans from early infancy, had lived in human houses until the danger of the situation had become disastrously apparent, and they were used to having their meals provided at regular hours. They would not leave; and if, instead, one were oneself to leave they would neither be able to fend for themselves nor to withstand the rigours of the Scottish climate without the heated sleeping quarters to which they were accustomed. It had been a different matter with the various Scottish otters we had kept at Camusfeàrna; we did set them free, and miraculously they appeared to have survived, for years anyway, the peril inherent in a wild animal's trust of man. I saw them occasionally; more often, however, I received letters from English tourists visiting the West Highlands telling me that at some point which was always within fifteen miles or so of Camusfeàrna an otter had come out of the sea, and had approached them unafraid, and sniffed at their shoes. Was this, some of them asked, the normal behaviour of an otter? Each of these letters gave me a tremendous lift of heart, for they told me that the creatures we had taught to trust humans had not yet been murdered because of it.

But with Edal and Teko there could be no such simple solution, and I had made up my mind at last. To love animals as well as humans increases one's capacity for suffering; sometimes I have envied those who are indifferent to mammals of other species than their own, but perhaps it increases, too, a general perception and understanding, the compassion and tenderness that is all too latent in most of humanity—so latent that by now we threaten the survival even of our own species. These things which constituted my attitude towards the two otters made my decision the outcome of a painful struggle, more painful than I would care to describe. But the struggle was over, the decision made. The otters were going, Camusfeàrna would be closed; somewhere I would find a new life.

Nothing is ever as definite as that. If you love a human or an animal there are great ropes pulling you back to the object of that love, and the hands that haul upon the ropes are your own. But it was a little late for loving.

I started down the hill towards the lights of the house. In the darkness the night seemed wilder even than the dusk had been; the rain, driven in from the sea by a full gale, slashed and battered at my face. The tide had turned, and I could hear the roar and hiss of the incoming breakers pounding on the beach below the house. It was an apt enough setting for a long farewell, a farewell that I knew would be not only a personal one but shared in varying degrees by all those who had written to me and identified my small and unimportant tragedy with something, perhaps much greater, in their own lives. It was, after all, the end of an era, and that comes with greater or lesser shock to every human being who ever lived. To these people it was as if my powers of resilience were symbols of their own; if I broke the pattern of my life as they had imagined it to be I would be betraying them, and they would break theirs too. I have never understood how I had acquired this unwanted responsibility, just as I had never understood why my first account of Camusfeàrna, *Ring of Bright Water*, had appeared to touch upon some unacknowledged need in those who read it. To me it had been no more than a kind of personal diary, the diary of a few years of much happiness and some sorrow, and most certainly not one of a great or outstanding man with whom others might identify themselves to the extent of sharing my grief in departure from Camusfeàrna. I remembered the actual words of letters from people whom I had never met. 'Whatever you are going to do, please never say that the Camusfeàrna of *Ring of Bright Water* never was. Say that it's gone, if you like, but not that you lied. I couldn't take that, because it was the only evidence I had that Paradise existed somewhere.' . . . 'Whatever you say,

Camusfeàrna will always be for me the Camusfeàrna you described. I want to keep that image, even though I will never see it—take it away from me and I don't think I have anything left' . . . 'Your book *The Rocks Remain* shook me. Not because I thought it good —I didn't—but because it destroyed my great illusion, that somewhere there was happiness, contentment—a world I have never entered in sixty-four years of life' . . . 'I am thirteen years old and I've read your book. Yours is the only kind of life I want to lead. Please, how does one start? Please tell me how you begin and how to leave towns, and live rough in country places away from other people, particularly parents and relations' . . . 'If you want to know, I think you're a lousy writer who sends one to the dictionary all the time. I'd rather read almost anyone else Bond's my favourite but I sort of want the way you live if it's like you say' . . .

Well, it had been like I said, but it wasn't any more, and it was nobody's fault but my own.

I passed between the rowan tree, its form just visible against the hurrying nighted clouds, and Teko's enclosure. Teko would by now be in his sleeping quarters, the little lean-to slate-roofed outhouse built on the northerly wall of Camusfeàrna cottage. There he had an overhead infra-red lamp, a raised platform, and a bed consisting of a large lorry tyre filled with blankets. As I passed by, I visualized his sleeping form; I did not expect ever to see him again, because I did not think that I could have borne to visit him in a zoo.

A dog suddenly nuzzled at me in the dark. Something huge, at waist level. I put my hands down and recognized my deerhound bitch Hazel, wet and draggled like I was, but warm and welcoming. Since the Pyrenean Mountain Dog, Gus, had been killed, Hazel had been my familiar; her vast form sleeping on top of my bed, to our great mutual discomfort but to her great delight. Many people may think that I should be ashamed to write that at this, that seemed our last meeting, I was near to tears. She put her paws on my shoulders, and her head was a foot above mine, I said goodbye to her and I let her into the house to warm and dry.

I had said goodbye to Hazel, and now I wanted, obsessively, to say goodbye to Teko. For some minutes I stood there in the dark and the rain and the high wind, knowing that what I wanted to do could only make things worse; but perhaps with a subconscious knowledge of what was going to happen, with a subconscious will to change what was happening to Camusfeàrna and to change all decisions I had made, I turned and opened the high wooden gate to his little house. I closed the gate behind me and switched on the electric light in his sleeping quarters. He wasn't there—and small wonder. The gale had dislodged slates from his roof; the entire floor was under something like an inch of water; the blankets were soaking, and the infra-red lamp had fused. I called him, and he came through from the big enclosure which contained his swimming pool, wet and draggled and miserable.

He greeted me as might a castaway on a desert island greet his rescuing ship. All his language which I had come to know so well over seven years he employed in welcome, in rebuke, in renewed hope for the future. The mustelline access of emotion that may turn to such terrible violence was now all affection and desire for reassurance; he squirmed and writhed and put his fingers in my mouth and ears; he put his mouth to mine and sought the animal exchange of saliva.

I called at the top of my voice for dry towels and dry blankets; when these arrived he took pleasure in being dried as he had when he was an infant, and when I had furnished his tyre with warm blankets he entered it at my gesture and composed himself to sleep on his back, his head resting ludicrously upon my forearm, his mouth open and snoring slightly.

I disengaged myself and left him sleeping, knowing now that I could not send him to a zoo, and that somehow or other he must be taken again to the waterfall, to the rock pools, to the sea and the river, to roam free as he had once become accustomed long ago. I did not know how this might be achieved, but I knew that it must happen; that if it did not I would be a betrayer, and a betrayer of animal loyalties becomes a betrayer in human situations too.

I lacked courage; I asked someone else to telephone to the zoo to which Teko had been destined, saying that whereas Edal now appeared relatively independent of human company and might settle there, Teko would not, and I would keep him. I did not know how; I knew only the necessity. I had become committed. I wanted to spend the next summer giving back to this animal the joy and freedom that we had once shared in Camusfeàrna. My own future had become dim and blurred by multiple problems; his, at least, I could restore for a season.

So when I left Camusfeàrna for North Africa in December 1966 I was not saying a true farewell as I had planned and prepared. I was returning, come what might, hell and high water. I felt that by now I was acquainted with both.

2

A Little Late for Loving

Some of the history of Camusfeàrna after the publication of *Ring of Bright Water* I tried to write of in *The Rocks Remain*, but it was necessarily an incomplete story, and I treated much of it in a semi-farcical vein that I should find difficult to do today. Then I saw the happenings as isolated and episodic, however bad the worst of them had been, rather than as part of a trend that was leading steadily toward the end of Camusfeàrna and all that it had stood for. With hindsight now each seems a logical step on a stairway of decline; though even with that hindsight only a few would have been avoidable.

In August 1961 the female otter, Edal, had almost literally chewed off two fingers from her keeper Terry Nutkins; in time even Jimmy Watt, who had known her for so long, lost his trust in her, and she was totally confined, as is any animal in a zoo. This in itself was a heavy enough hammer blow, but it was only the first, so that as time went on I came to expect nothing but blows.

In October of the same year there was the wreck of the *Polar Star*, a night such as I hope never to pass again.

In November I became engaged to be married, and in December the male otter, Teko, savagely attacked my fiancée's son Simon, then aged thirteen. In January 1962, while I was in London preparing for my wedding on 1 February, Teko attacked Jimmy Watt, and after that both otters became animals living under zoo conditions.

By the last months of that year the stresses of an incompatible marriage had become too great for me to write, and the sequel to *Ring of Bright Water*, which should by then have been completed, had hardly been begun. A friend offered to lend me an empty villa in a remote village of Majorca, and I went there meaning to shut myself off from all problems at home, and to concentrate upon working as I had never done in my life. On the day of my arrival my car was stolen from Palma dock, and within half an hour had been irreparably crashed. The whole of my time in Majorca was taken up by legal and police formalities, and by the time I returned to England the book was little further forward than before my departure.

When I came back I found that Terry Nutkins had left; Jimmy Watt was alone, and there were not enough hours in the day to deal with all the responsibilities that the management of Camusfeàrna now entailed. This was the beginning of a series of temporary assistants, nearly all of whom, each in his own way, brought the end of Camusfeàrna perceptibly nearer.

Some six weeks later my wife and I separated, though we were not divorced until July 1964. It is with the end of *The Rocks Remain*, in the spring of 1963, that I take up the story of Camusfeàrna—or perhaps some may choose to think of it as the story of the rowan tree.

On 24 June 1963 I left Camusfeàrna for the south. I was going to spend a fortnight at my brother's home in Greece. Normally I would have looked forward keenly to this visit, but now I did not want to leave my own home—or what little was left of it—for I was trying desperately to hold it together.

At the top of the hill I transferred my luggage from the jeep to the big Land Rover in which I was going to drive to Inverness to take the train south. This Land Rover was one which I had used in North Africa, and had a number of special features. Amongst others was one that a few minutes later probably saved my life—a BBC hard roof, designed to carry the weight of men and equipment. I remember that it was a sunny morning with no wind, and that the sea in the Sound of Sleat below me was brilliant blue. There were big white cumulus clouds high over the purple hills of Skye.

The first seventeen miles of road from Camusfeàrna is single-tracked, with passing places every two or three hundred yards, and for the first five miles to the village it is very narrow indeed. Barely wide enough, for example, for car and a bicycle to pass abreast.

I had driven half a mile or so, and I was going uphill at perhaps twenty miles an hour, when from behind a heathery knoll on my right a stag jumped across the road right under my wheels. I swerved instinctively and just missed the stag. He was bounding down the bank below me on my left and I was in the act of righting the steering wheel when a second stag followed him. I could not avoid this one, but I suppose I must have tried. I felt the dull thud of contact; then I felt the car lurch over, and I knew that I was overturning. My head hit the roof as the car completed her first somersault, then something heavy hit me in the ribs as she rolled over again.

If I lost consciousness at all it must have been for moments only. I was still in the driver's seat but I was lying on my right hand side, and grass and heather were pushing through the window into my neck and cheek. The engine was still running, but I could not reach the switch with my left hand because of a big suitcase that had been on the passenger's seat and was now pinning my left arm to my side. There were two full jerry cans of petrol on the front end of the Land Rover, besides a full tank; I was in no condition to assess rationally the likelihood of fire, but I knew that if it started while I was in this helpless position I should at the least be very badly burned. I struggled to get the suitcase off me, but I could only do this by half turning upward in my seat so as to be able to push with my left hand. This was made the more difficult because my left foot was somehow caught between the pedals, so that it would not turn with me and give me purchase. I struggled, squeezing my foot enough to hurt a little, but it would not move. Though I could not shift the suitcase I managed at last to worm my left arm through below it and reach the ignition switch. Then there was absolute silence, and I lay there getting my breath back.

I could move the suitcase only by butting it simultaneously with my head and left shoulder; at each butt it bounced, until one, stronger than the rest, toppled it over to lodge behind the gear lever, in the passenger's foot-well. Then I had both arms free, and I started to try to climb out. Because, like other Land Rovers, there were three seats in front, the door through which I had to make my escape seemed a very long way above me. I tried to haul myself up by the gear lever, and it was only then that I realised that my left foot was truly trapped and that it would not follow me. I writhed and squirmed and twisted it, but it was still held fast. At last I gave it one terrific jerk, which hurt only in the sense that a bad graze hurts, and I was free. I climbed awkwardly out of the horizontal passenger's door, jumped down to the ground and lit a cigarette.

There was hardly a mark on the visible portions of the car. There was no sign of the stags, though the second had left a big tuft of hair on the bumpers. There was no blood. It seemed to me as if neither the stag nor I had received serious injury. I was very wrong.

I did not understand then, and I have never understood since, the causes of that accident which had such far-reaching consequences, which changed, in fact, my life for years to come. To begin with, the stags had run downhill, straight at the forestry fence a bare thirty yards or so below the road, and a stag in summer would do this only if suddenly surprised from above by a human being. Even then they would have heard the noise of the Land Rover approaching. I climbed the knoll with a sort of anger, thinking that there really was someone up there, someone who had seen the car rolling over and over down the bank and had been too indifferent to help me while I lay there trapped and thinking that I was about to be roasted.

There was nothing; only the slot marks of the stags in soft black peat a few yards from the road, and, higher up, a few sheep grazing scattered and undisturbed. That ruled out the possibility of a dog, for the sheep would have bunched together. I began to walk back the way I had come.

When I reached Druimfiaclach, the cottage on the road above Camusfeàrna, I turned in to see my old friends the MacKinnons; I felt I could do with one of Morag's cups of tea before I started down the hill to telephone about having the Land Rover restored

1 Above: Camusfeàrna in 1958
Below: Camusfeàrna in 1966

2 Not infrequent scenes on the Camusfeàrna track

3 The author at Camusfeàrna, 1963

4 'Calum Murdo MacKinnon'

5 Teko with a beach ball

6 The goalkeeper

7 The author
and Edal

8 The author and Edal

to the road. Calum Murdo was as puzzled as I was about the behaviour of the stags. 'It's not like the beasts at all,' he said. In fact I think he did not believe me until he saw the tufts of stag's hair in the joints of the bumpers.

While I was sitting in the MacKinnons' kitchen the doctor came in. She was comparatively new to the district, though it had been many years since the village had had a male doctor. She had seen the Land Rover as she passed; she had been puzzled, as anyone would have been, as to how the accident could have happened, and she had stopped at Druimfiaclach to ask if anyone had been hurt. I told her briefly of the sequence of events. 'And you're not hurt?' she asked.

'No, not at all.'

'You're sure?'

'Quite sure. Only a bruise or two, and a graze on one foot. I feel fine.' I believed this completely, so that when the symptoms of damage began to appear I did not at first connect them in any way with the accident.

'Well,' said Calum Murdo, 'I don't know whether to say you're lucky or not, Major' (my war-time rank had stuck to me in the district, despite every effort on my part to rid myself of it). 'You get away with driving that Mercedes at a hundred and fifty miles an hour and you and the population of the British Isles seem to survive it, and now you leave the road in a Land Rover doing less than twenty. They say the devil looks after his own; he's got a lot of different ways of doing it, and maybe he employs stags as well as special roofs built on to Land Rovers. Anyway one thing's certain, we none of us get it before our time—"I have a rendezvous with death at some disputed barricade"... You'll pardon me if I'm carried away by the exuberance of my own verbosity...'

Five days later I arrived at Athens airport. As I left the aircraft and began to walk down the gang-stairs the heat seemed almost to push one down into the ground. The passengers began to walk across the tarmac towards the airport buildings some two hundred yards distant, and after a quarter of the way I could feel the sweat trickling down every inch of my body. I was halfway when I became aware of a curious cramping pain starting in my left foot, a dull pain like the feeling of a bruise, but growing steadily in intensity. To my enormous surprise it became so bad that I had to stop. I put down my hand luggage and wriggled my foot about, thinking that perhaps I had sat for too long in one position in the aircraft. After perhaps a minute the pain receded, but it was back with me by the time I had reached the Customs. As soon as I was standing still—and there was nothing else to do for quite a long time—it wore off. My brother was there to meet me at the airport with his car; after that I had no more walking to do, and I forgot the episode completely.

My brother owned a yacht and two beautiful small villas, adjoining each other, on the island of Euboea, their brilliantly-creepered and vine-trellised terraces a hundred feet or so above the sea. Throughout the whole of the summer he was in the habit of chartering the yacht with the larger of the two villas; only very occasionally, when, as now, there was a last-minute cancellation of a charter, did he have the use of the yacht for himself and his friends.

In a sense of format, set in a different climate, and a different, harder beauty, my brother's home at Katounia was curiously like my own at Camusfeàrna; the little seaside village five miles to the north; the port, the nearest shopping centre, seventeen miles to the south.

We drove from Athens to the port, Chalkis, where a bridge spans the narrow fast-flowing channel between the mainland and Euboea, and where the yacht was berthed to meet us. It was dark when we reached Chalkis, and my brother decided to spend the night there and sail in the morning. Again I had had no walking to do, and I had not given another thought to the curious behaviour of my foot at Athens airport.

We ate at a restaurant table on the waterfront, the narrow strip of water between us and the mainland bright with multicoloured slivers of reflected light that wriggled like eels on the running tide. We drank retsina and ate hot roasted crabs. Fortunately I had finished eating before I saw just how they were cooked; even then I was forced to move my chair so that I did not have to watch it any longer. A few yards from our table a girl, a gentle-faced little creature of ten or eleven years old, stood before a charcoal grill, and beside her was a big tray full of octopus arms and crabs. From time to time she would take a pair of tongs and place something new upon the grill in front of her. The grid on which she put them was surrounded on three sides by upright sheets of glass like a vivarium; I wondered idly why this should be so, and then I suddenly saw that the legs of the crab nearest to me on the grid were waving slowly, that the only completely motionless things on its whole surface were the octopus arms. After some minutes I realized that the crabs were being roasted alive, very, very slowly, but those that I was watching were in the later stages of cooking; lying there on their backs with the glowing coals below them, this protest of lingering life was all that was left to them. After a very long time all movement stopped, the girl inspected them and signalled to a waiter. He brought a tray, and to it with her tongs she transferred the hot crabs and octopus arms until the grid was bare of bodies. It was only then that I understood the significance of the glass sides. With her tongs she selected a fresh crab and placed it carefully, back downwards, upon the grid. For a few seconds it remained without movement; then, as the heat from the glowing coals penetrated through the carapace the crab suddenly twisted right side up and literally shot into the air. It struck the glass side, fell back on to the grid and began to scuttle around it at fantastic speed. One of its legs went through the grid, touched the embers and was burnt off. The girl caught the crab again with her tongs, and patiently replaced it on its back. She had to repeat this three times before only the legs waved helplessly and she could turn her attention to the next victim. This one actually scaled the glass with the force of its first leap and fell to the pavement where it scuttled about on scorched legs. Someone at the next table noticed it and laughed. Then I moved my chair so that I couldn't see the little girl any more, and there was only the delicious smell of hot crab coming from behind me.

When we sailed north in the morning the cares, the worries, the pressures and emotional strains of my life at home seemed to slip from me like a sloughed snake-skin. Here in the fresh breeze streaming south, ruffling the sea to the hue of dark lapis lazuli and striking miniature rainbows from the white upthrust of our bow wave, with the sun not yet too hot for a bare skin nor the deck planks too scorching for bare feet, I felt free and exhilarated as I had used to feel always at Camusfeàrna. Perhaps, I thought, the secret of keeping one's vision was always to be a nomad, never to remain long enough in one place to allow time for the deadly clouding of sight, the creeping cataract, that is composed of preoccupation with past mistakes and their present results. I felt the salt spray on my face and I was happy.

> I think Odysseus when he dies forgets
> Which was Calypso, which Penelope;
> Only remembering the wind that sets
> Off Minos, and how endlessly
> His eyes were stung by brine;
> Argos, a puppy, leaping happily
> And his old father digging round a vine.

On our starboard bow the great pale mountain cliff of Candeli towered three thousand feet out of the sea, a pair of eagles wheeling in steep arcs on the hard blue sky above. Just beyond its foot was a little flat calm bay where the water was emerald green backed by wild flowering pink oleanders. I said to my brother, 'God, you're lucky to live here.'

'You think so?' he said after a moment. 'I don't know why. You live by the sea too, where you chose to live, and you've got a boat too, and I suppose an income bigger than I've ever had. There are worries and troubles here too; it's only because you're a visitor without responsibilities for them that you feel like that. I daresay I'd feel the same if I came to Camusfeàrna—except that I couldn't stand the climate.' I had no answer, because he had put into words exactly the thoughts that had been mine a moment or two before. Instead, I asked, 'How does one get mail here? Is it regular and punctual?' He replied, 'Neither. If you're here for a fortnight you may not get a single letter, no matter how many are written to you', and I said, 'Thank God for that!'

In the afternoon we took the small inflatable rubber speedboat called Grishkin and roared down the coast to the little calm bay I'd seen at the foot of Mount Candeli. We beached her there on the roasting hot pebble beach below the giant cliff, and I set off to cruise with a Schnorkel. I cannot swim without it, so that this is not only my favourite water sport but my only one; rarely indulged, because to me it is essentially a leisurely pastime, and the sea at Camusfeàrna never becomes warm enough for a swimmer to be leisurely.

I swam slowly, entranced as always by the shoals of bright, multicoloured fish, the waving weeds, the host of marine life that passed unobscured below the clear glass of the mask. I swam out to the edge of the shelf, the sea's floor so far no more than ten feet below my face, and looked down into the great dim murk where the shelf ended and the depth plunged down an unguessable distance. There were huge shadows moving down there, too indistinct for identification, but I thought they were tunny. I turned for the shore; there is no more reason for a Schnorkel to jam in a hundred fathoms than in one, but even strong swimmers tell me that they experience the same illogical fear when looking down suddenly into the shadowed mysteries of the sea's abyss.

When I came back into shallower water I saw the brilliant mother-of-pearl gleam of an angel shell lying open and empty between the black spines of two sea urchins on a rock. I was trying to dive for it when the same thing happened to my left foot as had happened at the airport, but this time it took place much more quickly. I was in real pain in less than a minute. I remained long enough to get the angel shell, then I headed for the shore as quickly as I could. I landed on a smooth rock and took off the Schnorkel. I sat down and examined the foot carefully; I looked at it and prodded it, but at first I was none the wiser. It looked the same as its fellow but for the scab of a long graze across the arch of the instep. There had been enough dried blood, I remembered, to make it necessary to soak the sock from the foot when I had got back to Camusfeàrna that day after the Land Rover accident. There had been a bluish bruise, too, but it had soon disappeared. This was the first time that I connected what was happening with the recollection of my foot jammed between the pedals of the car; something sinister and unseen must be taking place below the marks of that graze. The rock was so hot that I had to move my foot; and simultaneously I realized that the pain had stopped.

I had enough medical knowledge to grasp the implications. I

had not emerged from that ridiculous accident unscathed; the blood supply to the foot was impaired. Heat caused a temporary alleviation, but the foot itself was in the very first stages of dying. Without supply of blood it could not live.

Even if I had acted then and there the situation was already beyond my control; I was probably right in wanting, for the duration of my brief holiday, to forget that something terrible and far-reaching had happened to me. I walked back to the speedboat, carrying my angel shell, and telling myself that this was a temporary obstruction that would clear itself. I could not bring myself to believe in any real sense that I might become a partial cripple; I had been too long used to strenuous physical exertion and the full use of my muscles and limbs, as a necessary part of my existence, to accept the idea of any change other than as a purely intellectual concept.

The next day we began a cruise of the Aegean islands, Skiaros, Skiathos, and Skopelos with its steep, chalk-white town and echoing marble sea-caves where the mud nests of a thousand swifts clung to the remote vaulted ceilings. By now the limitations of my physical activity had become exact and predictable—a hundred yards' slow walking before I had to rest and allow the pain to wear off, five minutes in the sea before I had to land and warm the foot on a hot stone until the cramp slackened.

When I got back from Greece to England I went at once to see a doctor about my foot. His opinion was somewhat vague, but generally encouraging. The temperature of the foot was considerably lower than that of the other, indicating a reduced circulation, but he did not think a natural cure impossible. He gave me pills to take, which were arterial dilators, and asked me to watch progress carefully. In the case of deterioration he advised me to see a specialist, and not to be content with only one opinion.

I returned to Camusfeàrna. Once there it was obvious that without the heat of a Greek summer sun upon a bare instep to aid circulation I was now virtually crippled, whether or not the crushed vessels might eventually re-channelize themselves naturally. I was scarcely able to walk at all, and when I sat writing at my desk I had to keep my left foot upon a hot water bottle to avoid the cramp setting in even without use of the muscles. All feeling of freedom had gone from Camusfeàrna now, and it was a wildly unsuitable place for someone in my condition to live, more than a mile from the road. I felt as much of a prisoner as the otters that were now confined to zoo conditions. I had always worked hard there, writing for long hours every day; now there was nothing for me to do when I had finished work, nothing to do but go on sitting at that desk and worry about the infinite problems that seemed to form the future of Camusfeàrna. The staff problem was acute. Jimmy Watt, who had then been with me for five years, had originally looked after one otter and a very small uncomplicated household; now he had under his charge the running and maintenance of two Jeeps; a Land Rover; the forty-foot speedboat *Polar Star*; half a dozen dinghies and outboard engines; and our recent purchases, the two lighthouse cottages of Isle Ornsay and Kyleakin, besides two cottages I had bought near to the village. In varying degrees all four of these houses were in need of more or less extensive renovation or alteration, and if I was to go on writing the responsibility for every detail had to remain with him. A gale would blow up, and someone would have to go out to *Polar Star* at her ill-sheltered moorings north of the islands, nearly a mile away, to pump her bilges and secure her tarpaulins. Every so often someone had to take her seventeen miles south for refuelling. Someone had to order household stores and collect them and the mail from the road at the top of the hill. Assistants came and went, leaving behind them diverse trails of disaster, but it was plainly impossible to run this microscopic but infinitely complex empire without Jimmy and two assistants. An accountant's analysis had shown that, excluding wages—but taking into consideration all other expenses, such as light, heat, transport fuel, vehicle repairs, human and animal food, laundry, insurances and telephone— each human being at Camusfeàrna was costing nearly twenty pounds a week. Wages included, the total sum was well above a hundred pounds a week. Even at that comparatively early date the cottage of Camusfeàrna itself was costing five thousand pounds a year, and the only way in which to meet this charge was for me to forget all the joy that I had once found in its beauty and its freedom and to remain immured between the walls of my little bedroom-study and write day long. Casual visitors, often strangers who wanted to see the otters, could not be expected to understand this situation, and my work was constantly behind schedule.

The only freedom now lay in *Polar Star*, and on the days of holiday when all conditions were right and we would take her to visit the lighthouses or just cruise the long winding sea lochs that, like Norwegian fjords, fray the mainland coast between high hills, I experienced a feeling of liberation and exhilaration as complete as I had on my brother's boat in Greece. The glory of summer days on *Polar Star* is with me still; days when the sea was so utterly smooth that the groups of guillemots and razorbills would leave spreading circular ripples as they dived before our bows, and our foaming white wake lay like a furrow far astern of us; the deep, pulsing throb of engines almost inaudible in the forward wheel-house; the pull and suck of the whirlpools in the tide race of the narrows at Kylerhea tugging at the rudders; the screaming, hovering, plunging hoards of gulls feeding upon fry forced up to the surface by great shoals of mackerel beneath them, and the fluttering pull of a darrow line on which danced a dozen or more fish as bright as fine blue and green enamel; storms when the ship would buck and slew in the waves like a bronco, and a terrifying white wall of water would pile up under her leeward bows so that she lay over to sixty degrees or so and I would be fighting not only with the wheel but with cold fear; all these, but perhaps most of all the quiet evenings when we returned her to her moorings at sunset and we would sit for long in the open after-cockpit. The sun going down behind the Cuillin of Skye, scarlet streamers of cloud reflected as a great path of blood across the Sound and staining the small wavelets that slapped lightly at the boat's side with a fluid changing mosaic of pale fire and jade. We would sit there until the hills had become black silhouettes against an apple-green afterglow, the only sounds the water lapping against the hull and crying of the seabirds, the colonies of gulls and of Arctic terns on the islands beside us. Those moments of peace and stillness at *Polar Star*'s moorings had come to represent to me what the waterfall once had, the waterfall now disfigured by pendant lines of black alkathene piping that carried the water supply to the house and to the otters' enclosures. Enclosures; the whole of Camusfeàrna by now seemed to me an enclosure, the sea the only freedom. The house and its surroundings were as much a prison to me as to the otters confined behind fences.

As the weeks went by it was impossible to disguise from myself that the condition of my foot was deteriorating rapidly. But a sort of inertia, born perhaps of a subconscious fear of the future, blocked me from taking any positive action. By October, when the deep sunburn of Greece had worn away and the true colour of the foot was revealed, it was a cold bluish white, and a cratered ulcer had begun to form near the base of the big toe. One day the doctor called to visit another member of the household, and inspected my foot. She said, 'Now you've got to do something; you can't postpone it any longer, unless you're prepared to lose the foot. When I say that I mean that there is now a possibility of future gangrene and total amputation at the ankle. This is no place for you now.' It was indeed no place for me, physically or mentally; it seemed a dead-end, without even the peace and quiet associated with a cul-de-sac.

So in late November I went back to London and saw specialists. The first said that it might be possible to replace the crushed vessels with artificial ones; the second said that the vessels were too small to replace satisfactorily, and in all likelihood would anyway be cast off by the system in the course of a year or two. There was no alternative, he said, to lumbar sympathectomy. Sitting behind his big desk he adjusted his spectacles, placed his fingertips together, and leaned forward, speaking slowly and carefully.

'The lumbar sympathetic nerves lie against and on each side of the spine at about the same level, we may say, as the kidneys. Amongst all other functions they control the blood supply to the lower limbs, and they could be described as taps which are permanently half turned on. By removing the left one entirely the blood tap itself is removed, so that a full, unregulated flow of blood pours down instead of what we may call the tap trickle. Nothing but the surgical removal of the left lumbar sympathetic nerve, the operation we term lumbar sympathectomy, can save your foot now. This, I know, sounds an alarming operation. It is, however, carried out frequently, and with a preponderance of success. If there are no complications you should be in hospital for no more than a fortnight, with a convalescence of, say, a month to two months. I am sorry to have to emphasize that in my opinion you have no choice between this operation or eventual amputation of the foot, which is already showing initial symptoms of necrosis.'

I did my best to evaluate this situation which, from seeming wholly unreal, had suddenly begun to bear true relation to me. I did not believe in his time factors, not because I mistrusted him, but because of an aphorism I had once composed for myself in North Africa and which I had found to contain unvariable truth. 'What you think will take five minutes will take an hour; what you think will take an hour will take a day; what you think will take a day will take a week; what you think will take a week will take a month, and what you think will take a month is impossible of achievement.'

I said, 'How long have I got before this operation becomes urgent?'

'That is a very difficult question to answer. Prognosis is not always clairvoyant, you know. In my opinion not very long— two, three months, possibly four if you were lucky, judging by the present rate of deterioration. Have you ever seen gangrene?'

'Yes.' I had indeed; I remembered with sick horror Terry's fingers after they had been chewed off by Edal; the stench, the amputation, the realization that parts of a young human body had gone forever, lying there blackened in an enamel basin, and that nothing in the world could ever restore them. In some way they had been to me more terrible to look at than a corpse.

'Then you realize that, after the initial onset, the progress of the condition may be very rapid. An emergency operation is always undesirable. I take it that you are now reconciled to the necessity of surgical interference?'

'Yes.' Reconciled was not quite the appropriate word, but this was no time to discuss finer shades of meaning. I did not feel then that I could ever be reconciled to any of these things that had so changed my life, even though I might recognize their menacing aura.

'I understand that you live in Scotland. Would you prefer to have the operation there or in London?'

The problems of Camusfeàrna babbled at me as I sat there in the calm, clinical atmosphere of the Harley Street consulting room with the muted rumble of traffic outside; I couldn't separate myself from them by five hundred miles. I said, 'Scotland.'

'Very good. Do you wish me to arrange things for you, or do you have adequate methods of doing that yourself?'

I said, 'I think I can fix things up myself, if that is not a breach of etiquette.' I enjoyed the acquaintance of perhaps the greatest surgeon in Scotland; now that I believed that I knew the worst I intended to place myself unreservedly in his hands. I was, however still far from knowing the worst; mercifully, neither humans nor other animals can ever do that.

From London I went to Scotland. The examination I received from the great surgeon was even more detailed and more searching than those that I had undergone before. When it was over he said, 'Tomorrow morning I am going to take you to the hospital for an X-ray. This, my friend, will hurt; it is only fair to tell you that. In order to determine at what point the blood supply to your foot ceases we inject the arteries with a substance which appears opaque on X-ray. This is injected at the groin, and it is uncomfortable. . . .'

It was much more than uncomfortable. There was a big room milling with nurses and students and other unidentifiable hospital personnel, and I lay naked and miserable and ashamed on a table in the midst of them all. The modesty that is innate in the greater part of our western culture made me close my eyes, so that at least I could not see reflected in theirs an evaluation of my helpless nudity. After what seemed a long time the X-ray camera closed in and a white-coated figure hovered above me with a needle that looked as thick as a pencil. 'Just try to keep still, now,' he said, and plunged this monstrous instrument into the artery of my left groin. It was all I could do not to scream; the pain was, I think, the most acute that I had ever experienced in my life. The needle was in and the opaque fluid was being forced in through it; to move my pelvis even in a reflex action of terror could only increase the agony. I wanted something to bite on, and unfortunately the only thing available was my tongue. I bit on it, deeply, and felt the blood slowly fill my mouth.

Just as the degree of tolerance to pain varies between individuals

—and notably between males and females—I think that the *perception* of pain varies too; in some the threshold is very high and even gross injury is felt as no more than acute discomfort; in others, where the threshold is low, the same physical situation may produce an agony so acute as to produce loss of consciousness. I didn't actually faint, but while I was swallowing the blood from my bitten tongue I wished very much that I could have done so. I had wondered why I was brought down from my bed in a wheeled chair; on the return journey I wondered no longer.

While the surgeon was driving me from the hospital, back through the crush of twilight city traffic to my hotel, I was thinking about these things and about the operation to which I was now committed. I tried to explain to him; I think I said that if the operation was going to hurt as much as that and for a much longer time I would rather lose the foot. I don't know whether I meant this seriously, but it was certainly what I felt at that moment.

'My friend,' he said as the big car came to rest at a traffic light, a drizzle of rain blurring the windscreen and sliming the black road ahead with muzzy reflections of street lamps, 'my friend, there will be no pain. None at all. There will be a long scar across your belly—it has to be long for a surgeon to get both hands in—but it will be a hair-line scar, and you will feel nothing, and your belly will be as flat and hard as it is now. And you will be able to walk again; in a short time the whole thing will be an incident that you will have forgotten.'

I have never stopped thinking about that short homily that proved, through no fault of his own, to be so far from the truth. Several years later I was reminded of it by a letter from my brother in Greece. It carried a postscript: 'Have you read that an Anglican clergyman in the south of England is holding, after his sermons, frank discussions of them in a nearby café, discussions held under the title of Where I went Wrong? One may picture a similar informal fork luncheon to discuss the errors in the Sermon on the Mount.'

Even without the threat of gangrene and amputation it was very plain that I could not go on as I was. It was December now, and since I was in a city I thought I would do my Christmas shopping there. I found that I could hardly walk at all. I limped about the streets more slowly than would a blind man. After the first half hour I had to add an unexpected item to my list of purchases—a walking stick. I remember that it rained incessantly and that it was very cold.

3

The Third Fall

I was admitted to hospital on Boxing Day 1963. I was afraid, but I suppose I had by then come near to the consultant's adjective 'reconciled'. In fact the institution did not call itself a hospital; it was a vast nursing home, built, it seemed, with utter disregard for cost. I was slightly disconcerted to find a nun behind the reception desk, in a spacious hall where a notice requested visitors not to wear stiletto heels. I wondered just what a visitor so shod was expected to do after reading this. The pallid, wax-work nun took down the usual particulars with a chilling impersonality, and without once raising her eyes from the form that she was filling in. 'Next of kin? Religion?' Because my own beliefs are eclectic and personal, I suddenly found that I could not answer this question. I hesitated for so long that at last she did look up, and her expression was icy, her thin lips pressed together. 'Religion?' she repeated in her small expressionless voice. I knew there was a word for what I wanted to say, but I just could not find it. She laid down her pen and waited, while I felt like a prisoner of the Spanish Inquisition. I said, rather desperately, 'I'm afraid I don't subscribe to any orthodox religion.' 'Non-denominational,' she murmured, managing to convey an infinity of distaste in the words, and I watched her inscribe them in a handwriting as anonymous as her face and voice. Then she rang a push-button bell, and passed me on to another nun who was as human and welcoming as a well-greased cog wheel.

The procedure, which must of logical necessity be routine, seemed to me grotesque. I was put to bed, my temperature and pulse duly recorded, and I was told that in the absence of doctor's instructions I might not even walk across the passage to the lavatory. The nuns who were on duty had no knowledge whatsoever as to why I was there, and when I tried to explain to one of them that I was to undergo left lumbar sympathectomy resulting from an injury six months before, she merely replied, 'What is this operation you mentioned?' I tried to supply the information she lacked, but she said, 'That has nothing to do with me; I am not a surgical nurse.' Indeed, as I discovered later, she was not a qualified nurse at all; in common with the great majority of the nuns who helped in the huge building she was merely fulfilling a supposed vocation. In many cases the vocation was considerably less than obvious.

Later, a night nurse came on duty, who, although a Catholic, was not a nun. 'What a lot of nonsense!' she exclaimed; 'of course you can go to the lavatory, or walk up and down the corridor all night if you like. These nuns just stick to rigid rules that double the work for everyone. What's the sense in someone having to bring you bed-pans and things when you're quite capable of doing everything for yourself? After you've had the operation—that's a different matter, and a nurse's head would be up on a charger if she put a foot wrong that way. But now, when you've just been admitted for an op like that, it's crazy. They make me sick, the lot of them—they're just not human, and no one's going to tell me it does a patient any good to be treated like a corpse from the moment he gets into hospital. Would you like a cup of tea?'

'Well, just at the moment what I'd ask for if I wasn't in hospital would be a drink.'

'You mean the hard stuff? I can fix that for you too—but keep it out of sight. I'll be back in five minutes, and don't take more than ten drinking it, because I'll be back to take the glass away.'

Oh, hard stuff nurse—I shall remember you with gratitude and affection for the rest of my life. I hope you will accept this tribute and be proud of a truer vocation than was apparent to me in the Order.

The next morning the barber arrived, and after half an hour's very conscientious work left my body smooth and hairless as a baby's. He actually used a magnifying glass to make certain that the perfection of his work was unquestionable. It was strange, I thought, how the whole routine from the moment of admission could be taken by a stranger, some anthropologist observing a new tribal ritual and unfamiliar with its reasons, for a deliberate reduction to a dependent and infantile status of helplessness; this childish hairlessness the visible symbol of submission. Even the word 'nurse' was one belonging essentially to childhood; and here there were yet others added to the hierarchy of the nursery, the 'Reverend Mother' and the 'Mother Superior'. . . . I was the patient inferior.

I was heavily sedated when I was taken down to the operating theatre; from my supine position on the trolley I saw the surgeon in his shirt sleeves in the adjoining passage. He smiled down at me and said, 'You're a little early—we don't usually let the patient see us down here without the full witch-doctor's uniform!' Then I was wheeled on into the theatre, and a few moments later there were nothing but anonymous white-masked faces surrounding me. I saw the pentothal syringe, and exactly as I felt it enter the vein a voice said, 'Count to ten.'

I only reached three. When I came to I was in the corridor outside my ward door, looking up at what seemed swarms of unfamiliar faces, among which I saw that of the nurse who had given me the hard stuff after I had been admitted. There was an appalling pain at the left side of my belly; I tried to reach for it but found that I couldn't move my hands. I suppose they were tied. I was unaware of saying anything, but she told me later that I gasped at her, '*Rectus abdominis! Rectus abdominis!*' and that she had answered, 'Well, that's all right dear, so long as it isn't *rigor mortis!*' What was actually going on in my head was something quite different. I had spent the greater part of the war in S.O.E., the organization responsible for the Resistance Movement in occupied countries, and for training and arming agents to be parachuted— often to their death under torture—into enemy territory. There had been a Glaswegian instructor in unarmed combat and knife- fighting, and he would begin his instruction of each new group with an invariable verbal formula, chanted rather than spoken, in his high sing-song voice: 'Ony o' youse fellies ever seen a felly killed wi' a knife? *Ah* harvn't—I seen a felly slarshed wi' a razy tho'.' It was this litany that was repeating itself over and over again in my head; dragged out of my subconscious, no doubt, by the jumbled associations of industrial Scotland and knife wounds.

36

As I have said, I believe my perception of pain to be unusually acute, and from then on it was difficult to imagine anything hurting more than what was happening to me. It seemed to me that the nuns were ungentle, unsympathetic and infinitely clumsy, as they went through their routines of making the bed and moving my now unfamiliar body that felt as if it were held together at the waist by an agonizing strand no thicker than a wasp's. Implicit in their attitude appeared to me the view that suffering was good for my soul. If I groaned involuntarily, one in particular, I remember, would say brusquely, 'Your wound's in a bad place, that's all.'

Unfortunately, it wasn't all. I woke one evening to find the hard stuff nurse beside me and the thermometer under my arm. 'How are you feeling?' she asked gently. 'Like death,' I said, 'what's gone wrong?'

'You're very ill. You've got a hospital staphylococcus. They've isolated it—*Staphylococcus aureus*. The surgeon's coming to see you in a few minutes.'

By the time he arrived I was being sick, oceans of black bile, and each retch seemed to tear the wound wide open.

'My friend,' he said, 'I am very, very sorry about this. The operation was perfect—I have never done a better sympathectomy, I assure you, I could not have foreseen this complication.'

The anaesthetist, whom over my protracted stay I came to look upon as my guardian angel and my best friend, entered my room with a vast trolley, and again I heard, 'Count to ten'. When I was next conscious there were three drainage tubes protruding from my wound.

Altogether, I now realize from the detailed hospital bill, I was returned to the operating theatre thrice, but time and sequence is now confused. I no longer had any resistance left to what was being done to me; I had made a complete surrender. Camusfeàrna and what it had once been was a dim dream, sometimes a night-mare. On the rare occasions when I thought consciously of the future, there was only one clear image before me—that of being able to walk again, that of setting the clock back to the time before those two stags had bounded across the road. Beside this one target, which demanded complete submission, the problems of Camus-feàrna now seemed insignificant except in troubled sleep.

But the worst was still to come. In all surgical operations which necessitate the actual handling and moving of the intestinal mass a condition called *ileus* may set in by which the normal gentle and rhythmic contractions, the peristalsis by which the digestive system is maintained, react by complete paralysis. All movement is arrested, in what is now considered by many schools of thought to be a protest by the whole entity—(for the psyche and the soma, the brain and the body, form a single entity that cannot be arbitrarily separated from each other)—against outside interference by something subconsciously interpreted as a hostile power factor. The net result, anyway, is that the gut ceases to function, and because of this cessation, gases form which have no route of escape, as happens in a corpse. One's belly swells and swells until one lies there like a stranded whale—or, in my case, like an inflated set of bagpipes, with the drainage tubes sticking out like the drones and the chanter. If this enormous distension is straining against a long wound, tending to force it open by mechanical principle, the result is pain and confusion. Until quite recently this condition was a frequent cause of death. I believe that several drugs were tried upon me without avail. I was grateful that the surgeon did not treat me as a child; he explained the whole concept, adding that he would go on trying until he found the effective drug. He did not disguise that in its absence my life would be in danger. I was intensely grateful for this absolute honesty.

Certainly the first drugs did not work. The mountainous hill of my belly would appear to subside slightly for a very short time and then it would swell again to its former monstrous proportions. I cannot pretend to remember now how long this grotesquely bloated condition lasted.

One night I was awoken suddenly by a sound in the room, the sound of somebody breaking wind noisily. I could not understand this; I was in a ward by myself, and I could hardly imagine a night nurse committing such a breach of decorum. Then it came again, thunderous, earthshaking, the longest, loudest and most superbly stupendous fart that I had ever heard in my life, a sound of such magnificent and prolonged volume as to appear utterly beyond human capability. With a shock I realized that it was I who was the author of this elephantine and sonoric flatulence; I put a hand on my belly and felt it deflating like a punctured barrage balloon. They had discovered the right drug at last, and the result had been so spectacular (or auricular) that I found myself wishing that the manufacturers might have had a tape-recording for publicity purposes.

The rest of my seemingly interminable time in hospital ran the course of a normal though somewhat protracted convalescence. I found that not all the nuns who staffed the establishment were as inhuman as had seemed the two who hauled me about after the operation. Some were saintly, efficient, and warm hearted, plainly devoted to their work, though the general organization remained to me an enigma. A day or two after my grand explosion I rang the bell for a bed-pan. A strikingly beautiful fair-haired girl, seeming no more than a child but wearing the uniform of a probationer, answered the bell. She appeared slightly disconcerted by my request, but brought what I wanted. She kept her eyes averted as she helped me to position it, and she appeared acutely embarrassed. Later, when she came to take it away and perform the usual offices of a nurse, she was in a state of pure confusion. I determined to find out more about her, and when an hour or two later she brought me my lunch (the quality of the food, like the quality of the building and its equipment, was magnificent) I managed to detain her in conversation. She was just sixteen, the orphaned daughter of a fishing family in Connemara, who had been rescued by this nursing order of nuns so that she too should become a nun herself. From the age of ten she had been part of the crew of her father's small fishing boat, and she could handle nets and ropes as well as any boy. She had been brought from Ireland the week before; she had been in the hospital for precisely three days. Before that morning she had never in her life seen a man with no clothes on; no wonder the child had seemed embarrassed. I asked her what her other duties were.

'Well, first thing in the morning I have to help the nuns put their head-dresses on. They can't do it themselves, because they aren't allowed to see their own faces in a mirror.'

'*What*? Never? What happens if they see themselves reflected in a shop window, for example?'

'They're supposed to look away. Well, doing their head-dresses takes quite a lot of time, and then after that I come to the hospital from the convent, and I'm just at call to fetch and carry and do odd jobs.'

'But when you become a nun will you never see your own face either?'

'No, never. It's a rule of the Order.'

'You'll be missing a lot,' I said, and she blushed deeply again. I could think, on the other hand, of some of the hospital nuns to whom this rule must have been the greatest gratuitous good fortune of their lives. I said so.

'You should not speak like that,' she replied in her gentle Irish brogue; 'it is uncharitable.'

'But do you want to be a nun?' I asked; 'don't you want to marry and have children and be a woman?'

'No. The Mother Superior has convinced me that I must renounce all earthly things, and it is my dearest wish to become a member of the Order. Nothing will ever alter my intention now. I shall be given a new name, and I shall forget my life before I was brought to the convent.'

Forget the sea and the salt wind and the sunshine and the great open sky, I thought; forget the feeling of wet sea sand and weed beneath bare feet, forget the pitching of a boat in the waves; the crying of gulls; the rasp of frayed and dripping rope on childish palms; forget the lovely little face that she must have studied and appraised in some cracked mirror with the awakening longings and doubts of adolescence. A blind anger took hold of me at what seemed the suppression and diminution of a human life.

I said, 'But you're only a child—how can you be certain that these are the things you want? What happens if you fall in love with a boy or a man during the next month or two?'

'I am in love with Christ,' she said, so simply and gently that I could find no words to answer her, though my anger did not die. The only hospital nun whose name I knew, and who must once have been as beautiful as this child was now, was called Sister Teresa of the Bleeding Heart. Whose heart was bleeding, I wondered; by her face it was her own.

There was one curious thing about my convalescence while I was still in the hospital. I was working, as soon as I had recovered the energy and application necessary to work at all, on the autobiography of my childhood, which was published in 1965 under the title of *The House of Elrig*. I realized with absolute certainty that my helplessness and dependence, my hairless body, my reduction in middle age to a childhood status, had performed for me some miracle of time transposition, so that I was able to think as a child and to recall images and attitudes that would otherwise have been lost to me. In some sense I did really re-enter childhood, so that to write of it was not an effort of memory, but an actual reliving of those early years, because I was required now to conform to that distant authoritarian pattern. The re-creation was strangely complete; I had passed through the stage of acute illness, corresponding to the dependent infant years, and gone on to impatient and resentful convalescence which found its exact parallel in the intolerant protest of puberty and adolescence. In this way and because the sequence of the writing followed these stages faithfully but unintentionally, long lost scenes and feelings, dialogues and mental directions, became things of the present and not of the past. The images, I suppose, were random, but they were real and uncontrived. The dedication

> This book is for the house
> and all I kissed
> But greatly more than these
> For children like I was
> If they exist

was, in my mind, rhetorical; I did not really believe that they did exist, and I was genuinely amazed when many children's letters began to arrive telling me that they were exactly as I had been, that I had put their own thoughts and confusions into lucid words. It is a terrible indictment of parents or otherwise responsible adults that children should feel driven to seek the confidence, and by implication the absolution, of a total stranger. I know that I owe this inestimable compliment to the two stags who caused my trivial motor accident, and the crushing of my left foot. Perhaps even to the curse upon the Camusfeàrna rowan tree; historically, curses seem often to have back-fired, and if I had not written the story of my childhood as honestly as I was allowed I should not now have the host of vicarious sons and daughters that brighten my world.

4

The Captive and the Free

When at last I was discharged from hospital the temperature of my left foot had been restored—indeed it was slightly higher than that of the undamaged one—but I seemed no nearer to being able to walk. The same cramp would come on after the same distance as it had before my operation; no one seemed to be prepared to say just when mobility might be regained, but I understood that it would be a few weeks at most. I left the hospital doubly crippled, because besides the cramp in my foot my wound had not healed; there was still one drainage tube in position, and my belly felt as if it contained a collection of spiked golf balls that bounced at each hesitating step. My brother, who was home for a time from his house in Greece, came to fetch me. I remember the long drive to our family home, Monreith, in Wigtownshire, because it was the first time for weeks that I had seen anything but the hospital walls and the drab view of industrial brickwork from my ward window. Now there were green fields, and moorlands and budding trees, and air that smelled of them instead of disinfectants.

In this kind of minor restoration to freedom, this first flap of wings long flightless, there is an uplift causing witticisms that might perhaps otherwise pass with a smile to seem flashes of extraordinary brilliance. I remember that as we drove through suburbs, past rows of small semi-detached houses, on each invariable television aerial surmounting their roofs was perched a single rook. I pointed this out to my brother, remarking that since there were trees all around it was extraordinary that the normally gregarious rooks should choose to perch singly on the antennae of television aerials. Without even the momentary pause that customarily precedes an impromptu *bon mot*, he replied, 'One can only suppose that each householder is determined to have a crow over his neighbour.' I think it must have been a long time since I had really laughed at anything, for the jagged pain it caused in my belly was quite unexpected.

I had gone to Monreith not only because it had been my family home and my brother had said that I might recuperate there, but because I had to be under daily medical supervision, and the local general practitioner, Dr Gavin Brown, was a close friend of very long standing. He had come to the village when I was little over twenty, and he was only a few years older than I. He was one of those rare members of the profession whose abilities could have carried him to practically any height he chose, but he preferred a remote country practice in which he could know each of his widely scattered patients individually and intimately, giving them as much help, perhaps, by his sympathy and deep understanding of human nature as by his medical skill. He it was who came every morning to swab out the wound and change the dressing, and to stay, when I could persuade him, to recount anecdotes of his profession, sometimes horrifying but often hilarious.

When he looked at my wound on the first morning he said, 'Well, you've got an awful mess of a belly, Gavin. One thing's certain—that'll never be a hair-line scar, and unless you want a cosmetic operation you'll never have a flat stomach again. There'll always be an unsightly bulge there.' He was right, as usual. (When, two years later, the question of a cosmetic operation came under review, I was too cowardly to consent to it. The prognosis, though it was in French because I was in Switzerland, was too terrifyingly verbatim in meaning with that of the great surgeon in Scotland before my lumbar sympathectomy—the same time in hospital, the same period of convalescence. I just couldn't believe any more that things would go smoothly, and because of that hideous wound I still cannot show myself in a bathing slip without acute embarrassment.)

After the first week or two Gavin Brown suggested that I

should try to walk down the half mile drive to meet him every morning. 'One of these days,' he said, 'I hope I'll find you waiting for me at the lodge gate.' But I never reached that gate, though I lingered long at Monreith, until the snowdrops were gone and the primroses out, and the woods full of the sound of courting woodpigeons. It was a sad house, reflecting my own mood of an epoch over and not to be regained; more than half its rooms were closed, the garden over-grown, and a great gale had swept the woods during the winter, smashing down the rare rhododendrons and collector's trees that my grandfather had planted along their rides nearly a century before.

It was a good deal more than a year before I was able to walk the distance of that drive without constant pauses for rest—more than two years after the stags had bounded across the Camusfeàrna road. By that time my muscles had become flabby with disuse, and in an effort at some degree of resignation I had almost acquired a sedentary, invalid habit of mind. In fact, though by 1965 I no longer looked upon myself as a cripple, and was able to walk ten miles at my own now very leisurely pace, I would never again in all my life regain the absolute use of the foot as it had been before the accident. The time limit within which total recovery was theoretically possible has now long expired.

When at length I returned to Camusfeàrna in the late spring of 1964 I was completely helpless. I could not walk, and even to be driven in a Jeep up the hill track with its rocks and potholes hurt my wound so much that I left the house as little as possible, and then almost always by boat. It was the beginning of a curious interaction between myself and those who staffed Camusfeàrna. Their solicitude and their desire to relieve me of every kind of task and responsibility, other than that of writing, worked upon me psychologically to increase my helplessness and dependence; at first I felt myself to be a cypher in my own household, and by degrees that is what I became. They were, the young and healthy, really and actually the masters; never had an adolescent rebellion so complete and satisfying a success with so small an expenditure of force. I could take no part in the activity of the others; I wrote for increasingly long hours every day, working simultaneously on

The House of Elrig and *Lords of the Atlas,* but with an ever growing sense of frustration—and, I believe, a growing petulance and ill temper. At some unremembered stage of my upbringing I had been taught to believe that self-pity is one of the most despicable of human emotions, and no doubt my surliness and irritability were substitutes for the state of mind in which I really wanted to indulge. I felt like an aphis, immobile but solicitously kept alive in a cell by ants who tended me assiduously for my daily excretion of written words. Had my thoughts been less fogged by frustration I should have realized then that it was folly to try to perpetuate a mutant phase of Camusfeàrna that had proved in an evolutionary sense to be an unpleasant dead end, and instead of spending huge sums on the conversion of two isolated island lighthouse cottages I had bought in October 1963 I should have sold them and bought some house with a road to it, and thus minimized the effects of my crippledom. But those lighthouses became my chief distraction, both because I could reach them by boat, and because they seemed then to represent something emergent and hopeful in the general muddle of my personal situation.

The two otters Edal and Teko were, like myself, by now confined. The Scottish otters, Mossy and Monday, which we had liberated early in 1963, had lived for months under the floor of the house, but at length they had decided in favour of less noisy quarters. They had taken up residence on one of the nearby islands, and we saw them increasingly rarely. At some time during my convalescence at Monreith, however, there had arrived at Camusfeàrna one of the strangest otters in what was by then a long series.

It had become customary for anyone who had come into possession of an unwanted otter in Scotland—and sometimes very much further afield, even in South Africa—to communicate with us. Of the otters actually sent to us, owing sometimes to their extreme infancy and once to a malady carried from a far country, few survived.

This new otter, whose owner had named her Tibby, was the companion of a bachelor cripple who lived alone on the island of Eigg, and who was unable to move without crutches. His increasingly frequent visits to hospital made him anxious to secure Tibby's welfare in the future by finding her a permanent home where she could live free as she was accustomed, and he at once thought of Camusfearnà. So Tibby had arrived, accompanied by her owner, during my absence. She was thought to be about a year old; she was small and friendly and domesticated, and in appearance almost indistinguishable from Monday at the time when she and Mossy lived under the coat-room floor.

Tibby's owner stayed at Camusfeàrna for a few days, and when he left Tibby was confined to the house for a week or two so that she might become accustomed to her new surroundings. At the end of that time she was placed in Teko's enclosure, for Teko had never displayed animosity towards any otter that had shared his premises either by chance or design. So that she should have some inviolable refuge from him if she wanted it, she was provided with a separate shed with an entrance so small as to preclude the passage of Teko's bulky form. This was the situation when I returned from Monreith to Camusfeàrna.

The arrangement worked well enough for a short time, but Tibby suddenly discovered, as Monday had before her, that stone walls do not a prison make nor iron bars a cage. Nor, she decided, would she take these for an hermitage. She simply climbed out, and having done so she did not head south-west towards the distant island of Eigg from which she had come, but north-east towards the village, the direction in which her master had left, unseen by her, weeks before. At that time a local resident, Alan MacDiarmaid, who had spent his childhood at Camusfeàrna before I ever came to it, was working for us before setting up as an independent builder and contractor in the neighbourhood. He lived now in the village, and drove his car every morning to Druimfiaclach, the cottage on the road a mile above Camusfeàrna, and walked down the track to us. On the first morning after Tibby's disappearance he arrived with her trotting obediently at his heels. He had found her on the road near to the village, caught her without difficulty, and put her in the boot of his white Riley. Liberated at Druimfiaclach, she had followed him down the track to Camusfeàrna without question or demur. We found the place from which she had escaped and made it, as we thought, impregnable. Alan spent the whole day working on the enclosure, and when he had finished it seemed that not even Monday herself, that Houdini of the otter world, could have escaped from it.

Two days later Alan again arrived with Tibby bouncing along at his heels. Again he had found her near the village, caught her, put her in the boot, and driven her to Druimfiaclach. I can't remember how often this farce was repeated before Tibby made up her mind that she would not be caught again. She decided to remain at the village. She located the only man who resembled her late master, in that he too was a cripple on crutches, and she tried to attach herself to him. She carried up grass and began to build herself a nest under his house. Unfortunately he was not otter-minded, and viewed her proposal of partnership with less than enthusiasm. Repulsed and no doubt bewildered, she forsook the immediate area, and it was some long time before I had any real evidence that she was alive. A month or two later an apparently tame otter appeared on a rock by the pier of Kylerhea ferry, a mile or two from the village, and sat down unconcernedly to eat a fish within a few yards of a number of tourists who were waiting to cross the ferry with their cars, but this may as well have been Monday. Months later I received a telephone call from a slightly inebriated gentleman who informed me that he had caught a 'half-grown' female otter and would I like to buy it. As far as I could make out, the call came from a village some twenty miles to the north. I asked him how he had caught it. He had been gathering shellfish on the shore and it had come up to him and sniffed at his shoes so he had 'thrown his coat over it'. I pointed out that this could not be a wild otter, that it must be one of mine, and suggested that he set it free at once. But, he protested, otters were worth money—even the skin would fetch £4. I said that I would pay him double that sum to liberate her. He demurred, and said that he would consider the question and telephone back after a few minutes. Half an hour later he informed me that all negotiations were now at an end, because the otter had vanished. As this power of evaporation was common to both Tibby and Monday I could not be certain which of them this had been, but I thought that Monday was by now far too wary to sniff at a stranger's feet.

The next time, however, there could be no possibility of doubt. The telephoner said he had actually been followed to his house by an otter. The otter had tried to come in, but he had been afraid and had driven her away. Acting on a sudden inspiration I asked, 'You don't by any chance use crutches, do you?' 'Yes,' he replied, with astonishment in his voice, 'but how in the world could you know that?' I told him the story of Tibby, and he promised to tell me if she came back, but I never heard from him again, and as I had not caught his name I could not enquire myself.

Perhaps if I had never had the operation, and had lost my left foot by amputation, I should have earned Tibby's allegiance for life.

Another wildcat came and went. One summer's afternoon I heard coming from beneath the coat-room floor, where the two otters Mossy and Monday used to live before they left us, unmistakable sounds of feline distress. It was a thin, wailing cry, pitiful, and clearly produced by a kitten rather than a cat. I fetched an old fishing net and laid it to cover all exits; then I went to the kitchen and searched for suitable bait. An open tin of pilchards was the strongest-smelling object I could find, and I placed this on the ground outside the net at one of the most obvious exits. I stood back a few paces to wait, but it was not for long. Within one minute the kitten was entangled in the net, so thoroughly enmeshed that it took me another five of patient work to cut it out with a scissors. Then I held in my hands a small and extremely emaciated wildcat kitten. It must have weighed ounces rather than pounds, and through the soft fur every bone in its body was hard against my hands. Even in this state of extreme weakness it was a ferocious little creature, spitting and snarling and clawing in the best tradition of its race.

It was already weaned, as I discovered when it began to eat within a quarter of an hour of capture, but it was also plainly unable to find food for itself. Somehow or other it must have become separated from its parents and the rest of the litter—not recently, to judge by its condition—and been drawn to the house by the smell of the otters' fish. I had no alternative but to keep it for the time being, and when I learned that the Edinburgh Zoo was in urgent need of a female wildcat, as mine proved to be, I decided to keep her until she was fully restored to health, and then to present her to the Zoo's wildcat den and a waiting mate.

This I did, but like so many wild animals taken by humans from their natural surroundings, she came to a violent and untimely end. She was in temporary quarters in the Edinburgh Zoo, awaiting introduction to her future mate, and in the adjoining compartment was a Honey Badger, that most dynamic and unpredictable of all the mustellines. The cat, who had been named Feàrna, because she came from Camusfeàrna, found just enough space to push an arm through into the Honey Badger's cage, and as a result she was so badly mauled that she had to be destroyed.

Mossy and Monday, I am almost certain, brought up three cubs on the island off Camusfeàrna where, in earlier years, there had always been an otters' holt. Here some big boulders lay together in such a way that beneath them there were commodious but, to a human, inaccessible chambers. We knew that the holt had been untenanted during the time that Mossy and Monday had been first captive and then free but living under the house; we knew also that it became occupied once more at some time soon after they left us. In the late summer of 1964, while I was writing in my room at Camusfeàrna, I heard the extraordinarily penetrating sound, something between a whistle and a squeak, that a young otter makes when it is trying to regain contact with a lost parent. The sound came from the waterfall; I limped across the field and peered cautiously over the shrub-grown bank that screens it from the direction of the house. All I saw at first was Mossy, the male; no other otter, I thought, could look quite so stupid, so silly, so unaware of any intruder. He was sitting on a rock ledge at the side of the falling white water, below where a small holly bush grew from the steep bank at the water's side, and he was, as usual, doing nothing in particular. Then the penetrating call came again, nearer at hand, and below my line of vision. I raised my head a little more, and three very small cubs came into view, cubs of about the same size as Mossy and Monday were when they first came to us. One was on a stone in midstream below the waterfall, and the other two were on the long, smooth, steeply sloping rock that formed the opposite bank from that on which Mossy was sitting. As I watched, one of these half slid, half tumbled down into the water; splashed around for a moment, climbed back out again; and then, looking to the top of the waterfall, called again. I looked up too, just, but only just, in time to glimpse a small sharp face like Monday's peering round a rock at the lip of the fall where the water began to spill over in cascade. The inference was obvious; she had climbed the fall and the cubs could not follow; Mossy, as in all other situations in which I had known him, did not know what to do about it. I was reminded of a *New Yorker* cartoon, in which a family of rats were attempting to board a ship by means of its berthing rope, and had been brought up short by the huge disc of a rat-stop. The little rats were fussing about on the rope behind their parents, and the mother was looking at them over her shoulder and saying, 'Oh, do for heaven's sake stop chattering and let your father *think*.' Mossy was presumably thinking, but as usual without result.

I was determined to secure a photograph of the family; I did not think Monday had seen me, but in case she had, and decided to take her cubs downstream again before I could return with a camera, I fetched a length of net and stretched it across the stream at the wooden bridge below the house. Then I went back to the waterfall with a camera. As I crossed the field I realized that the calling had stopped before even I had laid the net, and when I peered over the bank again there were no otters and no otter cubs. I walked downstream to the net, but they had not passed that way, for there was soft sand at each side of the stream, and if they had bypassed the net on land they would have left their prints there.

It was foolish of me to think that I could outwit Monday, who had proved so often and so conclusively in the past that she was master of any situation I could devise. She must have seen me at once, and somehow contrived in the first minute or so after my departure to convey her cubs and her dumb spouse up over the waterfall and into the inaccessible reaches of the cliff-walled stream above it. Monday, with much experience of human ways, was free, and she intended that she and her cubs should remain so.

Yet two and a half years later, in the spring of 1967, she hobbled into Camusfeàrna kitchen with a foreleg broken by a gin trap, and remained in the house until it was healed and she was again on the point of giving birth. She trusted us in her trouble, the highest compliment a wild animal can pay to humans who have once been its captors, and that she trusted Camusfeàrna and no other house was evident by her survival during the absent years.

9 The author and Dirk

SANDAIG
PET OTTERS
ALL DOGS
ON THE LEAD
PLEASE

PRIVATE

14 Gus—'reputedly savage and untameable . . .
in reality as soft and soppy as a spaniel!'

15 Gus and Jimmy Watt

16 Teko

5

Bitter Spring

The year 1965 opened with a succession of body-blows so massive that, although I had by then come to expect nothing but what a boxer might call severe punishment, I came very near to being knocked clean out of the ring altogether.

Nine years before, in 1956, I had published the results of long and arduous researches into the life and mysterious death of the Sicilian named Salvatore Giuliano, whom the Italian government had labelled a 'bandit', but whose deep political involvement—beginning with the Allies before Italy capitulated and became a co-belligerent—was obvious even to the most superficial enquirer. The book was published in England in 1956 under the title *God Protect Me From My Friends*, and in the United States as *Bandit*. It was translated into several other languages, and appeared in Italy in 1957 as *Dagli Amici mi Guardi Iddio*, the exact Sicilian equivalent of the English title. It was also serialized on the front page of the Italian national daily newspaper *Il Tempo*. As a result of the Italian publications a certain Signor Bernardo Matarella, at that time the Rome Secretary of State for Post and Telecommunications, instituted criminal libel proceedings against myself and my Italian publisher in Italy. After the customary and prolonged legal delays the case was heard in Milan. I found it impossible to follow the proceedings but at all events I lost the case. I was sentenced to eight months in prison, and fined a substantial sum of money. I had this money in Italy, and so lost it, but from my prolonged researches I knew enough of the horrors and perils of Italian prisons to have remained in England throughout my trial, I only had to be certain not to set foot upon Italian soil, which included ship or aircraft, to avoid arrest. I had one bad moment aboard a French airliner when, owing to some minor engine trouble, it landed unexpectedly at Rome airport, but the passengers were allowed to remain on board, and though I passed a very worried half hour I was safe.

The Italian publisher, co-defendant with myself, was dismissed from the case on a plea that he personally had not read the book his firm had published. The whole trial and sentence caused great sensation in Italy—mainly because of the mystery surrounding Giuliano's strange death—and it was front page news for the majority of daily papers. In 1959 there was an amnesty for "political prisoners', and I was free to return to Italy. I did so, but briefly, and with a beard, for by that time I was aware of enemies more dangerous than the law. The beard was less helpful than I had hoped. With its aid and that of dark glasses I made my way to a trattoria which had once been an habitual haunt and ordered some pasta. The owner made no sign of recognition, but he disappeared for a long time. He had not, in fact, re-appeared, when two carabinieri entered and approached my table. One of them said, '*Il Capitano Inglese, il Maxwell?*' I was all ready for the game; I said, 'My name is Maxwell, but I was a colonel for a few days; anyway I'm a real major.' 'Roll up your sleeves, please.' My passport has written under the heading 'distinguishing marks' 'birthmarks right forearm'. There are five large strawberry marks, and it would take major surgery to remove them. I rolled up both sleeves and put my arms on the table, but I was not quite prepared for what followed. I was handcuffed in less time than it would take to say any of the fearful oaths I know in any language. It is an undignified position to be in wherever you may happen to be, and some tourists had just come into the trattoria. I put my hands under the table and tried to seem as if I were studying the menu. I said, 'You're making fools of yourselves—I'm under amnesty, and there are no charges against me. You'd better go and check with headquarters before this becomes a scandal.' One of the carabinieri was dominant and aggressive, the other a novice and uncertain. The dominant one said to the other, 'Wait here and watch the prisoner. I shall return.' I asked my gaoler if I could have a newspaper on the table so that I could appear to be reading, and he complied politely. At the end of twenty minutes his boss came back, unlocked my handcuffs, and said, 'The English could never take a joke.' I said, 'I don't like Sicilian police jokes', and he replied, having ordered drinks for all three of us, 'It's not *us* you have to worry about—it's *them*. *They* don't like you here, and they know you're here now—

my fault. If I were you I'd get out—quick.' I am a coward, and I did.

The original episode appeared to be over, but it was not. In February 1965, nine years after the first appearance of the book, and eight years after the Matarella trial, a certain Prince Gianfranco Alliata of Montereale brought an action against me in the Queen's Bench Division in London, briefing a famous Q.C. He explained that the delay in instituting proceedings had been due to the fact that he had never read the book in Italian, nor the newspaper serialization; the first he had known of it was when he was shown a copy of the English edition in the U.S.A. The distinction is important, because it enabled him to bring an action against me in England rather than in the U.S.A.

His claim against me and my British publishers was for damages for libel. No one, as far as I know, had much doubt beforehand about our winning this case; the passages particularly complained of were not my views at all but were quotations from evidence (later discredited) given at the Viterbo trial of Giuliano's men, and would thus be held to be privileged. The hearing was protracted and extremely costly, and we lost it. The judge ruled that whereas a fair and accurate report of proceedings at a British trial was privileged, this principle did not necessarily extend to trials in other countries; nor did my account amount to a 'report'.

The whole trial was to me a sort of nightmare; I found it difficult to believe what was happening. However, I have now before me the report in *The Times* of the hearing to assure me that I have not misremembered.

He [Prince Alliata] had not proceeded against the . . . publishers of the Italian edition of *God Protect me from my Friends* because another person mentioned in the passages complained of, Signor Matarella—a Minister —had brought an action and had succeeded. This action had been reported in the Italian newspapers, and he [the witness] thought that it would be superfluous on his part to bring an action.

And then, after four questions and answers concerning the extent of damage to the Prince's reputation:

The witness [Prince Alliata] agreed that between 1956 and 1960 nobody had drawn his attention to the book.

There may have been linguistic confusion here since Prince Alliata was testifying through an interpreter. The Matarella trial had taken place in 1958.

I began to suffer an acute sense of unreality, doubting my ability to add up even a number of years that would fit on to the fingers of one hand; this did not increase my own coherence in the witness box. The work I had done was all so long ago that the most exact reply to most questions put to me would have been, 'I do not remember.'

He [myself] was saying that the book was not concerned to emphasize certain sensational features of the Viterbo trial. He had cut the description [of a horrific poisoning] down to three or four lines; the man had screamed for twenty minutes, and he could be heard outside the prison.

Later the question was raised of a potential witness at the Viterbo trial having paid a large sum of money not to be called in evidence at that trial.

COUNSEL: Do you believe that?—I apparently did believe it at the time.
Do you believe it?—No.
The witness [myself] said that that did not imply that —— had anything to hide. If he [witness] had 50m. lire he would certainly have paid it to be kept out of the trial. [*This I would have done—potential witnesses in that and similar trials tended to be short-lived and died unpleasantly.*]
HIS LORDSHIP: Do you realize what you are saying!

Counsel later asked me what was the purpose of a reference to Prince Alliata.

HIS LORDSHIP: To blacken his character, is that not right?
WITNESS: No. That is not correct.

And so it dragged on day after day. Soon I felt that I was not enjoying the Judge's sympathy and after a while that I had lost the jury's too. There were occasional moments of farce:

Mr Hirst [my Counsel] asked whether he might mention a matter not at issue between counsel. He had been asked by *The Times* reporter to point out that, in the report of yesterday's proceedings, by an unfortunate mishearing of a phrase of Mr Maxwell's evidence, the phrase 'General Luca'—this had been checked with the shorthand writer's note—became unhappily transmuted, the word 'General' into 'criminal'. He [Counsel] had been asked to make it clear that the reference was to General Luca.

His Lordship—Thank you very much.

On 20 February, the seventh day of the hearing, His Lordship ruled that 'the words were not published on an occasion of qualified privilege'. In layman's language that meant that my assumption that I could not be successfully sued for quoting words given in evidence at the Viterbo trial was false. According to Mr Justice Glyn-Jones, while this defence was available in respect of other reports of English trials, it did not always apply to reports of foreign trials—and my account of the Viterbo trial was in any event not, in legal terms, a 'report' of it. At last came His Lordship's summing up.

His Lordship, addressing the jury, said that each counsel had said that he might have formed a view about the case and, if he had, that view might, as Mr Hirst said, peep out when his Lordship addressed the jury. In his Lordship's view a judge could hardly help forming a view as he sat and listened to a case, and he was entitled to tell the jury what it was. . . . As so much of the evidence was really devoted to the issue of privilege and also the plaintiff's reply alleging malice, his Lordship would tell the jury why he had ruled that publication was not an occasion of privilege.

It had been the law for a very long time that we were all interested in judicial proceedings in this country, and, therefore, a fair and accurate report might be published in the public interest. If, in the course of evidence, somebody said something defamatory about somebody else, then the person defamed must, unfortunately, put up with it. That principle, however, did not extend to reports of trials in foreign countries. It was only some foreign trials that were thought to be of sufficient interest to us here in which publication might be said to be an occasion of qualified privilege: where, for example, the trial was of a British subject, or the proceedings were such that a report of them ought to be published here. . . .*

And yet the world press had published more than three million words about Giuliano. Clearly, I thought, an island must remain insular in his Lordship's view of the law; also I seriously believe that he would have testified at the Viterbo trial in all innocence and integrity, and that his own death would have come as a great surprise to him—if he had had time to consider the matter at all.

There only remained the amount of damages. 'His Lordship was not allowed to suggest any figure. Some people thought that a pity because it might be of help to suggest, within wide limits, an appropriate amount, because the jury were not bound by what the judge said.' I remember at this point the same curious feeling of loss of *sequitur*—this, to me, made as little sense as the dates involved.

The jury, after a little under two hours' absence, awarded Alliata £400. Our side had paid into court £325—we were thus liable for the costs of both sides. Total costs approached five figures; I walked out of court knowing that it would be years, if ever, before I could pay my share. I hope I shall meet his Lordship in an after life—if we are heading in the same direction

The events may be as confusing to the reader as they were to me. As a recapitulation, the jury had awarded Alliata only £400 damages, but this was £75 more than our side had paid into court, and under the rules of that curious chess-like game that is British libel law this meant that we were responsible for all costs—costs that were completely crippling to me.

Within a few weeks of the Alliata trial my mother died, after a protracted and distressing illness. When I returned to Camusfeàrna in April it was with a feeling of deep foreboding. It would have been better if I had paid greater heed to this and closed Camusfeàrna then, but the desire to resist and to fight against misfortune

* *Gatley on Libel*, 6th edition, 1967, makes numerous references to this case, and notes 'no privilege for publication of interest to students of history'.

was still strong in me—accentuated by indignation at the course which the Alliata trial had taken.

There was only one encouragement, and it was brief. The wild grey geese came back to Camusfeàrna for the last time. Year after year, since we had brought a brood of unfledged goslings from the diminished flock on the great loch at Monreith, these and their progeny had been wont to return to us in the late spring; having wintered, miraculously unscathed by human hand, in some southerly region unknown to us.

Their origins went far back in my life, to the days before the war, when I had built up at Monreith a collection of the wild geese of the world; when Snow geese from North America and Bar-headed geese from Tibet grazed the grassy slope below the old castle and the garden itself held exotic rarities. There had been the little Lesser Whitefronts that I had myself brought back from Lapland the last summer before the war; they would answer to their names with a shrill clamour that reminded me of the vast tundra and of the shine of still lake water under the midnight sun, of the sour tang of reindeer grease and the smell of trout cooking over a camp fire.

There had been a Cape Barren Goose, I remember, who would walk in through the open French windows of the library and squat in front of the fire, her delicate dove-grey argus-eyed plumage quivering with contentment, and at the hour of the evening flight the air would be full of the wild wings and the desolate music of the Greylags and the Snow geese from the loch. During the war, when all good grain was needed for human consumption, there had been terrible mortality among the rarer species, nearly half of their number dying in twenty-four hours of aspergilosis caused by a consignment of mouldy wheat. Despite this disaster, mine had been the only collection in Europe to survive the war somehow, and it was thus, though somewhat depleted, unique. By then I had transferred myself to the North West of Scotland, and Peter Scott had decided upon Slimbridge as the perfect site for what is now the world famous Wildfowl Trust. He had acquired the site, but there were no very obvious means of acquiring quickly anything but the British-wintering species of wild geese to stock it. He came to Monreith and found some twenty species still surviving, three-quarters of them the sole representatives of their race upon the European continent. It would have been hard to resist his eagerness even if I had had any real reason for refusal, which I had not. So they went to Slimbridge—all, that is to say, but for the flock of full-winged breeding Greylags, the descendants by many generations of birds that I had wing-tipped on Wigtown Bay in the days when I was an ardent wildfowler.

So the Greylags were left, and they bred about the loch shore and on the island until the numbers which were grazing the agricultural land of the estate drew adverse attention. At times there were more than a hundred, though the flock may have been augmented by truly wild birds wintering on the estuary of the Cree and the Bladnoch rivers. Their fate, in any case, was the same; they were treated as vermin, and their comparative tameness made their destruction the easier. By the time that I brought the brood of unfledged goslings to Camusfeàrna there were only four breeding pairs left on the loch at Monreith, and now there are none.

In due course the Greylags began to breed at Camusfeàrna, always on the little reedy lochan a mile above us, across the road from Druimfiaclach. Morag MacKinnon used to feed them and make much of them; she had names for them all, even when the original five had increased to thirteen. That was the highest number they ever reached; not only because there were always more geese than ganders, resulting in a proportion of infertile eggs, but because there was never a spring in which the whole flock returned from their unknown wintering haunt, and once we had to bring a fresh brood from Monreith to prevent our stock dying out. Some must inevitably have been shot; others, perhaps, remained with the flocks that had adopted them, and flew north in the spring to breed in the wild laval mountains of Iceland.

We had become used to wait for their return to Camusfeàrna late in April or in May. It was always a dramatic event; someone, while we were about our usual tasks either in or outside the house, would suddenly call, 'I hear geese!', and we would gather together searching the sky for confirmation. Then the sound would come again, the wild, haunting call that seems to hold within it the image of vast windswept spaces, mountain and salt marsh and limitless sky, the very utterance of the north and of untamed places; a lone voice first, like a bugle on a falling cadence, then joined by others in a tumbling cascade of silver trumpets, and the small flock would come into focus still high and far off but with wings set for the long spiral glide down to the greensward of Camusfeàrna. Then they would circle the field low over the house, the great wings audibly fraying the air each time they passed; and at last with a great flurry of pinions beating as the flock braked steeply to alight, they stood again before our door, as unafraid as if they had never encountered a human hunter. One of us would go to the kitchen to bring them bread, and the old gander who was their leader, the one whom Morag used to call George, would ruffle out his plumage and advance towards us with his neck held low and parallel to the ground, setting up a great gabbling clamour before beginning to guzzle the bread from our hands.

It was thus that they returned for the last time in the late spring of 1965. We heard them far away, thin and clear at first, then fainter and buffeted by a stiff southerly breeze that drove before it big shapeless white clouds above an ink-dark sea beginning to break into a chop of short steep waves. The little flock of five passed high over Camusfeàrna, heading inland in a perfect V formation; they checked in answer to our call to them, but resumed and held their course, so that there was nothing but that brief hesitation in answer to our voices to tell us that these were the Camusfeàrna geese. They passed out of sight in the direction of Druimfiaclach; then, five minutes later, they came back in a single straight descent on stiff outstretched wings, slanting steeply down from the horizon hilltop above the house.

There were two ganders and three geese; the third goose, whom Morag had in previous years named Cinderella, was unpaired, and remained at some distance from the others; she had always been small and silly-looking. There was nothing to show that this was the last time the wild geese would ever come back to Camusfeàrna; but their epoch, which had been part of the idyll, was over.

George and his mate took up residence, as they had in previous years, on the lochan at Druimfiaclach, and from there they paid us irregular but almost daily visits. The other pair flew further inland and we assumed that they were nesting on one of the many hill lochs above us. We never saw them again. Cinderella stayed alone about the Camusfeàrna beaches, until one day we came upon her remains, eaten by a fox or a wildcat.

Then one day, visiting Druimfiaclach to collect stores (the cottage was now empty and shuttered, the MacKinnons gone) we saw that George had a broken wing. It trailed out from him on the water as he swam, and he tried constantly, both by its own helpless musculature and by his beak, to put it back into position. We carried a small fibre-glass dinghy up to the lochan, and approached him closely enough to assess the damage. It seemed a simple fracture of the ulna, caused, I thought, by striking the telegraph wires in a half light, and I thought it would heal by itself. But it meant that George could sire no goslings that year, for the act of copulation takes place in water and requires the use of both wings to maintain balance.

In fact his female did not even lay, and a few weeks later I was told that George was dead, his carcass floating near to the edge of the reeds. We went up and launched the fibre-glass dinghy again and recovered his body. The wing had set perfectly and he had been able to fly, but there were twenty pellets of No. 5 shot in his neck and that was that. The concentration of shot showed that he had been killed from very close range, and since he had no fear of men this was in no way surprising. His mate lingered about the lochan for a week; then she too disappeared, and no wild goose ever came back to Camusfeàrna again. With their absence something, for me mystic, had gone forever.

6

Isle Ornsay Lighthouse

The two lighthouses, which had been my main focus of attention in all leisure moments since I was crippled, had become my property by curious coincidence. Camusfeàrna itself stands on the mainland shore of the Sound of Sleat, and from it leads north-westward a mile-long chain of small islands, some grassy and some heathery; on the furthest out of these, the largest, is a minor lighthouse erected in 1909. There was no house attached to this; the light was operated by gas cylinder, and tended by the occupant of Camusfeàrna croft, a shepherd; for the work was far from being a full time job. When, before my arrival, Camusfeàrna had stood empty, the light had become the responsibility of Druimfiaclach, the cottage on the road a mile up the hillside. When I came to the place in 1948 the incumbent was Calum Murdo MacKinnon, who was also the local roadmender, and he held the post until he and his wife Morag left the district in 1965.

Three miles away, W.S.W. across the Sound of Sleat, is Isle

Ornsay Lighthouse, on the Isle of Skye; at night its signal, a double flash every seven seconds, were the only lights in sight from Camusfeàrna shore. This was a much larger lighthouse than the one on the Camusfeàrna island, built at the seaward extremity of a small green islet, and it possessed a big cottage to house two lighthouse keepers and their families. I had never landed at Ornsay Light, though one of the keepers was an acquaintance, for on calm evenings he would sometimes visit us after he had been fishing for mackerel. On one such still summer evening in 1963 when the peaceful evening light had lingered long on the hill-tops, he came in at dusk, bringing a present of fish, and as we sat in the kitchen living-room he said:

'I'm afraid this is the last dram I'll be taking with you—Ornsay Lighthouse is to be made fully automatic, and I'm being transferred to Ardnamurchan. I'll be sorry to leave; I'd got kind of fond of the place, but in our job you have to go where you're sent. Anyway, I'm glad it's not Hyskeir or any other one of those rocks where there isn't room to stretch your legs if you step outside the house. They say Ardnamurchan is not a bad place at all, and it's certainly an important one, being the most westerly point of the whole mainland of Scotland. Still, I'll miss Ornsay.'

I asked him what was going to happen to the house.

'Oh, the Northern Lighthouse Board will put it up for sale, no doubt, and it'll be a lucky man who gets it. They put a whole new roof on it a year or two back, and that cost them several thousand pounds. It's quite a big place too, built for two families, though I suppose anyone buying it would need to do a bit of alteration, because in a manner of speaking it's got two front doors and there's no connexion between the two halves of the house. There's a big walled garden, too, though we haven't done much with that for the last few years back, since tinned vegetables came into fashion.'

All this had touched off in me an immediate train of thought. I was a grace-and-favour tenant of Camusfeàrna, with no ultimate security of tenure; the terms of the lease stated specifically that there would be no compensation for improvements, and that at expiry the house must be left as I had found it. I had brought in the telephone and electric light—the latter at great cost—and during the time of my marriage a great deal of money had been spent in the way of extensions to the house: bathroom and sanitation (neither of which it had possessed before), deep-freezes, and other bulky and expensive electrical appliances. I had realized that if I were required to leave Camusfeàrna the removal of all these things by land would present insurmountable problems; they could only be taken out by sea, and even then only by a considerable number of journeys in *Polar Star*. All this added up to looking for an alternative cottage on the coast, and I had already found out that this simply did not exist. Isle Ornsay, only ten minutes distant from Camusfeàrna at *Polar Star*'s maximum speed, appeared an ideal insurance policy against possible future homelessness.

Anonymous enquiry to the Northern Lighthouse Board elicited three salient facts: that the prospective purchaser must meet with its approval; that the house would not necessarily go to the highest bidder; that, other factors being equal, preference would be given to someone who would also buy the houses of Kyleakin Lighthouse, eleven miles north of Camusfeàrna by sea. Kyleakin was a major lighthouse on a narrow shipping thoroughfare, connected by a causeway to a substantial hilly island of rock and heather in mid-channel between Skye and the mainland at Kyle of Lochalsh. The lighthouse keepers' cottage, also built for two families, stood high on this heathery island, with a fantastic view northwards to the Red Hills of Skye and southward right down Loch Duich to the hills called the Five Sisters of Kintail.

At that time my earned income was almost indecently large, so large that if for no other reason than fear of disbelief I shall not mention the sum. This strictly temporary affluence had not in any essential changed my way of life or thought, but it did mean that for those few short, foresightless and improvident years I just did not have to think about money at all. It is an interesting experience to have had once in a lifetime, even though the lack of foresight brought the disastrous consequences my *hubris* deserved. With this attitude of mind, which fully deserved the good Scots noun 'fecklessness', I should have bought the lighthouses even had the Northern Lighthouse Board asked me a considerably larger sum than they did.

Each had an entirely different atmosphere and character. I went first to see Isle Ornsay, with Jimmy Watt and Alan MacDiarmaid. We took *Polar Star* across from Camusfeàrna on an early summer's day so glorious that even a grim Glasgow slum in the Gorbals would have seemed transfigured. At *Polar Star*'s moorings the still air was full of the sound of nesting sea birds, the white wheeling wings of the gulls patterning a blue and cloudless sky; the slender terns, the sea-swallows, with their dancing, ballet-like flight, screaming their disapproval of human intrusion in a series of swirling sallies from their breeding rock a hundred yards away. A big bull Atlantic seal showed his head above the smooth surface a stone's throw distant, stared, and submerged with a heavy splash. An eider duck and her brood of fluffy ducklings made a pattern of spreading ripples on the clear shiny water, and there were black and white oystercatchers with their brilliant red beaks piping from the weed-covered rocks at the sea's edge. All this was the essence of Camusfeàrna as I had known it in the early days of the idyll, before the clouds formed and the storm broke, before the days of disaster and diminished vision.

We found that it took twelve-and-a-half minutes to reach Isle Ornsay Lighthouse, keeping *Polar Star* at a high cruising speed but not at her maximum. We timed this carefully because with the engines burning nine gallons of diesel fuel an hour we wanted to estimate probable future expenses. We went to anchor a few hundred yards north-east of the lighthouse and rowed ashore in the dinghy. The lighthouse, the cottage and the walled garden, all dazzlingly white-washed, stood on a small, rocky, tidal islet, the very green grass grazed down to lawn length by Black-faced sheep and their bleating lambs. We drew the dinghy up at a little concrete slipway, and began to walk up the short steep grass slope to the house; a sandpiper flew twittering from her nest of four eggs a yard from the pathway, and stood bobbing on a stone.

I had lived in the West Highlands and Islands for many years by then, but never, except perhaps at my very first sight of Camusfeàrna sixteen years before, had any view affected me as strongly as the splendour and purity of the immense panorama spread before the islet. Looking eastward, directly across the Sound of Sleat, one could see far up Loch Hourn, its entrance guarded on the northerly side by the mighty conical peak of Ben Sgriol that rose behind Camusfeàrna, a vast scree slope plunging more than three thousand feet from its pinnacle into the sea, diminishing to doll size the tiny houses at its foot. On the southern side of Loch Hourn rose the great hills of Knoydart, Ladhar Bheinn, Ben Ghuiserein and Sgurr na Coire Choinneachain, huge and mysterious in the haze of summer heat; further to the south the huddled houses of Mallaig made a faint white blurr above miles of sea as smooth as pale blue satin. Beyond Mallaig, dim in the still blue distance, was the point of Ardnamurchan. To the north of Loch Hourn, Camusfeàrna Lighthouse looked tiny and insignificant on its island that seemed no more than a promontory, dwarfed like all else by the vastness of the hills that formed its back-cloth.

It was as though I had found Camusfeàrna once again, the same sense of sudden freedom and elation, the same shedding of past mistakes and their perennial repercussions. Here, it seemed to me, where the rocks and the white stone buildings were the only solid things in a limitless bubble of blue water and blue air, one might be able to live at peace again, to recover a true vision long lost by now in the lives of other humans and in the strifes of far countries; here one might set back the clock and re-enter Eden.

Alan looked around him over the sea and the hills and the open sky and said, 'To think I've lived all my life just across there on the mainland and seen Isle Ornsay light flashing and never knew that this paradise was just across the Sound! Look, you've got another colony of terns on a rock a hundred yards away, and no big gulls to bother them. And seals too—just look at their heads coming up round the *Polar Star*. And if you wanted to have the otters here— look at that walled garden—plenty of space, and not even Monday could get out of that. This is a paradise right enough!'

It seemed paradise indeed; I did not know, though I was already in middle age, that you cannot buy paradise, for it disintegrates at the touch of money, and it is not composed solely of scenery. It is made of what many of us will never touch in a lifetime, and having touched it once there can be no second spring, no encore after the curtain falls. This is the core of our condition, that we do not know why nor at what point we squandered our heritage; we only know, too late always, that it cannot be recovered or restored. I did not know it then; this was paradise, and I was going to buy it for hard cash. But Isle Ornsay had no rowan tree, no guardian, only the four wild winds of heaven, no shelter. 'She had put her hands upon the trunk of the rowan tree and with all the strength of her spirit she had cursed me, saying, "Let him suffer here as I am suffering." Then she had left, up over the bleak hillside.' I had not known this when I bought Isle Ornsay, all unprotected, and if I had known I should not have been much disturbed.

> Because I see these mountains they are brought low,
> Because I drink these waters they are bitter,
> Because I tread these black rocks they are barren,
> Because I have found these islands they are lost;
> Upon seal and seabird dreaming their innocent world
> My shadow has fallen.

I remember the very first time that I ever landed at Isle Ornsay, and the first time that I was aware of the place other than as a lighthouse, twenty-four years ago as I write now. I had bought the Island of Soay and was preparing to start there the shark fishing industry which I believed would solve the problems of the island's small and isolated community. The factory, with its pier and slipway for hauling by steampower ten-ton carcasses on to a flensing yard like that of a whaling station, its oil-extraction units and fish meal plants and glue tanks, its salting vats and laboratory and all the other costly follies, consisted still of plans on paper; and in those days, at the war's end, all kinds of equipment were difficult or impossible to come by. I landed at Isle Ornsay village from my little thirty-foot lobster boat the *Gannet*, that gallant little craft that after the Island of Soay Shark Fisheries Ltd became fact rather than fantasy was the most successful harpoon-gun boat of them all, and killed nearly two hundred sharks of almost her own length. Isle Ornsay was a dead place by then, a few scattered cottages, the mansion house ruined and nettle-grown, the pier in need of repair; there was little enough to tell a visitor that this had once been a prosperous place; indeed I did not know myself that it had been a great port crowded with ships, the industrial centre of Skye and all the adjacent mainland coast.

Soon after I had landed, my predatory eye was caught by a large rusty hand winch standing near the head of the pier. I went over and examined it; it was intact though obviously in long disuse, and a little probing with a knife showed that the rust was not too deep for the winch to be restored as a functional item. At Soay I should need many winches, large and small, ranging from huge steam-driven things to little toys like this one. I looked around me for some sign of human life, and saw a middle-aged man in tattered oilskins sitting on the ground with his back against a wall. He was smoking a pipe and eyeing me with some curiosity; strange visitors to Isle Ornsay must have been a great rarity in those days of fuel restrictions and disrupted communications.

I went over to him and asked him if he knew to whom the winch belonged. He looked me up and down speculatively, without moving or taking the pipe from his mouth. Clearly I presented a problem; though I was dressed in a torn seaman's jersey and dirty old canvas trousers and had several days' stubble on my face, my voice must have told him that I wasn't a fisherman as he understood the term. Few West Highlanders will ever give a direct reply to a question as it is first put to them, any more than an Arab merchant will give the final price of his wares on first demand. Fact is something to be approached circuitously or tangentially, to go straight to the heart of the matter would be clumsy and unrefined. In this case my question about the winch had anyway to be subsidiary to his own as yet unspoken question as to my identity. So he looked me up and down from untidy head to shabby, patched rubber-booted toe and back up again, and then said, 'You'll be a scrap merchant?'

I said I wasn't a scrap merchant. I didn't want to elaborate, to tell him that I was the man who had bought Soay and whose projects for it had been widely reported in the newspapers, because if he chanced to be the owner of the winch this knowledge would send the price soaring. So I said I just happened to need a winch like this one, and could he tell me who it belonged to. After a long pause, and with patent mistrust, he replied, 'There hasn't been a scrap man here for a long time. There's some old iron lying near the beach in Camuscross down there, but I couldn't rightly say who owns it. It's been there as long as I can remember

—but it wouldn't be easy to shift. The half of it's bedded down in that black mud, and you couldn't get your boat in there except at high springs, and then the iron would be under water. Ay, it would be a problem right enough.'

I gave up, and wandered away to explore the ruins of the mansion house. Early seventeenth century, I thought, with later additions; it must once have been magnificent, with a high-walled garden stretching away behind it, and a real curiosity of a lavatory —a beautiful little stone structure built on the rocks directly above the sea, so that no drainage system was necessary.

Unfortunately I found, among the nettles that flanked the old gateway to the mansion house, a pile of lorry tyres—another thing that it was difficult to obtain in those days, and which I badly needed as boat fenders for the big Stornaway drifter I had bought, the *Dove*. With resolution but not without misgiving I went back to the man with the pipe, who watched my approach out of the corner of his eye, without turning his head. I asked, diffident but defiant, about the tyres. He took his pipe from his mouth and looked me straight in the eye. At length he said:

'It is a scrap merchant you will be.' This time it was an order, not a statement; it sounded like an army directive.

I left Isle Ornsay empty-handed; the winch and the tyres were still there, in exactly the same positions, when I bought Isle Ornsay Lighthouse cottage just twenty years later. But by then the winch was rusted away, and I had no use for the tyres.

It was between Isle Ornsay Lighthouse and Camusfeàrna, too, without knowing that I should ever have any connection with either, that I had my very first encounter with a shark, an incident that in retrospect seems to have led slowly but inexorably to my tenure of both. I wrote of this incident in *Harpoon at a Venture*, my story of the shark fishery, when it was still fresh and focused in my memory; now it and many other once clear images are like the trunks of great trees where lovers long ago have carved their names with Cupid's sign, but where round the initialled hearts the bark has split and blurred the lettering to anonymity. But it was from this first encounter that the Shark Fisheries grew; it was the Shark

Fisheries that brought me to Camusfeàrna, and Camusfeàrna that led me back to Isle Ornsay after so many years.

I had with me a Morar man, who looked after the boat for me; 'Foxy' he was called, both by his friends and his enemies.

We were returning from Glenelg; it was late afternoon, the sky paling, and the hills turning to deep plum, their edges sharp and hard, as though cut from cardboard. We were about a mile off Isle Ornsay Lighthouse, heading southward over still, pale sea, when I noticed something breaking the surface thirty yards from the boat. At first it was no more than a ripple with a dark centre. The centre became a small triangle, black and shiny, with a slight forward movement, leaving a light wake in the still water. The triangle grew until I was looking at a huge fin, a yard high and as long at the base. It seemed monstrous, this great black sail, the only visible thing upon limitless miles of pallid water. A few seconds later the notched tip of a second fin appeared some twenty feet astern of the first, moving in a leisurely way from side to side.

It was some seconds before my brain would acknowledge that these two fins must belong to the same creature. The impact of this realization was tremendous and indescribable: a muddle of excitement in which fear and a sort of exultation were uppermost, as though this were a moment for which I had been unconsciously waiting for a long time.

I could only guess at what was beneath the surface. In common with the great majority whose lives have not been lived in fishing-boats, I had no idea what Basking Sharks looked like. Once, years before, I had seen them from the road bordering Loch Fyne, three great black sails cruising in line ahead—heavy with the menace of boys' adventure stories and ship-wrecked sailors adrift in the Caribbean. I knew nothing of them, their size or their habits; to me all sharks were man-eaters. That was my state of knowledge as I looked at those two fins and guessed wildly at what must lie below them.

Foxy's knowledge, though not encyclopaedic, was less sketchy than my own. He knew the name by which the fishermen called them— 'muldoan', 'sailfish', 'sunfish', and the Gaelic name *cearbhan*; he knew that they played havoc with the herring-nets; that their livers contained large quantities of valuable oil; that they were immensely powerful and could damage small boats; that long ago the people of the Islands used to harpoon them from massed formations of small boats, to get a winter's supply of lamp-oil. He assumed that they fed upon the herring-shoals, because they were usually to be found where the herring were.

All this he told me as we closed in to the fish. I scrambled up on to the foredeck and stood in the bows, hoping to see clearly what lay below the surface.

The first Basking Shark of which one has a clear and entire view is terrifying. One may speak glibly of fish twenty, thirty, forty feet long, but until one looks down upon a living adult Basking Shark in clear water, the figures are meaningless and without implication. The bulk appears simply unbelievable. It is not possible to think of what one is looking at as a fish. It is longer than a London bus; it does not have scales like an ordinary fish; its movements are gigantic, ponderous, and unfamiliar; it seems a creature from a prehistoric world, of which the first sight is as unexpected, and in some way as shocking, as that of a dinosaur or iguanodon would be.

At ten yards I could make out a shadow below the surface; at five, as Foxy slipped the engine into neutral, I could see the whole form clear in transparent water. The body was brown, with irregular python markings upon it, a vast barrel that seemed to get steadily wider towards the incredibly distant head. The head was perhaps the most unexpected thing of all. The gills were by far the widest part, frill-like and gigantically distended, like a salamander's or a Komodo Dragon's. The upper jaw was a snout, the tip of which was now breaking the surface; the mouth was held wide open, and a child could have walked upright into that whitish cavern. As we began to sheer off, our wash slapped across the dorsal fin, and the shark submerged with a slight flurry of water about his tail.

Mounted in the bows of the *Gannet* was a Breda light machine-gun, which I carried to shoot up drifting mines, and also in the rather ridiculous hope of engaging a U-boat, since they had been sighted as near as Eigg. A Danish seaman had told me that a small launch, accurately handling a light machine-gun, could permanently damage the periscope and also command the conning-tower if a U-boat surfaced, since it would be unlikely to waste a torpedo on so insignificant a target.

Foxy said, 'Try him with the gun, Major.'

When I had finished loading two extra magazines, the fin had reappeared, apparently stationary, and within a stone's throw.

We circled it widely and approached from astern—the technique we later used for harpooning. I waited until the fin was abreast of me and not much more than a yard away; the boat was almost scraping the shark's side. I fired thirty rounds in a single burst, straight into the huge expanse of his flank, and saw a mass of small white marks spring out on the brown surface. A great undulating movement seemed to surge through him, and near the stern of the boat his tail shot clear of the water. Its width was a man's height; it lashed outward away from the boat and returned, missing Foxy's head by inches, to land with a tremendous slam upon the gunwale of the stern cockpit. It swung backward and hit the sea, flinging up a fountain of water that drenched us to the skin.

He was back on the surface in less than a minute. Six times we closed in; I had fired three hundred rounds into what was now a broad white target on his side. At the last burst he sank in a great turmoil of water, and it was ten minutes before the fin surfaced again. Now it seemed to me as though he was wallowing and out of control, the fin lying at an acute angle. I thought that he was mortally wounded, if not actually dead.

Foxy suggested that we should try to make fast to the fin with the *Gannet's* boat-hook. He stood up on the foredeck, and I steered him as close to the fish as I could. I felt the bows bump against the shark's body; then Foxy took a tremendous swipe with the full force of eighteen stone. I could see the hook bite deep into the base of the apparently helplessly rolling fin. There was just time for Foxy's triumphant shout of 'Got the b——,' then the boat-hook was torn from his hands, and those gorilla-like arms were waving wildly in a frantic effort to keep balance, as shark and boat-hook disappeared in a boil of white water.

After the next encounter—quite suddenly—without, I think, any conscious build-up—I thought that here was the industry for Soay, the occupation I required, new and utterly absorbing.

It was just so that I thought of the lighthouses of Isle Ornsay and Kyleakin when I returned to Camusfeàrna as a cripple in 1965.

7

Kyleakin Lighthouse

We went next to inspect Kyleakin Lighthouse, in the same splendid summer weather of cumulus clouds and calm seas; up the cliff coast and past Glenelg village on our starboard side, on into the narrows at Kylerhea where the spring tides run at nine knots, past the mouth of Loch Duich and into Loch Alsh. Only at two points does the Island of Skye almost touch the mainland of Scotland, at Kylerhea and at Kyleakin, and Kyleakin is very much the narrower of the two channels. Here a chain of shaggy, heathery islands reaches out from the mainland, so that the last and highest of them, on whose rocks the lighthouse was built, almost closes the channel, leaving less than three hundred yards of water between it and a high rocky promontory of Skye where Kyleakin House stands upon the summit sheltered by a crown of trees.

We came up Loch Alsh leaving Kyle on the starboard side, dodged between the crossing ferry boats, and came in slowly to the southern side of the island, where between steep rocks there was a bay at the foot of the slope. Here a runway on the beach had been cleared of boulders, and at its shoreward end a small shed for an outboard engine showed pale against the dark heather. We anchored the *Polar Star* clear of the tide's current and rowed the dinghy ashore.

Every new island or islet upon which I have ever landed for the first time holds a mystery of its own, a feeling of discovery that is some small echo of the wonder and anticipation with which the early navigators set foot upon greater unknown shores.

The lighthouse itself is an imposing structure, seventy feet high, and connected to the mass of the island by a bridge. From the bridge a steep path leads up to where the joined cottages are perched high on the south-east-facing slope of the island.

Deeply though I had been impressed by Isle Ornsay, I felt drawn to Kyleakin as I had to few places in my life—and this despite its nearness to the summer tourist scene. I have since tried to analyse this feeling of profound attraction; at first I thought it might be due to nothing more complex than the fact that Camusfeàrna, with all its echoes of past unhappiness and loss, was out of sight. But I think now that it was a far call back to childhood, for the long, rough heather, the briars and the outcrops of bare rock might have been those surrounding The House of Elrig where I was born, the house that obsessed my childhood and adolescence and came to represent for me the only refuge in a frightening and unfamiliar world. The land surrounding Elrig was a wilderness in which the close-cropped green turf of Isle Ornsay would have found no place, but at Kyleakin I felt as if I were coming home. It was here, I decided, that I would live if ever I left Camusfeàrna.

Even in the early years after the war, when I first came to live at Camusfeàrna, both Kyleakin on Skye and Kyle of Lochalsh on the mainland shore—from which the mail for our district used to arrive by a thirty-foot motor launch in every wind and weather—were very quiet little places, and seemed to retain much of an earlier flavour. Though the crossing was the only car ferry to Skye (for the Glenelg-Kylerhea ferry was not renewed until 1963, and the Mallaig-Armadale service carrying many cars at a time did not come into being until 1965) there was little tourist traffic, and correspondingly few shops and hotels. Those that there were had for the most part a modest, old-world atmosphere; in Kyle of Lochalsh, for example, the Pioneer Stores—which is now a sort of miniature Marks and Spencers, essentially of this decade—was a dim little premises run by two elderly ladies, and it smelled of Harris tweed and tallow and such homely things; it had an indefinable personality of its own, like the Post Office in Glenelg, which sold cheese as well as postage stamps. The Marine Stores, less massively equipped than it is today, had a sort of nostalgic quality crystallized for me by a pair of bellows which I bought there in 1952. Bellows were a necessity at Camusfeàrna, and I had none. There seemed to be only one pair in the Marine Stores, and they were, I remember, hanging from the ceiling; they were sturdily constructed of beechwood and leather, and ornamented with brass studs. When I asked how much they were the proprietor unhooked them from the ceiling and looked for a price-tag. An expression of mild surprise crossed his face as he saw what was plainly written on the smooth white board of one side—four shillings. 'Four shillings,' he said; 'that's pre-war stock left over from the good old days. It takes a thing like that to remind one what they were like.'

If one drove from Camusfeàrna to Kyle, a distance of almost forty miles by roads that were then entirely single tracked, one would meet hardly another vehicle, even in summer, and if one did it would be, as often as not, a local car or a lorry carrying sheep or Forestry Commission timber. Just when all this changed, just when Skye and the mainland coastline became a great summer holiday resort thronged with cars and caravans I find it impossible to remember accurately, but now that stretch of road—mercifully widened for at least a small section of its length—often carries a nose-to-tail procession of cars for miles on end, and the Kyle sea frontage has been modified to contain vast car parks for tourists awaiting their turn on the ferry. (Before these were constructed the queue of stationary vehicles would occasionally stretch for a quarter of a mile or more inland.) New shops and new hotels had sprung up at Kyleakin to deal with new demands, and though it is still a small fishing port, with the emphasis upon prawns and lobsters, the atmosphere in summer is that of a village geared primarily to touristic requirements.

But the lighthouse island was untouched by these changes, and it seemed to me an enchanted place. I bought both lighthouses in October 1963. In the Deed of Sale of Ornsay I was curious to notice a specific clause excluding mineral rights in the land purchased. I knew that the rocks were of hornblende schist, and contained large garnets and other crystals, but that was not the reason for the clause; a far more precious metal underlies that rock. There was no mention of anything invisible at Kyleakin.

Before describing in detail the ghosts that seem indisputably to haunt Kyleakin Lighthouse island they must be shown in perspective, separated from the great host of their more dubious and debatable relations common to the whole area of the West Highlands and Islands.

Superstitions of every kind—witches, the evil-eye, omens, mermaids, fairies, kelpies (water horses), sacred waters, trees and stones—were at the very core of the Skye man's life. There were propitious days to begin a task (Monday was the most favourable) and disastrous days (Saturday was the worst). All action had if possible to follow the sun's course, and a boat putting to sea would initially row sunwise no matter what its real destination. Fishermen would ensure a heavy catch of herring by walking three times sunwise round a sacred stone. Crops were planted and harvested by the phases of the moon—the sowing on the wax and the reaping on the wane. A waxing moon was held to communicate power of growth, so that sheep-shearing, and even a human haircut, could only take place during this phase. Anything that must dry, such as wood, peat, hay or corn, was cut only on a waning moon, so that it could not be re-vitalized by the moon's strength.

Among the old people, and not a few of the younger, the world of the 'supernatural' is accepted as unquestioningly as the 'natural'. Until very recently the belief in witches was universal. A witch could take the form of an animal at will, usually that of a hare or a cat, but sometimes horses, cows, or even whales, and whereas she could be killed only by a silver bullet any injury inflicted upon her while in animal shape left corresponding marks when she resumed her human identity. A hare would be shot at and wounded, and the next day some old woman would be found to have gunshot wounds in her legs or arms.

Many of these stories from the district are very detailed; these are samples. A Kyleakin man was troubled by a cat that consistently raided his kitchen. He succeeded at last in catching it, and cut off one of its ears; soon afterwards it was discovered that a local woman had lost an ear, and for the rest of her life she had to wear a shawl over her head to hide her shame.

A fishing family suffered from the attentions of a small whale that constantly tore their nets and freed the fish. At length one of the boat's crew armed himself with a sharpened three-pronged potato fork and hurled this at the whale as its back showed passing the boat. The whale sounded and did not reappear. The next day a woman, already believed to be a witch, died in great agony, calling down curses upon the name of the fisherman. An examination of her dead body showed three terrible wounds in her side, corresponding to the prongs of the fork. The whale was never seen again.

Kelpies were held to inhabit many lochs; they waylaid maidens by night and carried them down into the cold deep, so that they were seen no more. Loch na Beiste (Loch of the Beast) at Kyleakin is said to contain a creature that some describe as having a head covered with a mane, while others who claim to have seen it refuse utterly to give any description whatsoever. Two fishermen in a rowing boat were almost submerged by an unknown animal which they described as about twenty feet long, as thick as a man's thigh, and with a maned neck. The carcass of some apparently unknown creature with a mane is said to have been found in the Boom Defence Net off Camusfeàrna Lighthouse island during the Second World War, but no scientist ever examined it, and it remains a story. However, we should perhaps remind ourselves that serious scientists are still looking for the Loch Ness Monster.

The mermaids of Skye, called in Gaelic Maighdean Mara (sea maiden) or Maighdean na Tuinne (maiden of the waves), seem to be less frustrating to the male sex than the rest of their kind; instead of remaining fish from the waist down they become wholly human after their capture. A Skye man caught one in his nets and took her home. She shed her tail at once, and, delighted with this co-operative metamorphosis, he hid it in the rafters of the barn, and made the most of what had replaced it. She lived with him many years, and bore him children. At length one of these, playing in the barn, chanced upon the tail, and came running to his mother to ask what it was. 'It's my tail!' she cried in wild delight, 'My long lost tail!' and without a backward look she hurried down to the sea with it and was never seen again.

Another, less amiable mermaid, was captured in different circumstances. An old boat-builder who worked on the shore near a cave found that every morning the work he had done the previous day had been maliciously undone during the night. At length he decided to hide himself near to the boat he was building and catch the destroyer red-handed. He was watching landward, but it was from the sea that the wrecker came at midnight, and it was the sound of her tail slithering over the wet stones of the beach that drew his attention. He watched as she began to undo his labours; then he crept up on her stealthily, and after a brief struggle he overpowered her. He demanded to know why she should want to harm him when he had done her no hurt, and she replied that she had felt compelled to do so because he did not at the close of each day bless the work he had done, and that by neglecting to do this he was endangering the lives of all who would sail in the vessel after it put to sea. 'But if you will let me keep my tail and set me free,' she said, 'no boat that you put a single nail into will ever sink or cause a man to be drowned, and this I swear to you.' He carried her down to the sea and watched her disappear into the waves. When he told his story boats came to him from far and wide so that he might set a single nail in the hull and thus come under the mermaid's oath of protection. But one owner of a new boat sent for the boat-builder, to save the tedium of a long voyage, and the boat-builder was unable to leave his work. The unblessed boat suffered disaster after disaster, and many of her crew were drowned before her owner decided that she was cursed, and took her ashore. He did not think, however, to remove the bung, and slowly the hull filled with rain water to the gunwales. She remained as deadly ashore as she had been at sea, for two small children at play fell into her and were drowned. Thereafter she was smashed and her wood burned, for it was held that the mermaid had cursed the boat and that her curse was as potent as her blessing.

A local laird became worried over the apparently failing health of his young man-servant, who had rapidly grown so weak that he could hardly carry out his daily duties. He refused explanation or examination by a doctor, until, at the edge of collapse, he sobbed out his story to his master. He was possessed, he said, by a witch. Every night she would come into his quarters outside the big house; she would put a rope halter around his neck, murmur an incantation which he now knew by heart, and change him into a horse. Then all through the night she would ride him at tremendous speed through the air; often they went to Norway, and sometimes to Spain. At morning, when she returned him to the house and restored his human shape, he was too exhausted to work; it was, he said, weeks since he had slept. The laird deliberated long, and then asked his servant if he was quite certain that he knew accurately the words of the incantation. Assured of this, he said, 'With her own words, then, you can defeat her. When she comes to you tonight you will have a rope halter ready, and before she can do anything you will throw it over her neck and recite those words. This, I think, will change her into a mare. Early in the morning you will take her to the smithy and have her shod. Then you will recite the words that she uses to make you human again. The horseshoes or the marks of them will remain upon her, and we shall know who she is.' All these things the servant did. The next morning the laird's wife was screaming in terrible pain and would not leave her bed. Her husband sent for a doctor, who found that to her hands and her feet were nailed bright new horseshoes, and she died from loss of blood before they could be removed. The Freudian significance of this tale needs no underlining.

Most Skye men would laugh at such stories now, but I think there are few who would deny absolutely the existence of 'second sight', whose possessor is able, often most unwillingly, to see into the future—not all the future, but isolated happenings usually of a calamitous nature. A possessor of this ability is feared, but also fears his or her own powers, so that a ritual of exorcism was devised; at the very first vision the seer must recount all that he saw to an intimate friend who meanwhile holds a Bible before his face and turns the pages rapidly. However open a mind one may try to keep as to the possibility of 'second sight', the credibility of this as a remedy must rank with the mermaid's tail.

Whatever is foreseen, the image is said always to be of great detail, never a blurred impression. Often it is a funeral, and the face of every mourner is recognisable, together with knowledge of the time and the place; sometimes it is a photoflash, but of equal intensity and shock. One Skye woman, drinking a cup of tea with neighbours, suddenly fainted. When she was again conscious she at first refused any explanation, but under pressure she whispered that she had had a sudden and instant vision of the corpse of a boy whom she had seen ploughing in a nearby field. The boy died by drowning within a week.

A whole volume could be filled with such tales; they vary little, and for the most part concern simply the prophetic vision and its fulfilment.

Apart from the specific gift, or curse, of the 'second sight' any unexplained phenomenon is held to *presage* some event that is yet to come; the very opposite, if one may put it that way, of the more familiar European conception that a house is haunted by humans or happenings belonging to the past. The following are strictly local examples.

Two men were sitting talking in a shed on Kyleakin pier when from outside came the sound of a splintering crash as of two boats in collision. They ran out, but found nothing to explain the noise, nor had anyone else heard it. A few days later an old and partially deaf fisherman, an octogenarian, had his launch at anchor in the narrows, hand-lining mackerel, and failed to hear the approach of the MacBrayne Stornoway-to-Kyle steamer, the *Loch Ness*. When he turned and saw her bows towering over him he knew that he could do nothing, for he was too late to get his anchor up; he stood and waited without flinching. Just before the impact a rope was thrown to him from the forepeak of the *Loch Ness*, and as he caught it his boat was literally sliced in two. Old as he was he contrived to cling on to the life line for many minutes before he was finally hauled aboard, and his life was saved. It was accepted as being entirely natural that the sound of the collision should have been audible days before to anyone attuned to hear it.

For some years the people of Kyleakin were puzzled by what appeared to be a mast-head light on the mainland side of the narrows, opposite to the Station Hotel and off the Kyle of Lochalsh pier—for there was reported never to be a boat about the place when the light was seen. Then the 'explanation' took place; a large boat was reversing out from the pier when a south-going fishing smack came into full collision amidships. Of the crew of the smaller craft one only was a powerful swimmer. For a long time he struggled to keep his companions afloat, swimming to each in turn and tying to him an empty paraffin drum, and at length all but he gained the shore. No trace of him was found until, three months later, his body was brought to the surface by the churn of a big ship's propellers. But the strange light was never seen again, and its mystery was considered solved.

Lights play a major role in the superstitious lore. The old people believed that to see an unexplained light near to a house foretold a death in its family, and if there was no dwelling nearby the light marked a future wayside 'resting place' of a coffin on some long journey from the death bed to the graveyard. The coffin-bearers and the funeral party would have often to trudge many, many miles to the place of burial, and at each halting place, where they would refresh themselves with food and funeral whisky, they were accustomed to build a small cairn of stones; lights, it seems, appeared with pin-point accuracy at the sites of these cairns long before they were built. A modern sceptical Skye man remarked to me that he would not be surprised if a beacon were to appear if anyone struck a match near to one of these cairns now, as owing to the enormous quantity of whisky consumed at each resting place the very air above them must remain inflammable.

An irresistible story concerning lights, modern and fully authenticated, tells of how a doctor was called out at night to attend a confinement in a remote croft that had no electricity. The doctor got together all that was necessary, including a very powerful electric torch, and was greeted by the elderly husband, who showed him into the dim room lit by a single oil lamp. When instruments and basins had been arranged to the doctor's satisfaction he turned to the husband and said, 'Now you hold this torch steadily so that I can see what I'm doing properly.' In due course he delivered a baby, and when it had been washed and swaddled, he said, 'Leave the baby there just now and hold the torch for me again.' After a moment or two he looked up and said, 'Do you know, you're going to be the proud father of twins—there's another one on the way! Now just keep that light steady—that's all you've got to do.' After a while the second baby lay swaddled beside its twin, and the doctor said, 'Well now, that's a great thing, two fine boys. Now we must do a bit of tidying up, and try to make your wife comfortable. Hold the light steady again.' The husband looked at the twins with distaste, and raised the torch again. Some minutes passed, and then the doctor straightened up and said, 'I didn't like to say so until I was certain, but it's not twins you have but triplets. There's still another one to come yet—just hold that light quite steady now.' Suddenly the torch was extinguished, and the husband's arm fell to his side. The doctor exclaimed, 'What's the matter, man? How do you think I can see to work without light? Just hold that torch steady for me, as you did before.' The husband did not move, and the doctor repeated impatiently, 'Come on now, and be quick about it—hold the torch so that I can see what I'm doing.' The reply was gruff, firm, and with a deep note of resentment, 'I will do no such thing, doctor! *Cannot you see that it is the light that is attracting them?'*

A Kyle man bought a fishing boat that had been long disused, and began the work of renovation and painting. This occupied several months, during which people told of strange sounds coming from within the boat when nobody was aboard her or near her. They began to say that this was an omen, and that some calamity would befall the vessel when she eventually put to sea. It seemed as if her owner was of the same mind, for he dawdled long over his work, as if loath to put the question to test. But at length the boat was ready for launching, and he collected a crew and sailed for the fishing grounds. It was a beautiful sunny morning with a smooth sea when, as they passed Camusfeàrna islands, one of the crew came up on deck from below and walked straight overboard. There was no reason why he should not have been rescued immediately—none, that is, but that he never once broke surface, and disappeared as though he had never been. Neither his body nor any part of his clothing was ever recovered; the old folk of Kyle when they heard the news nodded to each other and said, 'We knew it—the boat should never have been put to sea after the warning that was given.'

The best-known modern ghost of the district, both on Skye and on the adjoining mainland—and more particularly in the regions of Camusfeàrna and Kyleakin—is a phantom car. To understand how an apparently solid and normal small black saloon may be recognized as a phantom may require a reminder of the nature of the terrain and its roads. The whole country is mountainous, and the roads, taking the line of least resistance, are correspondingly winding, with many a blind corner formed by a bluff or outcrop of a hillside. They are single-tracked, so that two cars cannot pass abreast, and every few hundred yards there are 'passing places', marked by a white board on a post, into which one may pull to allow passage for a vehicle coming from the opposite direction. Thus one may often see an oncoming car say half a mile away, but as a rule much of the road between will be hidden. Drivers accustomed to these roads will draw into the nearest passing place as soon as they can see a car approaching, so as to avoid a head-on meeting at the next blind corner. This does, it must be admitted, quite often result in both cars doing the same thing, and waiting impatiently out of sight of each other until both decide to go forward, meeting at precisely the point where one or other has to reverse for the maximum distance. In the case of the phantom car, however, the impatient driver, having waited for a minute or two, goes cautiously forward and finds absolutely nothing before him— the road is clear. The other car cannot have turned round and gone back the way it came, for there is no room to do so; it has simply disappeared. I myself know people of the utmost integrity who swear to having had this experience, and who become positively angry if it is suggested that there may have been some optical illusion. Whole families travelling together claimed to have seen the phenomenon, and have even argued among themselves whether it was a Ford, a Morris, or a Wolseley, that had vanished into nothing. It was, in any case, a small black saloon, upright and pre-1939, and though there is no accurate agreement as to when it was first seen it is said to have been some time about the outbreak of the Second World War. It has not always disappeared in front of the onlooker; sometimes it has passed with two people inside it and vanished before it reached a second car a few hundred yards behind the first. Once, at six o'clock on a clear summer's morning, a Skye man saw a car approaching at a distance of a few hundred yards, but separated from him by a blind corner. He pulled into the nearest passing place, and waited. When the other vehicle turned the corner and came abreast of him he glanced into it to see if the driver was anyone he knew. He suffered from shock for a

84

long time afterwards—for there was no driver, no one at all in the whole car.

The 'explanation' was a long time in coming, some twenty-five or thirty years after the first appearance of the phenomenon. In the early 1960s a Skye minister was driving two women to some village on the mainland, and had to cross the Kyleakin-Kyle of Lochalsh car ferry. Some part of the ferry boat's mechanism failed, and the car drove straight overboard. The women were drowned, and only the minister survived. Since then the phantom car, which had been very active for some years, has never been seen again.

All my life my own attitude toward what is popularly called the 'supernatural' (but which may well prove to be an imperfectly understood aspect of the 'natural'—as was for example the phenomenon of electricity but a short while ago) had been cautious and strictly empirical. I had not once personally experienced anything that could not be rationalized and made to fit into the plainly minute and constricted framework of my own human experience and limited knowledge. I had recognized that what my senses could perceive and my brain understand was no more than a millionth, a billionth, part of even the human cosmos, but I was essentially of the faithless generation that waited for a sign. I had adopted a scientific approach which demanded unquestionable evidence before accepting and assimilating any new concept, and having read Spencer Brown on the theory of probability I had pigeon-holed several curious experiences under the temporary and pending label of 'coincidence'.

This broadly sceptical attitude changed in May 1964 with the undeniable arrival at Camusfeàrna of what is usually known as a poltergeist. It remained our guest—a very unconventional one— for two days, and when it departed I was disappointed, for I longed to go on studying those weird phenomena that were actually testable, though inexplicable, by my five senses.

They had begun one evening at about 10 p.m. There were three of us sitting in the kitchen-living room of Camusfeàrna. Along one wall there is a homemade sofa, above which are shelves holding groceries and tinned foods, like any small village store. I was sitting at the end of this sofa nearest to the actual kitchen, a small room whose door was on my left. In front of the fire-place, at forty-five degrees to my right, was an L-shaped sofa, also home-made. On the section facing and parallel to where I was sitting was a guest, Richard Frere, who later became the manager of Camus-feàrna and its small but complex dependencies. Richard is a moun-taineer of distinction, an extremely practical man, little given to fantasy. Facing the fire-place, and in profile to both of us, was Jimmy Watt, then aged twenty.

Among the grocery stores above my head—tins of green vegetables, pickles, jam-jars and so on—I suddenly heard a scrap-ing sound, but I only just had time to look upward before I saw an object flying outward from above my head. It landed about three feet in front of me; a glass marmalade jar smashed to pieces on the cement floor. It was curious that after a moment's pause Richard and I both said, simultaneously and somewhat disbelievingly, 'Poltergeist!'

I climbed up and examined the top shelf, a foot wide, from which the missile had launched itself. The woodwork was deep in dust, and the jar had been standing close against the back wall. From its original position there was a clean track of its own width, clear of dust, all the way to the edge of the shelf. There cannot have been more than half an inch between the jar and the wall, allowing no space for mechanical propulsion, yet somehow it had projected itself over a distance little less than six feet.

Our reactions varied; Richard and I were intensely curious, while Jimmy was irritated, almost angry. Nothing more happened that night. We discussed what little we knew about the recorded phenomena of poltergeists, and found that from our small reading we had each retained the same impression, that these demonstrations had always been apparently associated with a human, male or female, at the age of puberty. We had a candidate—a juvenile delinquent who was employed by us and in our charge, but who was, for reasons of temporary convenience, boarded in the village five miles distant. He had not liked this arrangement, and we made up our minds that, as we could not deny the phenomenon we had witnessed, the solution might lie in some projected protest of his personality.

About ten o'clock the following morning, while I was writing in my bedroom-study, Jimmy entered and said, 'The bloody thing's been at it again—come and look.' He led me through to the kitchen, and said, 'Do you see anything wrong?' I looked round me carefully, and I could see nothing out of the ordinary. I said so, adding that such things as we had seen the night before were only interesting if they were not confused by human imagination. In short, I made a fool of myself. Jimmy said, 'You really see nothing unusual?' I said I did not.

'Nothing odd about the window panes?'

I looked at them; they had been recently cleaned, and they all looked alike to me. I said so. Jimmy said, 'Try passing your hands over them.' I did so. There was one missing, completely missing, as though it had never been there. Outside, in Edal's enclosure, it lay shattered on a big stone more than five feet from the wall of the house. It had been somehow propelled outwards by force from inside the room, leaving almost intact the putty that had retained it. We took photographs, and telephoned to London for literature on poltergeists. I was trying, in common with so much of the scientific world, to confine happenings not understood within a known or assumed framework.

I was alone when the next incident took place, but unless I were to distrust my senses I must say that as far as I was concerned it really did happen. I was standing in the little kitchen waiting for a kettle to boil when I was aware of a curious rustling sound in the living room behind me. I turned to look, and saw a stack of long-playing discs fanning themselves out like a pack of cards over the floor from where they had been piled under a little table supporting a record-player. They slid outward in an orderly movement, and came to rest covering more than a yard of the floor, each neatly overlapping the next. I replaced them as they had been, and tried to produce the same effect myself by mechanical principle. It wasn't possible; as in the case of the marmalade jar, there was not room between them and the wall for a hand or any human artifice to propel them outward.

Jimmy had been out; when he returned a little later I described to him what had happened, and was about to resume boiling the kettle to make coffee. We entered the little kitchen together, and as we did so something shot off a high shelf opposite to us, hit my face lightly, and fell to the floor. It was a baby's plastic feeding bottle with a rubber teat, relegated, like other things for which we had infrequent use (this we used occasionally for orphaned lambs in the spring) to the high shelf above the cooker. It had cleared the cooker by two or three feet, and, like the marmalade jar, it had left a dust-free trail in its passage. This time I had the subjective feeling that this object had definitely been aimed at me; whatever was throwing things about was, it seemed to me, no longer random in direction.

What followed, the next day, was a classic example of how an imagination once attuned to the unknown can take an illogical control and blur utterly the outlines of true empirical experience. At about eleven o'clock in the morning Jimmy, the only other occupant of the house, said that it was now a long time since the dogs had been properly exercised, and asked whether I would object to his taking them for a long walk down the coast, which would mean his absence for about three hours. I said that would be perfectly all right.

About twenty minutes after he had left with the dogs I went to the lavatory, which was just inside the usual entrance to the extended house. While I was there I heard footsteps outside; the door beside me was opened and closed, and someone was breathing, panting, within a few feet of me. I said, 'Is that you, Jimmy? Is something wrong?' There was no answer, only the breathing. I tried the same question several times: no one answered. At last I said, 'Who are you?' There was utter silence for perhaps thirty seconds; then a voice that did not sound human uttered a long, desolate moan. It would be ridiculous to pretend that I was not frightened; the hairs of my head literally stood up with a colossal outpouring of adrenalin. Then I reflected for a moment; clearly I could not spend the next few hours locked in the lavatory with some strange and unknown presence waiting at arm's length outside the door. I tidied myself up and put my hand on the door handle, determined to see whether this creature—whom I was now convinced must be the author of the inexplicable happenings of the past twenty-four hours—was small and hairy, a sort of pre-man, or lank and glaucous with white eyes, and attenuated gibbon limbs, or just amorphous.

I flung open the door violently and all I saw was the familiar figure of our juvenile delinquent, looking at me with as much astonishment as I was looking at him.

He said, 'What the hell's up? You look as if you'd seen a ghost!'

I tried to take hold of myself. I said, 'Sorry, but that's just exactly what I thought I was going to see.'

'Oi, what's all this about? I was only trying to put the wind up you for a giggle 'cos you couldn't see who it was. I was told I could come back here 'cos there wasn't any work for me today. What's all the scare about?'

I hadn't intended to tell him anything at all about what had happened, the more particularly because we had assumed him to be the unconscious origin of these curiosities, but now it seemed unavoidable. I said, 'Come into the kitchen and I'll explain.' The kitchen door opened from the room in which we stood, a square hall or lobby hung with rows of coats and oilskins; on the floor below them there were dog beds, and rows of rubber sea-boots. In the corner of the room diagonally opposite to the lavatory door a large empty laundry hamper stood on a low table.

When we went through to the kitchen I did not close the door to this room behind me. We sat down, and I had just begun a carefully worded explanation, when there came a resounding crash from the lobby we had just left. There could be no doubt that the boy believed me now, even if he had appeared sceptical about my opening sentences; we both knew that there were no dogs in the house, nothing animate that could have caused that noise, and his eyes were popping out of his head.

I re-entered the coat room with a certain caution. It was not difficult to see what had produced the sound; the laundry hamper had been thrown from the table and flung more than halfway across the room. It lay upside down with its lid open, within a few feet of the lavatory door. It had evidently been propelled with considerable force, for it had sailed clean over two tall pairs of rubber thigh boots that stood in its path.

That, unfortunately, was the last manifestation of the Camusfeàrna poltergeist. I waited hopefully for the least sign of its continued presence, for I was profoundly fascinated by this first-hand evidence of an unknown world; but after that last splendid gesture of the laundry hamper it was years before anything ever happened again that was not capable of easy interpretation in normal terms. The brief visit had, however, broken through a lifelong barrier composed, if not of disbelief, at least of mild scepticism; and after that glimpse of the unguessed I could not, two years later, view the curse upon the rowan tree with the degree of scorn that I would probably have accorded it before. It was as if an enquiring mind of the eighteenth century had suddenly heard an invisible radio set broadcasting for a moment, with silence before and after, and thereby had forced upon his attention the existence of a world totally incomprehensible to him; as if he had known, as we know now, some of the astounding facts of animal 'homing' for which we can still find no explanation—that turtles travel unerringly over 1,400 miles of empty and featureless ocean to lay their eggs on the beaches of tiny Ascension Island, an island in those days difficult to find even with man-made aids to navigation; that a mouse who had never wandered more than fifty yards from his birthplace would return to it without detour or deviation if deposited a mile away; that a Manx shearwater, removed from its nest on Skokholm Island off the Welsh coast and taken by airliner to Boston, U.S.A., was back in its nesting burrow just thirteen days later; that albatrosses, causing hazard to aircraft on Midway Island, some 1,300 miles west of Honolulu, captured and flown a distance of more than 4,000 miles, far outside their range of possible experience, returned as directly. All these things would have been as inexplicable to the enquiring mind of the eighteenth century as they remain to modern science now, a reminder that as yet we have touched but the outermost fringe of knowledge, and should keep a very open mind about what Robert Ardrey has called 'that scientific shady lady, extrasensory perception' and all its allied phenomena.

It was soon after the lighthouse cottages became mine that a resident of Kyleakin, not born locally, said to me with a slight constraint in her voice, 'I suppose you know that the lighthouse island is haunted?' I said that I didn't, and she replied, 'Well, I was told about it in confidence, but as you've actually bought the place now I don't suppose there's any harm in telling you. There doesn't seem to be much doubt about it, anyway. You'd better talk to some past lighthouse keepers; I believe any of them can tell you all about it. It seems that it's not frightening, anyway, it's just there.'

I sought out the most easily available, and though he was a slow starter, as I should have been in the circumstances, he eventually gave me a wealth of detail that, coming from so clearly level-headed a source, left me with the conviction that there must be something on the island not explicable in ordinary terms. He referred not only to his own experiences, but to those of his former colleagues and his predecessors; for the purposes of this narrative I shall give them fictitious names, but no doubt they would be open to approach from serious enquirers.

There have been experiences which must be classified as individual, but there has remained a standard, unvarying pattern common to all who have occupied the house. From somewhere just *outside* the walls, never seeming to be within them, comes the sound of low-pitched muttering voices, as though intentionally subdued, but rising and falling in intensity, as if in hurried argument. This may be preceded or succeeded by loud metallic clangs; these have been variously described as the sound made by an iron poker raking out a stove, or, perhaps more fancifully, as the clash of claymores or broadswords. With one exception, which was after my ownership, these things have been puzzling but never frightening.

A Mrs Findlay, wife of a former lighthouse keeper, recalls a visit from the Northern Lighthouse Board inspection vessel. Only the inspector himself came ashore, and when he and her husband had sat long in conversation in the sitting room she herself went to bed. She believed herself to have been asleep for a long time when she awoke to find that her husband had not joined her, and that there were the sounds of several muted voices coming either from the next room or from some point near to it. She imagined that other officers of the inspection ship must have come ashore, and, reproaching herself for her failure as a hostess, she made herself respectable and went through to the next room. It was empty of any human; both her husband and the inspector had gone to the Lighthouse Tower itself to check upon a suspected defect in the system.

A keeper whom we may call MacLellan was on the island for seven years, and during that time became so accustomed to the voices and the metallic clang that he came simply to ignore them. He was a Gaelic speaker, and was certain that the language spoken bore no relation to Gaelic. He emphasized that the occurrence was always during the small hours of the morning. He told me, too, that a relief keeper who spent eighteen months there had followed the advice of a predecessor, with absolute success. If, on hearing the voices for the first time, one asked loudly, 'Who's there?' they would cease and never recur.

This was the audible aspect of the haunting, but there seems, too, to be a visual apparition. At the first light of a September morning a lighthouse keeper's wife went to fetch water from the catchment tank at the west end of the house. Standing beside her, lit by the rising sun, stood a man in ancient highland dress, leaning upon a sword and looking north towards Broadford and the Red Hills of Skye. She was in no way afraid, and waited, as if expecting it, for the man to turn towards her; but he remained immobile and silent, his head still turned toward the north. She stood holding her pail until he faded and dissolved in the growing light. This tale would not, perhaps be worth recounting had it not been in some sense duplicated during my brief tenure of the island.

This kilted figure was far from being the only visual perception to be unexplained. Dancing lights appeared round the Lighthouse Tower, and above the highest point of the island where the water tank gave gravity fall to the house. A big ship, brightly lit, moves fast into the channel from the north, turns inwards towards the lighthouse as though to crash on its rocks, and then simply disappears. There is variation as to just where it disappears; sometimes when the impact should already have been audible, sometimes before she could be aground anywhere. Likewise, a masthead light of some tall ship is seen in the lee of the island when no ship is there. A dog barks, heard plainly by the people of the village, when there is no dog on the island.

I daresay I should have paid little enough attention to these stories if I had not had more contemporary evidence. At first, having bought the lighthouse cottages, my idea was only to maintain them in good condition until I should need to occupy one or the other myself. This negative scheme developed, through the project of furnishing them minimally in order to obtain a minimal summer rent, to converting them completely into comfortable, even luxurious, houses which could avail themselves of the tourist boom in the West Highlands. There seemed to be no immediate prospect of my being required to leave Camusfeàrna, and here might be a source of income that did not necessitate my writing at a desk for eight hours a day. I went into this, as I always have with any new project, with enthusiasm.

I had recently made the acquaintance of Richard Frere, alias Marquis de la Union, Vizconde de la Alianza—Spanish titles which had been conferred upon his forebears and which he disdained to use. He was a man of independent means, who lived near Inverness; he was a paradox, and to such I have always been drawn. He had no financial need to work, and yet he was never happy unless he was working. He was a distinguished mountaineer, and excelled at all physical activities, yet he had a razor-sharp brain and a profound appreciation of literature. He had trained himself as a builder, a joiner, a mechanic, and much else. Work, physical or mental, was his food. When he offered to take over the structural conversion of the lighthouses, and his wife, a talented decorator, to make herself responsible for the interior décor of Ornsay, I had embarked on a programme that deserved better financial results for all of us.

This arrangement was infinitely more economical than I could have achieved from any contractor; for both of them it was a hobby, and by it I benefited enormously. On 15 May 1964 Richard and his wife Joan began the conversion of Isle Ornsay and finished early in August. By then it was a luxury house, though we continued alterations and improvements until April 1966.

In October 1964, Richard began a similar conversion at Kyleakin —to my own somewhat ambitious designs—at first with an assistant, and then alone for some weeks. (The first assistant was Terry Nutkins, who had temporarily returned to our employment, and who kept a pair of wildcats in the annexe building subsequently known as The Cat House.) Terry left in January and for some weeks Richard was alone at Kyleakin. I had regarded Richard as a test case for the existence of some unexplained phenomenon at Kyleakin, and had been careful to tell him nothing of the stories I had heard. If, I thought, so pre-eminently sane and level-headed a man were to experience anything unusual without preconditioning there would no longer be any doubt in my mind. Richard writes:

My appreciation that there was something beyond the bounds of the readily acceptable came slowly. While Terry was there I heard nothing. When X arrived (our juvenile delinquent) he was frightened from the first moment, and would not stay in the house by himself after dark. Even when I went down to the boat to confirm that it was secure for the night he would follow me, often in pyjamas, and would insist on coming with me. This was foolish, because there was never anything in the *house* to fear; the house was a haven.

You will remember the night when Terry and I took you and Jimmy by dinghy to Kyleakin, and then went on to Kyle for a drink. We were no longer than we had anticipated, and when we got back to Kyleakin cottage in the dark there was no lamp lit in the house, nor was X evident. We found him buried under a vast pile of bedclothes with a large spanner at his right hand; he had heard many voices, and he was very, very frightened.

After X's departure in January 1965 I returned to spend the night and subsequent nights alone. I had my dog Hedda (Dalmatian bitch) with me, and she was never at any time worried by atmosphere or voices. I slept very soundly for the first three or four nights. At first, the weather was calm with frost; on the fourth night a southwesterly wind was blowing, which kept me awake until after midnight, and when I slept it was fitfully. I was awakened shortly after 3 a.m. by a sharp metallic clang. I heard the first voices a few minutes later. The wind had dropped, and it was raining. The voices, a curious disconnected muttering, rose and fell and seemed to be travelling down the north side of the house from west to east. So kindly was the atmosphere within the house that my only fear was that I should *become* afraid. *Nothing* would have made me go outside, but I was strangely prepared to lie and listen. It went on for about ten minutes, the clang being repeated two or three times. The voices suggested the passage of many people past the house, but I heard nothing of their movement. Believe it or not, I went to sleep again before it was entirely quiet; though, as I say, the very audible part continued for about ten minutes. This performance was repeated often, but never in stormy conditions; or, if it was, it was impossible to hear it. I always had the impression (if one can accept it to be some captive echo from the past) that here was a warlike party, arriving stealthily to deploy on the island preparatory to some battle or skirmish. By March it was all over.

Many lighthouse cottage occupants have heard the voices, and all accounts seem to agree that they are low-pitched and incoherent, but I myself have heard sharp sounds and expressions which would be meaningful if I knew the language.

By 21 June 1965 the work was almost finished, and I had brought over to Kyleakin my wife and two friends of ours, Gordon Mackintosh, and Ian Cameron, who is now an instructor with Outward Bound at Applecross. Mackintosh, who is a clear-headed and successful business man, describes what happened to him as follows:

'At about 9 p.m. on a pleasant, mild summer's evening, I had just returned to the island by motor boat from Kyleakin village, and was met by Richard at the lighthouse jetty when I arrived. He told me that there were still a lot of odd jobs to be done; the first and most important was to move a forty-gallon paraffin drum up from the jetty to the site of the new electric generator on the summit of the island, near to the old walled garden. He had with him Noddy Drysdale, who was acting as his assistant on the island, and as they were both very strong I contented myself with giving advice rather than active assistance. They sweated away pushing the barrel up the hill, while I trailed along behind. When they finally got the barrel to the generator house I realized that in the confined space I was only getting in their way, so I volunteered to gather firewood. Richard's wife Joan and their six-year-old daughter had gone indoors by then.

'I had gathered a big armful of wood and was on my way down the path towards the main house when I saw a man come round the corner of the house and on up the path towards me. As I knew exactly who was on the island, I assumed that this was Ian Cameron, the friend with whom I had come there, but I did notice that instead of wearing a kilt as he had been he was now wearing trousers. This didn't strike me as very odd, because his kilt was new and we were all doing messy jobs; I thought he had sensibly changed to avoid getting it dirty. However, as this man came closer he somehow didn't look like Ian, and as he grew closer still I knew it was no one I had ever seen before. He was a young man—about 25, I should say—and he was dressed in normal clothing for that part of the world, a fisherman's high-necked jersey and dark trousers. Seeing that he was definitely a stranger I was wondering what to say to him when he passed—when absolutely suddenly he disappeared as though he had never been there. One moment he was only a few paces from me and the next he was gone. There was nowhere he could have hidden himself, though I did begin to look around as though there was. I was still questing round when Richard came down the path from the generator house. I asked him who else could be on the island and how someone who seemed perfectly solid could just disappear. He didn't seem particularly surprised, and at that time I wasn't at all frightened—just utterly bewildered. But as the evening wore on I began to get some sort of delayed shock reaction, and I did become really frightened, and if I hadn't been sharing a room with Ian I don't think I'd have got to sleep at all.'

There is one particular sentence in Richard's letter which ties up closely with my searching questions to a former lighthouse keeper. 'By March it was all over.' No one could remember having heard the voices during the spring and summer months; it appeared to be a seasonal haunting, limited to autumn and winter, though the visual phenomena might be encountered at any time of year. Morag MacKinnon, who used to be my neighbour at Druimfiaclach above Camusfeàrna, went to live in the house for a few weeks early in 1966, in company with a boy who was preparing the adjoining island for a further project which I shall describe later. She wrote, 'I personally heard the voices only once. One Sunday morning at about 8.15, lying in bed, I heard what I thought was the wireless turned low, but I was puzzled that I had not heard the boy getting up. The voices were pitched quite low, alternately strengthening and fading, and were speaking in some foreign language. I got up and found that the wireless was not on and the boy still sleeping, and then I realized that the voices had stopped as soon as I had left my bedroom. Everyone else who has heard this had told me that it is not frightening, and having now heard it myself I agree, but at the same time I can't any longer doubt that voices *do* speak, and that it is not in English or Gaelic.' (Morag is bilingual in these two.) 'It certainly isn't just an old wives' tale like a lot of the ghost stories in these parts.'

Kyleakin is named after King Haco of Norway who, just seven hundred years before I bought the lighthouse cottage, anchored his invading fleet in the lee of the lighthouse preparatory to his last and disastrous attempt to conquer Scotland. He left his name to Kyleakin—the Narrows of Haco—and perhaps he left some ghosts as well, for the invisible inhabitants of the lighthouse island speak no tongue that is known in Scotland now.

The only occasion on which I had almost, but not quite, first-hand experience of something out of the ordinary at Kyleakin was during the month of April 1965. Richard was going home for the week-end, and I went by car to Kyleakin to collect him. We left the house empty and firmly locked up. The electric wiring was almost complete, but the generator was not yet installed. On Monday, when I brought Richard back, we were immediately asked in the village who had been at the lighthouse cottage over the week-end. No one, we replied. But, we were told, there had been a light in the kitchen window all the previous night, not a bright light, but a yellow one, of the strength of a couple of candles, or a small oil lamp. There had been many witnesses to this and they had assumed that contrary to our stated plan we had left someone in the house over the week-end. I said to Richard that he must have left an oil lamp burning, but he was positive that he had done no such thing. We crossed to the island and examined the doors and windows. Everything was locked as it had been left. We went into the kitchen and examined it as carefully as if we had been insurance detectives, but there was no trace of anything what-soever that could have produced either a light or the illusion of one.

I never heard the voices myself, because in all the time I have owned the house until now I have only spent two nights there, in July 1965, with a party of friends. I was still at the stage when I felt that I had all the time in the world; I loved Kyleakin and everything about it, and I planned to live in it later.

Vizconde de
la Alianza

8

Something Old and Something New

Well-established habits and attitudes of mind persist long—long enough in my case to influence my outlook on the lighthouses.

During all my adult life I have had an almost compulsive urge to start something new; to try to be a pioneer; to essay fields either virgin or at least imperfectly explored. This, perhaps, has stemmed from an unconscious desire to avoid competition, so that nobody could say that I had failed where others had succeeded. 'Educated' as I had been, I had always been unequipped for any life that I wanted to lead; while I was essentially an amateur in every sphere, others bore upon their banners the strange but powerful device 'Qualifications'. Whereas they had degrees in zoology, psychology, medicine, biology, and enviable letters after their names, I had emerged from Oxford with a degree in Estate Management, and the very fact that this course of action had been dictated against my wishes precluded me from ever managing an estate or wanting to.

I had rebelliously followed my own interests, attending medical and zoological lectures, and trying to learn to paint at the Ruskin, with the result that I and a few others who had no interest at all in the subject they were officially reading failed in our preliminary exams at the end of our first year. We attended, and continued to do so during our second year, the absolute minimum of lectures at the School of Rural Economy; during discourses upon economic history, inorganic chemistry or soil science, we used to play noughts and crosses with each other, and emerged from each lecture as ignorant as we had entered it. A singularly pompous Old Wykehamist contemporary labelled three of us unequivocally as 'wasters', and once the word had become public we made virtue of necessity. When a fat little man with loose false teeth and a curiously oblique gaze towards a corner of the ceiling began a lecture with the words, 'This morning, gentlemen, I propose to tell you something of the properties of calcium chloride. . . .' we used to raise eyebrows at each other and whisper 'wasters?'. The words represented noughts and crosses; all we learned from our lecturers was an almost sinister ability to mimic their voices and mannerisms. So when our preliminaries came round for the second time, after an undeserved year of grace, we were in no better case than before. We held a conference. We all agreed (over our glasses of brown sherry and our Balkan Sobranie cigarettes in an oak-panelled room at The Old Parsonage) that as this was in no sense a competitive exam, existing only for the purpose of allowing us to remain at the University, we should be harming nobody if we cheated. We should, on the other hand, be saving our parents or guardians an infinite amount of distress in avoiding being sent down. This was, in essence, true; in any case it was the only side of the picture that we wanted to see, though I am not now particularly proud of our decision.

So we cheated. There were to be no half measures, no possibility of failure—the plan we devised was in the grand manner. We were going to steal all the examination papers by a series of faultless and undetectable burglaries upon four separate and dispersed houses. The timing would have to be exact, late enough before the exams to ensure that if any authority entertained suspicions after our burglaries it would by then be too late to change the papers. At the same time it must be long enough before the exams to allow us to profit from our theft. We decided that six days would be the ideal interval, and moreover that would give us a moonless night for our terrifying enterprise. Terrifying it certainly was for all of us, this calculated risk, for if we were caught it would mean a final and disgraceful end to our University careers, and much greater distress to our families than being sent down for idleness or inability. But it was especially terrifying to me, because, being very much the lightest and most agile of the four of us, I was selected to do the actual burglaries while the others kept watch or created diversions. We were, I think, very thorough for amateur criminals, we were masked, gloved, and equipped with pencil-beam torches; we had made the fullest possible use of reconnaissance; we had 'borrowed' two keys and had replicas cut. We knew exactly where each of the Board of Examiners was to be on the night in question. We had two cars ready with false number plates and the compulsory undergraduate green light removed from them. I remember the first house, at Minster Lovell, and how the heavy sweet-smelling June blossoms of wistaria impeded my palpitating progress up the long drainpipe. The car was waiting for me a field away on a different road, and I was to give the signal of a double owl's hoot when my work was done and I was on my way. I had miscalculated the time it would take to copy the paper (with trembling and gloved fingers) by the light of that tiny torch, so that the car's driver (false moustache and stage make-up good enough for a poor light) gave me his own owl's hoot which we had agreed was only to be used in emergency. This was so unexpected that I thought it a warning that he had found danger, and I wasted a quarter of an hour on an extremely cautious and circuitous approach to the car. Thus I was nearly half an hour late at the next house, and here I got my first really bad fright. I managed the drainpipe and the window and found myself in a pitch dark room with the just audible sound of someone else breathing within a few feet of me. This was something none of us had foreseen; my heart must have been as audible as the breathing, and I had no idea what to do. There should be a table, I knew, about four feet to the right of me, and the breathing was coming from straight in front. Very cautiously I reached to my right until I touched the table; then I laid the little torch upon it, snapped the beam on and straightened up in the same instant. There, staring with horror at the torch but not at me, was my confederate who should have been keeping watch outside. Because I had been half an hour late he had assumed that I had been caught and,

17 Isle Ornsay Lighthouse in winter

18 and 19 Four views of Isle Ornsay Lighthouse

19

20 and 21 Approaching Kyleakin Lighthouse in *Polar Star*

22 Kyleakin Lighthouse Island, *above:* from the eastern approach, and *below:* from the Isle of Skye

23 *Right:* Monday

Below: Tibby
on arrival with
her owner

deciding that half a loaf was better than no bread, he had broken into this particular house himself.

We had only one failure; the Economic History paper seemed to be contained in a safe whose opening was far beyond my amateur status as a thief. This was a formidable set-back, for failure in this one important paper might well make suspect our success in the others. The answer to this problem was almost supplied to us by the customs of the University. For the exams themselves we were required to be dressed in formal garments that might have been made for our purpose—white shirts with hard cuffs, and bow ties. We covered the hard cuffs with white drawing paper and inscribed upon them, in microscopic lettering with pale yellow ink, a shorthand version of every fact and date that we could assemble. This, together with high powered bifocal spectacles (which caused comment but seemingly no suspicion), enabled us to refer constantly during the exam to what was virtually an encyclopaedia of our subject. Without the magnifying lenses our cuffs looked only mildly stained.

So we passed our preliminaries in this disgraceful manner, and we remained at Oxford for a further two years of idleness or experiment in other fields before we were required to take our finals. We had still wasted our time by academic standards; one of our number was wholly preoccupied with almost clinical experimentation on the female pelvic region in all its phases of excitement (more than fifty case histories in two years); another had a similar absorption with male anatomy; a third essayed *la dolce vita* of gigantic cars, caviar, champagne and debutantes, with a nightly solace of Caruso discs and Cointreau ('it's wonderful stuff, but what a hangover') while I remained virgin and pursued my childhood hobbies of natural history and painting.

It is not an edifying story, but, academically, Oxford did teach me one thing. I did no work on my set subject during the next two years, and on the first day of my final term I contracted a bad bout of jaundice, cutting two full weeks from the eight theoretically at disposal. I appealed to my guardian to be allowed to retire gracefully from the scene on the grounds of ill-health, rather than face the apparent certainty of failure in my finals. The refusal was absolute, and held, also, sanctions; I was to sit for my degree, no matter what the outcome. I had no choice but to accept these terms. The final exam was competitive; for all of us 'wasters' conscience was strong, and there could be no question of cheating this time and possibly depriving some more worthy undergraduate of his just reward. So, for that brief period, we worked, and we worked very hard; indeed we hardly slept. We all passed with distinction; and in doing so we proved that a three-year course could be passed in six weeks' complete application.

Immediately after I had taken my degree I was offered the job of private secretary to Sir Archibald Clark-Kerr, then Ambassador in Iraq. It was, as he put it, a 'back door to the diplomatic service'. I wanted to leap at this opportunity, but my uncle and guardian Lord Eustace Percy, then Minister without Portfolio, disapproved of Clark-Kerr's unconventional approach to life in general and to the Establishment in particular (amidst much other strictly individual behaviour his marriage had been dissolved and he had subsequently remarried the same wife), and urged me strongly to refuse. It was a major turning point in my life. When I told Clark-Kerr he said, 'You're making a big mistake. I'm going to the top, and I could take you with me.' I asked what the top was, and he replied, 'Washington. Ambassador to the U.S.A. is the summit of my profession, and I'm going to reach the summit.'

He did. The following year, 1938, he was made Ambassador to China; in 1942 Ambassador to the U.S.S.R.; and in 1946, as Lord Inverchapel of Loch Eck, Ambassador to the United States of America. But my uncle had prevailed, and I did not accompany him through his triumphant career. He wrote to me occasionally; from Hong Kong, 'I feel as if I was in the pan of a lavatory. The reason for this illusion is that sticking through the broken ceiling above my head is the underside of a bath, looking obscenely like a bishop's bottom. I say a bishop's because I always think of them as having larger and whiter bottoms than anyone else's—though I suppose the Prime Minister could compete'; and from Moscow when Stalingrad was under siege and the war was at its blackest hour, 'Despite every possible appearance to the contrary I am as certain that we shall win this war as I remain certain of being the future Ambassador to the U.S.A. I could still get you out if you want me to apply for you.' But by that time I was absorbed in my work as an S.O.E. instructor, and I declined.

My degree was useless to me, though it looked well upon the letter-heading of the egregious agricultural firm for which I worked during the ensuing eighteen months. But I wanted to travel (more widely than my capacity as travelling salesman permitted—for that, despite resounding titular disguises, was really my work) and I did not feel suited to the protocol of Embassies, so I resigned from the company, and planned my life on what might well have been fruitful lines had the war not intervened. I wanted, in plain terms, to be an explorer; not in the grand manner as a member of mighty expeditions (my lack of qualifications precluded this, for it was difficult to see how a degree in Estate Management could find place in, say, a Polar or Amazonian expedition) but as a solitary, a lone wolf, using the minimum of my small capital for each journey and then writing about my travels after I had returned. Experienced friends warned me of the dangers that lay in too ambitious a start; I must begin, they said, with a comparatively short journey and a limited, definite objective that was within my own field of interests. In ornithology, for example, no one had ever proved whether or not the extraordinarily beautiful little duck called Steller's Eider, whose breeding grounds were along the Siberian coasts, actually bred in Varanger Fjord, where the northerly tip of the Scandinavian countries joined Russia on the 70th parallel, some four hundred miles north of the Arctic circle. Moreover, there were no known photographs of this bird in the wild state, so that book illustrations tended to be correct in colour only, characteristic pose being conjectural to the artist.

So there I went, to the tundra of East Finmark, alone and with precisely £100 to cover the whole journey, and though I never proved that Steller's Eider bred there I did succeed in taking a unique series of photographs of them, and, very much more surprisingly, in delivering a breech-presentation Lapp baby without killing it or its mother. It was a boy, and the father said he would christen it after me; perhaps somewhere among what remains of the nomadic reindeer people of Northern Scandinavia there may be a Lapp called Gavin. He would be thirty years old as I write in 1967.

It was, I suppose, the same desire to tread new paths that led me after the war to try to establish a Basking Shark fishing industry on the Isle of Soay in the Hebrides. Those three years, however, cost a good deal more than £100; they cost, in fact, every penny that I owned and a very considerable number of pennies that other people owned. But I had, however abortively, done something new, and I had added to scientific knowledge despite my lack of qualifications. When in 1956 an animal previously unknown to science actually received my name, Maxwell's Otter (*Lutrogale perspicillata maxwelli*), I felt that I had really begun to live down my degree in Estate Management at last.

With this long background of attempted, partial pioneering, coupled with the supreme need for some sort of regeneration that I felt after my return to Camusfeàrna as a cripple, it was perhaps not surprising that I looked at the lighthouse islands with a speculative eye, probing their possibilities for some new and improbable project. I had a plan for Isle Ornsay, but it was a distant and ambitious one, requiring more capital than I could outlay, even if the Northern Lighthouse Board were to grant their permission. I wanted, at some time in the future, to form there a porpoise pool, and to study captive porpoises as dolphins are being studied in the few great oceanariums of the world. There seemed every likelihood that the dolphins' extraordinary mental development and powers of communication were paralleled or even surpassed in the porpoise; yet, so far as I knew, the experiment had never been tried. The rock formations of Isle Ornsay lighthouse island lent themselves well to the construction of a spacious sea pool, but I recognized that this project must wait for a much later date and that it might be years before I could own talking porpoises.

For Kyleakin, however, I had conceived a much more immediate and practical scheme, something else that would be absolutely new. I intended to found an Eider Duck colony—or at least to establish whether or not it was possible to do so. If I succeeded I would have opened the way to a new industry for the crofting population of the West Highlands and Islands.

There will be some to whom the Eider will require no introduction; to others, perhaps, who have no particular interest in ornithology, the connotation of the word will be limited to the eider-down (which rarely contains eider-down) used upon a bed in cold weather. As a formal introduction, the Common Eider bears the scientific name of *Somateria mollissima*, and is perhaps the humblest of an exotic group of sea ducks that include the dazzling King Eider, Fischer's Eider, and Steller's Eider. The males of all the species are spectacular, and with the exception of the last (which is small, light and skittish) they are heavy, solid, flat-bottomed, ocean-going people; awkward on land, with their legs set too far back for a dignified gait, but deep divers and superb in the momentum of full flight that appears to gain impetus from weight like a runaway lorry on a steep hill.

Eiders are somehow more like animals than birds; perhaps it is this impression of weight and compressed bulk, or their peculiarly unavian voices, or the way their massive bills ascend in a straight line to the top of their skulls without any 'scoop' in between. Or perhaps it is their curious and very individual smell, which seems as if it could have nothing to do with a bird. They hold, anyway, some strange fascination for most people who have had anything to do with them.

The drake in breeding plumage is a superb creation, suggesting the full dress uniform of some unknown navy's admiral. The first impression is of black and white, but at closer quarters the black-capped head that looked simply white from far off seems like the texture of white velvet and shows feathers of pale scintillating electric green on the rear half of the cheek and on the nape; the breast, above the sharp dividing line from a black abdomen, is a pale gamboge, almost peach. From the white back the secondary wing feathers of the same colour sweep down in perfect scimitar curves over the black sides, adding immensely to the effect of a uniform designed for pomp and panache. The whole finery looks so formal that one has the impression that it must be uncomfortable,

restricting, and the sureness and grace of all movement that is not on land is disconcerting. One would expect, too, that this essentially massive and masculine image would be incapable of anything but gruff and curt utterance, yet the mating call, uttered as the drake flings his splendid head far back on to his shoulders, is a wood-wind sound, something between the lowest note of a flute and the highest of an oboe, a serenade so sweet and pure that it seems to become a part of the smooth, blue sea and the small jewelled tumble of wavelets upon white sand under a summer sky.

As with all the Eiders, the female is dowdy by comparison, but in a way no less impressive. She is of a warm vermiculated brown all over, bulky and thick-necked, increasing the impression of lead-like weight; her voice is appropriately bass, whether in content-ment or complaint. Above all she appears, with this voice and manner, competent to deal brusquely with any situation—but unfortunately this is not always true.

Eiders breed at Camusfeàrna, and over much of the north-west coast of Scotland and its thousand islands. They do so, however, in the most disastrous conditions, almost as if inviting the destruction of the species. They choose to make their nests where there is the maximum commotion of other breeding species; and this most often means that they lay in the very midst of their worst enemies, the greater gulls. Thus at Camusfeàrna lighthouse island, where there are some two or three hundred pairs of nesting Herring Gulls and Lesser Black-backed Gulls (to say nothing of a dozen pairs of that great vulture of the sea, the Greater Black-backed Gull) some thirty or forty female Eiders lay their eggs every year. One would say that on that island there could be nothing that they could desire—neither fresh water nor smooth beaches for their toddling young, nor safety for their unhatched eggs. It would appear a deliberately suicidal situation, since there are adjacent islands with none of these disadvantages or hazards. Yet the fact remains that they do limit their breeding territory to this and similar islands throughout the area, despite the destruction by predators of at least three-quarters of their potential offspring. Long before I had acquired Kyleakin Lighthouse this fact had puzzled me; there was an inescapable conclusion that the tumult and the shouting of other species, even if they were proven enemies, provided some necessary stimulus to the Eiders' reproduction.

From the time that the female has completed her clutch of five eggs, laid in a carefully chosen site amongst heather, bracken, dwarf-willow or goose-grass, she begins to pluck her own breast of the fine down underlying the firm, springy feathers, and with this she surrounds her nest. The down serves a double purpose. When she leaves her nest to drink (she eats nothing during the four weeks of incubation) she arranges the down with her massive bill so that it covers the eggs; thus at the same time concealing them from robber gulls and maintaining their temperature until she returns. If unexpectedly disturbed from her nest she will (under extreme provocation, for female Eiders are very tame while they are incubating, and will often allow themselves to be touched or even stroked) take off in a flurry, emitting as she does so a strong-smelling liquid which falls upon the eggs. This is not, as many people have thought, excreta; for, fasting, she has nothing to excrete. The inference is that when she has not time to cover her eggs she ejects this liquid as a deterrent to predators; to make the smell of her eggs noxious and unpalatable. It is a curious smell, very pungent, and resembling the smell of frying liver. For the few who may have smelled the cooking liver of a stag after the rut has begun the simile is almost exact. It is a warm, perhaps hot odour, suggesting its own colour of rich brown; most humans do not find it unpleasant, but feel that if it were increased to the least degree it would be nauseating.

Ever since the Gallgaels and the Norsemen had colonized Iceland, even long before King Hakon had come and left his name to Kyleakin, they had realized the immense value of the Eiders which bred in fantastic numbers in their new land; and, probably without recognition of the reasons, they had sensed that movement, noise and colour had something to do with the Eiders' basic requirements. They lured the Eiders away from the predator gull colonies, and for the wild white wings and raucous voices of the enemy they substituted an elaboration of fluttering flags, little wind-driven clacking propellers, and reeded wind instruments that would sigh, groan, or trumpet, according to the strength of the breeze. Over the centuries these traditional means became lore; and even without true scientific knowledge or controlled experiment they had been able to form colonies of several thousand pairs of Eiders, and to harvest from the nests a great quantity of the down—at first only for local household use, but later as an important source of income from export.

The island immediately adjoining Kyleakin lighthouse island, separated from it at low tide by only a few yards of water, was rough and heathery, and despite the presence of breeding Greater Black-backed Gulls and Hooded Crows, both the very worst enemies of the Eiders, there were already some twenty or more pairs nesting there; each probably raising to maturity a fifth of their potential offspring. From the lighthouse cottage this island could be kept under perpetual observation, and it appeared the ideal site for experiment. It was the property of the National Trust for Scotland, who gave their immediate and unqualified approval to my project.

It remained only to go to Iceland and learn, before I began, all that I could from those who had been colonizing Eiders for nearly a thousand years.

9

Slowly through a Land of Stone

So although no ghost was scotched
We were happy while we watched
Ravens from their walls of shale
Cruise around the rotting whale,

Watched the sulphur basins boil
Loops of steam uncoil and coil,
While the valley fades away
To a sketch of Judgment Day.

Rows of books around me stand,
Fence me round on either hand;
Through that forest of dead words
I would hunt the living birds—

Great black birds that fly alone
Slowly through a land of stone,
And the gulls who weave a free
Quilt of rhythm on the sea.

When the early Gallgaels of the Western Isles (men of mixed race
from the interbreeding between Scots of the Hebrides and of Skye
and their Scandinavian conquerors) sailed to settle in Iceland,
which is only our own corruption of the norse word Island, they
faced a hazardous sea voyage of 500 miles upon the open Atlantic

ocean, with the prevailing and often tempestuous westerly wind upon their port bows. In their high-prowed, low-decked galleons they carried sheep and cattle and horses, religious idols, and wood for the traditional framework of their turf-built houses. When, some thousand years later, Jimmy Watt and I set out on 11 June 1965, from the same region, we had only to motor to Glasgow and take an aircraft whose flying time to Reykjavik, the capital, was two hours and ten minutes. I had a curious sense of pilgrimage, not only because the history of Iceland had in the dim past been so closely linked with the part of Scotland that I had made my home, but because my own remote ancestors had been Scandinavians who had pushed westwards to Scotland, and probably to Iceland too.

I had written to the great Icelandic naturalist Finnur Gudmundsson (great in every sense, for he was more than six foot seven in height and very broad in proportion) and he had replied that whereas June was a little late in the season to see all that I might have a month earlier, he would do all he could to help us. He himself was working upon a long-term ecological study on an isolated island in the far north, an island called Hrisey in Eyafjördur, but he promised to arrange our reception by the Southern consultant to Eider farmers, Mr Gisli Kristjanssen, who would take us to see two colonies just outside Reykjavik, and he suggested that we should then go north either by plane or by car and visit him. There was, he pointed out, too much in Iceland of interest to a naturalist to limit our visit to a few Eider colonies near to the capital, and we should not only come to Hrisey and see his work there but also spend several days at the fabled fresh-water lake of Myvatn, where no less than fourteen species of duck were reputed to breed. We should, he said, try to spend at least three weeks in Iceland, and to be as mobile as possible.

As the aircraft took off and passed low over Loch Lomond we tried to keep our bearings and to recognize landmarks, for we believed that the route of the plane on its north-westward course led directly over Camusfeàrna. But the Highlands looked completely unfamiliar from the air; there seemed to be water everywhere, and the first time I was certain of our position was when the unmistakable figure-of-eight shape of the Island of Soay, where

I had once lived and founded the Shark Fishery, passed far below on our port side, ringed with a white edge of foam. After that I saw the Outer Hebrides, some particular bays and headlands that I remembered with an absolute and total recall from the days when I was fishing for sharks so fatally far from my base and the processing factory on Soay. There was time for an enormous succession of visual images from the past to come back one after another—here on our port side was Uishenish Lighthouse; and, to starboard after a few minutes, Rodel Bay where we had, so many years ago, so many adventures. I was back in the Tiger Moth aircraft in 1947, searching those same waters for sharks whose mighty submerged bodies looked from the air like a fleet of submarines. For the next hour I was reliving as never before those years of wild adventure.

From the air, as so many thousands of travellers see it, Reykjavik, which holds almost half the entire population of Iceland, has the appearance of any small, unpretentious modern town; clean, white, red-roofed, well planned, with green spaces and a lake at its centre. It was, in fact, the very first site to be settled by the Gallgaels and the Scandinavians, but until the last few decades it remained a small and primitive fishing village. Although there are only fourteen towns in the whole island (if one counts as a town a group of dwellings with no more than 700 inhabitants), into these communities is concentrated more than 70 per cent of the whole population; the entire remainder who inhabit this great island of nearly 40,000 square miles, an island of ice and fire, volcano and glacier, number no more than a total of 50,000—a population of little more than one per square mile. As these tend naturally to inhabit the few fertile valleys and coastal strips, there are vast areas of the country in which it would be difficult to find a single human being in fifty square miles. Only 1 per cent of the entire island is under cultivation.

Even a very short stay in Reykjavik reveals remarkable divergence between the image of a small new bourgeois town and the facts as they emerge. The first thing a stranger discovers is the almost incredibly high cost of living. This, I understand, is due to a wartime inflation that has never been solved; it does not affect the indigenous people, whose wages and salaries are perhaps four times the equivalent figure in the British Isles, but it makes life almost impossible for the foreign visitor. On that first evening we explored Reykjavik on foot, and, although attempting to be frugal, we could not have spent more in Monte Carlo or any other millionaire resort.

In the whole town there were only some three or four bars that served alcohol, at staggering prices and with staggering results for the majority of the patrons. The results of what may be termed a partial prohibition seemed to be total inebriation wherever alcohol was to be found. These bars were packed, crammed; and the majority of the clients were, by the time we arrived, drunk and uninhibited. That first evening we visited a bar above a *cordon bleu* restaurant, the bar decorated as the saloon of a sailing ship from a past era—portholes, heavy timber beams, ships' steering wheels, and imitation oil lamps. There were about fifty men present, and almost all were drunk to some degree. They were dark suited, white shirted, dark tied; their sartorial respectability only added to an intensely febrile climate. They were paying the equivalent of 15s. for a glass of whisky (58 Kroner for a Schnapps and a Pilsner); they were loving it and drunk on it—a very expensive drunk. (About 45 Kroner go to £1.) Fascinated, we visited later that evening a night club, close to the central lake and beside a huge and grotesque church, with a tall tower, built entirely of corrugated iron. Entrance to this night club cost 25 Kroner for each person. It was entirely empty, and the band was playing to an imaginary clientèle. One Pilsner and one Schnapps cost 65 Kroner each, and we were served with a positive hostility which a lavish tip seemed in no way to diminish. This, we found, was the enormous difference between the town-dwelling Icelander, as a rule rude, brusque and unfriendly, and the country-dwelling people whose kindness and hospitality was unequalled in any country that I have visited. There were notable exceptions to the first of these rules; the staff of Hotel Holt, for example, I remember for their remarkable helpfulness and courtesy, and the wholly delightful policeman who conducted our driving tests before we could hire a car. This was necessary, he explained, because foreigners had frequently arrived in the country possessing international driving licences and had subsequently proved themselves 'as ignorant and irresponsible as monkeys'. While he put us through our paces he talked of the town and the road conditions we were likely to encounter in the interior. Metalled roads, he told us, were confined to the purlieus of the few towns; for the rest the roads were constructed of lava clinkers and had 'soft shoulders' which could be very dangerous to the uninitiated. There are 6,000 miles of roadway, because there are no railways. All these roads had to be completely rebuilt every year after the devastations of the winter snow and ice. 'Iceland is a dangerous country,' he said, 'and here we respect human life. The roads are dangerous, the snows are dangerous, the sea is dangerous. So we ensure that all who drive cars are experts, we have highly organized winter rescue services, and it is compulsory for every child to learn to swim. They learn in heated swimming pools, for there are few inhabited parts of the island where there are not natural hot springs.' He chuckled. 'They say Iceland is a land of contrast, and it is true. No one is cold even in the worst of winters, if they stay indoors, because their houses are all centrally heated without paying a penny for it. Why, not far south of the Arctic circle we have big commercial greenhouses growing grapes, tomatoes, carnations, and even bananas. But we recognize that it is a dangerous country, and so with the precautions we take there are only seven deaths a year per thousand persons. But I can see now that you two will not increase this figure, and I will give you your licences.'

We hired a car—for a naturalist in any country to be dependent upon public transport is completely self-stultifying—for an unimaginable sum of money. This was a Ford Cortina; the first evening we drove down to the port to look at the ships that were in harbour. There was a French vessel *Valeur*, and a British Admiralty craft whose class I did not know. Besides these there were innumerable fishing boats of all sizes. Jimmy's hair was, due to distance from barbers rather than to any special inclination, long by Icelandic standards; as the Cortina was parked in the port, two small girls on bicycles constantly circled round us, and at length the elder stopped beside us and explained very seriously to the younger, 'Et en Beat-ell.' Then, the mystery solved, the creature classified, they rode away. We remained, watching fascinated as a big American saloon car was driven round and round the port, flat out with screeching tyres, in a seemingly aimless and suicidal exercise. A sailor from an Icelandic trawler passed by our stationary car and said, 'There are madmen everywhere—but I think in Reykjavik there are more madmen than anywhere, and that is to say a lot, yes?' We said yes, it was a lot. At last the crazy, screaming car disappeared, and we decided to go back to our hotel. We had to reverse because of a lorry in front of us, and immediately the gear lever broke off short at, so to speak, its root. I was left holding this ridiculous chrome-plated object in my hand, and no means of progressing in any direction. We returned to our hotel by taxi and with a tremor of anti-Icelandic feeling, which did not wear off until we were once more amongst country people.

The central lake of the town proved to be as surprising as the terra firma and its inhabitants. In the parks of London there are lakes with ornamental water-fowl, essentially artificial situations, and ducks and geese to be admired and fed by the lonely humans who have no other living contact. In Reykjavik the central lake, the 'Tjornin', contains a breeding colony of wild Arctic Terns, white wings dancing above their little green island, and a host of undomesticated wild-fowl, which seem to ignore the presence of the public.

Germany sent to Iceland a present of a pair of Mute Swans, the common, semi-domesticated swan of Europe, which, in England are still by ancient lore the property of the Crown. This pair was put upon the Reykjavik lake, but soon afterwards a pair of wild Whooper Swans, of which the Icelandic population is conservatively estimated at 10,000, arrived and challenged the foreign Mutes. The male Whooper killed the male Mute, and the Whooper pair, thus established, became so aggressive that they attacked children and passers-by and actually killed several dogs. The Icelandic government replied to Germany in kind, and, with a specifically Icelandic sense of humour, presented the two Whoopers to the West German Government as a return gift for the Mutes. Unfortunately I do not know the sequel to this mischievous retort, but it cannot have been less than hilarious. How many dachshunds defended themselves from the northern intruders, how many drakes and ducks died for the honour of the Reich, how many potential Ledas preserved their virginity in face of this preposterous bird, remains a subject for personal fantasy.

In the morning after our arrival we were met at our hotel by Mr Gisli Kristianssen, advisor to Eider Colonists, who suggested that he should drive us first to the 'hobby' Eider colony at Bessastaoïr, property of the President, Mr Asgeir Asgeirsson, and then on to a commercial Eider Colony at Bessastadir in the immediate vicinity.

We drove out through the straggling suburbs of Reykjavik and on over some seven or eight miles of featureless land to where the noble structure of the President's house, reminiscent of Dutch country architecture on a grand scale, stood alone at the base of a broad, low-lying promontory leading out into the sea. It was a cold morning with a drizzle of rain from a grey sky, and a bad one for photography. The President himself was indisposed, but we were greeted by his extremely attractive young personal secretary, who appeared to be as much at home in gum-boots and leaky boats as she obviously would be on occasions of protocol and state. She led us down to where, a few hundred yards from the house, a small brackish lake gave the impression of the site of some village carnival. There were several small artificial islands dotted on its surface, and on them under the dull sky flapped multicoloured flags and strings of red and white pennants and bunting. The whole composition had an almost surrealistic quality, for the islands were also decorated with white whales' ribs, and on the summit of one of them stood a gigantic vertebra. Across the water came the faint clacking of small wooden propellers as they turned in the wind, and all about the fringes of the islands and on the water surrounding them showed the black and white plumage of scores of Eider drakes. All the components of the picture seemed to bear so little relation to each other that I was reminded of a canvas by, say, Hieronymus Bosch.

As we dragged from the bank a shabby, flat-bottomed dinghy in which several inches of rainwater sloshed about above the floor-boards, the young lady began to explain the history of the colony. 'The President,' she said, 'is naturally not interested in the commercial side for himself. But this is what you might call part of his garden, being so short a distance from his house, and he wanted to have some Eiders on the lake for ornament and interest.' Here she insisted on taking the oars, and began to row with short, powerful strokes. 'He was advised that this would be very difficult, because you see we are less than a mile from the colony at Bessastadir which has been established for several hundred years, and the Eiders are very much creatures of habit. I think Mr Kristianssen is going to take you to Bessastadir as soon as you've seen our little colony. Anyway, the President was determined to try, and so three years ago he put up these little islands in his lake and the flags and all the other gimmicks. And sure enough we've got two hundred pairs already and they're still increasing. There's not really room for more than three or four hundred pairs here, but we think we'll reach saturation point in two or three years' time.'

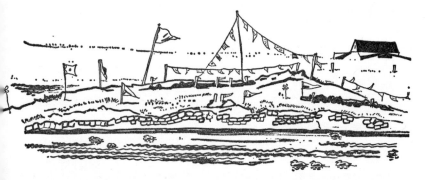

The boat grounded on the shore of a little island forty or fifty yards across, and we climbed out. 'Careful, now,' she said, 'just move gently and try not to disturb them.' They did not, in fact, seem very easy to disturb; the drakes pushed out a few yards from the shore, and a few ducks very close to us waddled off their nests, grunting petulantly, and just stood there looking at us. The whole island was a mass of artificial nesting sites, made, for the most part, from slabs of stone; these formed small rooms, little more than Eider-sized, some roofed, and some roofless, but all frontless. We walked slowly among them, and only a very few brooding birds moved at all. Their eggs were near to hatching now, and the ducks were loath to leave them.

It all looked absurdly easy—some slabs of stone, some string and pieces of bright-coloured cotton material, and you had an Eider colony. I wondered if this were really all there was to it.

From Bessastaoïr we drove over a mile of track between grassy fields, still at the base of the long flat promontory; and on it, but more especially on its seaward tip, was the Eider colony of Bessastadir farm. We left the car, crossed a fence, and began to walk over tussocky grass, each hummock roughly the size of a football. Here were neither flags nor pennants; the only visible sign of human interest in the colony was a single dead raven dangling from a stick, insignificant on the vast expanse. Soon we began to see brooding Eiders deep between the tussocks, scattered at first and then becoming denser and denser until near the end of the peninsula there was hardly room to step between them.

'No one knows how old this colony is,' said Mr Kristianssen, 'but it is very old, possibly even a thousand years old. That is why it is still thriving without any of the usual human assistance, but it's not giving anything like its potential output. The farmer's been ill all spring and summer, and he couldn't find anyone to take over the work. He had troubles last year too; I don't know what the weight of down will be this year, but I can give you last year's figures.' He pulled a notebook from his pocket and thumbed through it. 'Here we are—30 kilos of refined down. It takes sixty nests to make a kilo—so that means at least 1,800 pairs of Eiders. He took the down twice, once halfway through the brooding period and again after the young had left. In your money the down is worth roughly £20 a kilo, so you see he made £600 from the colony. I think he'll make about the same this year, for just two days' work. Not bad—£300 a day? But I believe that with careful management this colony could be worked up to yield £1,000 a year. I shall be very interested to see whether you can do it in

Scotland—it would certainly be a brand-new industry for your crofting population. It's funny that it hasn't been tried before—more especially when you think that it was the English who taught the Icelanders the commercial value of Eider down, when their trading ships first came here in the fourteenth century.'

Already I was calculating how many pairs of Eiders the Kyleakin island could hold with this degree of concentration; in my mind's eye it was already a flutter of flags and Eiders were jostling for position over every square yard of its surface. Dreams.

In the morning we left by car for the far north, to meet the fabulous figure of Dr Finnur Gudmundsson, some five hundred miles away upon his island fortress of Hrisey. We drove slowly, not only because we had little faith in our hired Cortina, but because on every side there was so much to see, so many new impressions to take in.

Harlequin ducks

The distances seemed enormous, because the road followed always the deep indentations of the coast line; on the west coast, skirting the long and circuitous indentations of the fjords, one was conscious of four enduring images: inland, vast barren hills, dark in colour, almost devoid of vegetation, plunging abruptly to a narrow strip of flat land between them and the sea, where grew small, delicate and brilliant flowers; ponies and sheep of every imaginable (and some unimaginable) colours; and the small wading bird called the Icelandic Redshank, whose perpetual trilling call was, together with the more haunting and poignant notes of the Whimbrel, the uninterrupted orchestra of our journey. Birds, birds, birds; Iceland has not one single indigenous mammal or reptile except the Arctic Fox, and even these are presumed to be the progeny of original individuals who, helpless, drifted south on floating icebergs broken off from the polar ice-cap. Occasionally Polar Bears have thus arrived involuntarily, but they have not survived, and apart from the fox there is nothing on the island but an unthinkable host of birds and insects—not even a frog, snake or lizard, not even a mouse, among this great throng of winged creatures who seem to dominate the whole landscape despite its vastness and desolation. The perpetual snows are always in sight, for they begin between two and three thousand feet above sea level, and most of the higher mountains are more than five thousand feet, many sheering down straight into the sea. All are volcanic in origin, a land of fire and lava, ice and glacier; a land in a constant state of change; a land with an atmosphere so clear that one can see, undimmed, a mountain a hundred miles away, every architectural detail of its structure and encrustation sharply defined.

Ponies and sheep—thirty thousand ponies running wild, and almost a million sheep. (I think the official figure is 850,000 sheep, but is held to be an under-estimate.) The ponies used to be a major source of export revenue; 20,000 went annually as pit ponies to Scotland alone. But now that the mechanized age has taken over and the sad life of a pit pony is mercifully something of the past, the Icelandic ponies are for the most part unused except for the bi-annual gathering of the sheep and the riding clubs which form increasingly round every community. But their use is over, and they are in truth an encumbrance to Iceland, though their ownership, in numbers, remains a status symbol. The sheep are fantastic, not only because they are of weird colours and often have three or four horns, but because they represent the original race taken from Scandinavia to Iceland perhaps a thousand years ago. Their fleece is silky and soft like that of the Shetland sheep; they live, apparently, upon nothing, grazing upon unguessed herbage among the laval clinkers of the mountain sides. They are ubiquitous, silent, suspicious; the only voices are those of the birds, sweet and haunting, trailing back to childhood and lost, beautiful wildernesses.

I feel I could write a whole book about our short stay in Iceland, but it would find no true place in what is essentially the story of

Camusfeàrna and my doomed plans for its expansion. The vivid impressions that I retain from all five senses were even then only a background to my eager project for Kyleakin, though they will

remain with me long. The great emerald icebergs jostling in the northern fjords, for the polar ice-cap had for the first time in forty years broken and drifted south to Iceland; the almost unbelievable stench of the whaling station where the lanky, cowboy-like figures of the flensers moved amid blood and blubber with a curious swaggering walk imparted by the long spikes in their boot-soles, and thousands upon thousands of Fulmar Petrels swarmed around the great carcases still in the sea; the geysers that were everywhere, some spouting scalding water and some crater-like, in which a grey substance, evil-looking and sulphurous, bubbled and plopped in a lunar landscape; the lonely white, red-roofed farm-houses, each with its tiny patch of green field vivid against the vast, dark desolation of the mountains, and each with its disused predecessor of the traditional green sods built with a pattern like a parquet floor; the incredible numbers and varieties of unfamiliar birds which stimulated anew my old interests and enthusiasms; the mighty waterfalls turbid and fluted, and the low midnight sun's rays turning a mountain ridge of laval clinkers to crimson and violet; a flight of Whooper Swans transformed to fairy-tale creatures with golden breast-plates—all of these were the distilled essence of the North as I had known it long ago in Lapland. This was the bleak, barren landscape that was paradoxi-cally the matrix for ideal and endeavour.

For a long time there was one ingredient mercifully missing—the terrible Black Fly of the tundra as I remembered them. I had told Jimmy of how I had been forced to go gloved and veiled, and of how they would form a mass in the air so dense that daylight would become dusk; of the stories I had heard of people driven literally mad by their bites; I had impressed upon him the necessity of taking on this journey liberal quantities of insect repellant and insecticides. As the days passed and we set eyes upon hardly an insect, Jimmy grew a little sceptical of my traveller's tales, and when on 16 June it was actually snowing at Myvatn I too began to think that this was one of the experiences of the low Arctic that he would miss. The next morning, however, it was warmer and only partially overcast, with a north-easterly breeze that left ragged gaps of blue sky and gleams of sunshine. We were exploring a tussocky promontory that reached into the lake when the sun came out and for a moment or two the wind seemed to drop away to nothing, and it was warm. Suddenly a sound started, a sound so intense that at first even I did not recognize it for what it was. It was not so much a humming as an all-pervasive high-pitched ringing tone that came from all directions at once—the sort of sensation one might experience if one could be actually inside a balloon glass whose edge has been struck by a spoon and is ringing. At first I thought this was some violent singing in my own ears, but then I saw that Jimmy was looking so startled that he must be hearing it too. I glanced around me and suddenly saw that the ground was no longer in focus—as far as the eye could see in all directions it appeared as if a flat grey sheet of muslin were suspended a foot or so above the grass, blurring all forms and outlines. After perhaps half a minute the sun went in and a gust of cold wind blew fresh upon our faces; the sound stopped, and slowly, as we watched, the grey muslin curtain seemed to dissolve and sink into the ground, leaving the coarse grass-stems as sharply etched as they had been before.

'Christ, what on earth was that?'

'Black Fly,' I replied nonchalantly; 'if the sun had stayed out and the wind hadn't come back they'd be at head height by now.'

He didn't propose to wait and see, but before we had regained the car in a hurry the performance had been repeated twice; the numbers were so gigantic, and we were so unprotected, that we both felt close to panic. After a quarter of a mile the car passed through a belt of them and though every window was tightly shut they somehow entered in their thousands and we were in their midst. After minutes of feverish spraying with insecticide they coated the floor and filled every cranny of the upholstery. There were no further references to the imbecility of my precautions.

By the time we left Iceland we had visited a number of Eider colonies, and I felt that we had learned as much as we possibly could have done in the short space at our disposal. I felt confident of colonizing Eiders at Kyleakin, and I looked forward keenly to the experiment. Back at Camusfeàrna I assembled my notes into the form of a Report, which I circulated—somewhat pared and much edited by The Wildfowl Trust—to all bodies who might be interested in a possible new industry for the crofting population of the West Highlands and Islands—though at the last moment I was persuaded of the inadvisability of asking for financial support at this stage, and the heading *Co-operation Required* became almost redundant. It remained, as a matter of form; it would read very differently now. Public bodies grant vast sums for stranger experiments than this, and for projects with less evident possible public benefit, so I might perhaps have been successful.

EIDER DUCK COLONIES
By Gavin Maxwell

Summary

Eiderdown is taken from the lining of an Eider duck's nest after completing its natural function in maintaining the critical nest temperature needed in the early stages of incubation. The down from 30 nests is worth about £10. Eider ducks have been intensively farmed for their down in Iceland, perhaps for as long as 800 years. By means of special techniques which unexpectedly include the planting of flags on the breeding areas, small colonies have been increased to as many as 10,000 pairs. The birds have even been encouraged to start new colonies in this way. Eider ducks breed in numbers round the coasts of Britain, and especially in W. Scotland, where Icelandic methods might be used to advantage. An experimental attempt is proposed to increase the colony of 30 pairs at present breeding on the island adjoining Kyleakin Lighthouse, Ross. It is estimated that the island, which is the property of the National Trust for Scotland, could support at least 2,000 breeding pairs.

No adverse side effects such as damage to fisheries are anticipated. The Wildfowl Trust has indicated its willingness to advise on the biological aspects of the experiment.

If it is successful, a minor industry might develop which could augment the income of the crofters in the region; and the numbers of a delightful, harmless, and decorative bird would be increased for the greater enjoyment of visitors to the West Highlands.

EIDER DUCK COLONIES

General

In Iceland Eiders have been farmed for their down since the days of the early colonists, possibly as early as the 11th Century. A farmer who has Eiders on his land draws considerable revenue from their careful management, and some farmers whose land held no Eiders succeeded in attracting birds to form a new colony.

Methods of establishment and management are traditional and very little work has been done to test the true value of some of the customary procedures, or to experiment with improvements.

In peak years Iceland has produced approximately 4½ tons (worth more than £100,000) of Eider down for export. A farmer receives approximately £10 per lb for the cleansed down. Thirty nests produce 1 lb. Until recently cleansing was done by hand, and it took one man a full day to cleanse 2 lbs weight. Now a small machine has been invented and is sold in Reykjavik. This has revolutionized the industry, and has encouraged many more Icelandic farmers to attempt the establishment of new colonies. Very rapid expansion is possible: on Hrisey Island (Eyafjord), for example, the breeding population has been increased from 60 pairs in 1960 to more than 1,000 in 1964—and this despite eminently unsuitable terrain.

There is no particular magic in the down of the Eider as opposed to that of other ducks, but the species is capable of a unique degree of concentration. Other down is used in Iceland—notably that of the Scaup and Tufted Duck—but not in sufficient quantity to be of economic significance. No synthetic insulating material has been found which can compete with this kind of down.

In the case of established Eider colonies the down is taken twice, once about the 18th day of incubation, and again after the young have left; in the case of colonies still 'under construction', there is only one taking —after hatching.

ESTABLISHMENT AND MANAGEMENT

(a) *Establishment*

Traditionally, Icelanders have relied upon a single item—flags set on sticks about 5 feet high and scattered over the area in which it is intended to concentrate the colony. The flag theme is capable of great variation, and may include longer flag poles with diagonal lines of pennants, small brightly coloured wind propellers, scarecrows, dead ravens, painted posts, and so on.

It is demonstrably true that Eiders will congregate round these things *where fresh water already exists*, but there is no proof that they will forsake a fresh water breeding site in favour of flags by which there is no fresh water. It is at least probable that the traditional Icelandic methods have underestimated the enormous importance of fresh water pools near the breeding site. During the 28 days' incubation period the duck does not feed, but she drinks daily, and access to nearby fresh water is of first importance. In areas of very high precipitation she may rely upon drinking the raindrops from her own feathers, but the provision of drinking pools is the greatest attraction the Eider-farmer can offer.

When fresh water already exists, flags are the first attraction. Ölfusa, a fresh water lake in S. Iceland separated from the sea only by a narrow strip of land, has tussocky shores outstandingly suitable for Eider nesting, and several small islands, very close to the shore, which are extremely unsuitable—close-cropped green grass without cover. The farmer has formed a strong colony on the islands solely by a vast elaboration of flags and pennants.

The Icelandic President's house near Bessastadir stands at the landward end of a low promontory into the sea. This promontory is the property of the farm of Bessastadir, and contains a badly-managed colony of some 2,000 pairs of Eiders. (The farmer has been ill, and has also had labour problems.)

There are no flags, and the nearest fresh water is a small lake below the President's house nearly a mile away. The President had small artificial islands constructed in his lake and set up the traditional flags plus artificial nesting sites (see below). Two hundred Eider pairs now use these islands, and the number is still increasing.

There may be some instinctive recognition by the Eiders that the flags etc. are a deterrent to predators, but there is at least some evidence to suggest that bright colours and inanimate objects in movement are a stimulus in themselves. Where the movement is not that of predators the attraction may extend to other bird species. Tern colonies, for example, appear to attract and stimulate Eiders.

Artificial nesting sites seem often to be used in preference to suitable natural sites. The commonest form in Iceland are built of stone or lava clinker, three sides of a square 18 inches each side and 18 inches high. Sometimes a roof, or lid, is provided, and from my own observations a very high proportion of the roofed sites were used in preference to their roofless neighbours. These sites are sometimes arranged in rows as 'back-to-backs', sometimes grouped as half circles, sometimes scattered. Peripheral nesting sites should have a view of at least twenty yards, but this is not important with central sites, which apparently feel protected by the peripheral sentries.

My own impression is that the birds have a natural liking for *variety* in all forms (terrain, vegetation, colour) and that this applies to nesting sites as well.

Windshelters, built like a very commodious grouse-butt, of stone or turf and furnished with artificial nesting sites, are usually colonized immediately.

Besides their function as a drinking supply for incubating ducks, fresh water pools are the gathering place for the breeding birds on their arrival, and the gathering place for each duck with her newly-hatched brood. I have certain suggestions (see under Management below) for prolonging the ducklings' stay on fresh water and under flags, and thus reducing the mortality rate through predators. Wooden decoy Eider drakes placed at the edge of the fresh water pools have been found to be of great use in attracting breeding pairs to a new site.

Whereas Eiders will colonize cliff-faced islands if their requisites are supplied, they prefer to be able to walk up from the water. Flat beaches, however small, are therefore of great value as an attraction, and the duck will also bring her young to these beaches as a communal roosting ground during the first few weeks after hatching.

The ideal site for a colony is an island in sea water, having small fresh water pools and at least one flat beach. Variety in terrain. Minimum predators—not in immediate vicinity of breeding—Greater Black-backed Gulls, Herring Gulls, or Lesser Black-backed Gulls. Eliminate local Ravens and Hooded Crows (Scotland). Set up flags, wind propellers, scarecrows. Provide artificial nesting sites and wind shelters. Minimum possible disturbance by human beings. Place decoy drake Eiders at the edge of fresh water pools. (N.B. no experimental work has been done with decoy eggs in the artificial nesting sites. No experiments with music, which Dr Gudmundsson thinks worth exploring.)

(b) *Management*

There appears to be a certain *mystique* about the management of a colony of Eiders. I am told that a change in ownership of a colony sometimes produces increase or decrease quite disproportionate to the apparent differences in technique used by the new owner, and the Icelanders have no explanation for this. Some men seem to have 'green fingers' with Eiders.

Minimum disturbance comes second only to control of predators. Ideally, only one man should visit the colony, and he should always wear the same coloured clothes, and avoid any quick movement. He visits the colony when he judges that the majority of birds have begun incubation, and marks each nest with a painted stick stuck into the ground a few feet from it. He may put a separate coloured mark on the stick showing his estimate of the length of incubation, which will guide him as to when to take the down for the first time. A different coloured stick is used for each year, and the previous year's sticks are not removed, both as a ready comparison in figures and choice of sites, and because it is believed that the sticks themselves have some sort of stimulus value to the birds.

He may take greater liberties with the older ducks (distinguished by paler plumage) than the younger; first year breeders may forsake the nest if disturbed while laying. Any dead Eider must be immediately removed from the vicinity of the colony.

No attempt has been made to prolong the stay of the ducklings on the fresh water pools where they are comparatively safe from predators, and in Scotland such a prolongation might be crucial. In the West Highlands and Islands it is not uncommon to see a duck with 5 newly-hatched young on, say, a Monday; on Tuesday she has 3; on Wednesday 1, and on Thursday none. I would propose suspending over the pools fish or other carcases which would become fly-blown, so that the maggots would drop into the water and be a continual attraction to the ducklings.

Mussels are of great importance, and if they are not present at the colony site they may be carted (which often results in the formation of a new mussel bed). The provision of mussels, even in small quantities, tends to concentrate Eiders, and to keep them concentrated after hatching. Mussels will survive for up to five days in fresh water, so that the weekly dumping of small numbers into the fresh water pools might be of great value.

Possible Significance of Eider Colonies in the West Highlands and Islands

Eiders are resident in large numbers throughout the great majority of the area. I do not know of any census of the breeding Eider population (West Highlands and Islands), but I would guess that an estimate of 25,000 pairs would be very conservative.

I do not know of any attempt being made to use this natural resource as a profitable adjunct to the crofting industry, and it is plain that whatever the existing figure is it could be very greatly increased by careful colonizing.

Proposal

To start an experimental colony on the island tidally separated from the island commonly known as Gillean Island (Kyleakin Lighthouse, which I acquired from the Northern Lighthouse Board and the National Trust for Scotland two years ago) and which is the property of the National Trust for Scotland.

This island has water near to the surface (but not yet any pools), small flat beaches, and good nesting terrain. It is perhaps 4 acres, and could certainly hold 2,000 breeding pairs. It can be kept under observation from Kyleakin Lighthouse Cottage, 200 yards distant.

Co-operation required

Permission from the proprietors to exclude the public from this island by written notice between April and July—(the flags will tend to draw curious visitors)—and to use the island for the experiment.

I don't know why, when I think of Iceland now, a single and seemingly insignificant image is the first to come to my mind—our last night at Myvatn. It was utterly still, and somewhere close by, alone under the pale immensity of the midnight sun, a single Redwing began to sing with a hesitant, creaking voice. It seems now like a threnody.

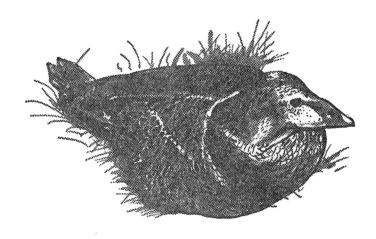

10

The Rocks of Kylerhea

Early in July 1965, a fortnight or so after I had returned from
Iceland, Richard Frere had finished his massive work of conversion
of the two Kyleakin cottages into one, his installation of a generator
and the electric wiring of the whole premises, and he left, warning
me that a certain amount of tidying up would be necessary before
my guests arrived the following week. These had been invited for
a week's cruise on *Polar Star*, using first Isle Ornsay Lighthouse
and then Kyleakin as a base. So the day after Richard's departure I
set out from Camusfeàrna in *Polar Star*, carrying a work party
to spend a full day preparing the house for its very first residential
occupancy since I had bought it.

I was immensely proud of the house and its furnishings, for
while the décor of Isle Ornsay had been largely the work of
Richard's wife Joan, Kyleakin had been my particular project, my
own unaided concept. Against the advice of both architects and
friends, I had created, on the southern side of the house, a single
room more than forty feet long, its windows looking down the
long reach of Lochalsh and Loch Duich to the distant peaks of
The Five Sisters of Kintail. In that loch lay perhaps the most
spectacular piece of architecture surviving in Scotland, the ancient
island stronghold of the Clan MacRae, Eilleann Donan Castle.

Because the room I planned would be little more than eleven
feet wide, all my advisers were unanimous in saying that it would
look disproportionate, like a corridor, and that, furthermore, it

would be impossible to heat adequately. I believed that the corridor effect could be obviated by using neutral-coloured furniture against the inner wall, the only strong colours being bright cushions which would draw the eye away from the four large windows, and one large wall mirror would reflect the sea and the ruin of Castle Moille. There were to be no pictures other than Michael Ayrton's vast and splendid, almost colourless wax of the falling Icarus, dominating the far end of the room as one entered it from the kitchen-dining room. The heating problem I proposed to solve by two very wide open fireplaces, one under the Icarus and one at the near end of the room, against the inner wall; these would be supplemented if necessary by electric heating from the generator we had installed. I had made watercolour sketches of this room as I visualized it and hoped that it would become, and all the furniture had been chosen to correspond as exactly as possible with these drawings.

The project had been entirely successful; I bought the furniture with great care in London and finally transhipped it to the island with a surprisingly small list of breakages. The house itself was now all and more than I had ever hoped for, and I had exact plans for the formation of a wild informal garden where flowering shrubs and rare honeysuckles would grow in the shelter of the rock crevices and buttresses on the northern side of the house.

With all having gone thus far so smoothly in the face of such formidable obstacles it was with an unusually high heart that I set off from Camusfeàrna that morning carrying five others with me to clear away the last traces of reconstruction and to arrange the furniture in its final positions. It was a fine summer's morning; we reached Kyleakin in thirty-five minutes; we anchored *Polar Star* in the south bay of the island, and we worked all day. Even the tide had been in our favour, the north-going flood as we set out and the south-running ebb when we started home at just after eleven o'clock in the evening.

That night I put *Polar Star* on the rocks for the second time; and because it was the second time I may perhaps be forgiven for protesting that it really was not my fault. The whole experience was so sickening that even now, more than two years later as I write, it is a painful and confusing effort to try to reassemble the

25 Icelandic waterfall

26

26 and 27 Four
Icelandic
farmhouses

28 and 29 Icelandic ponies

30 Whale Fjord

31 Icebergs and Eiderdrakes

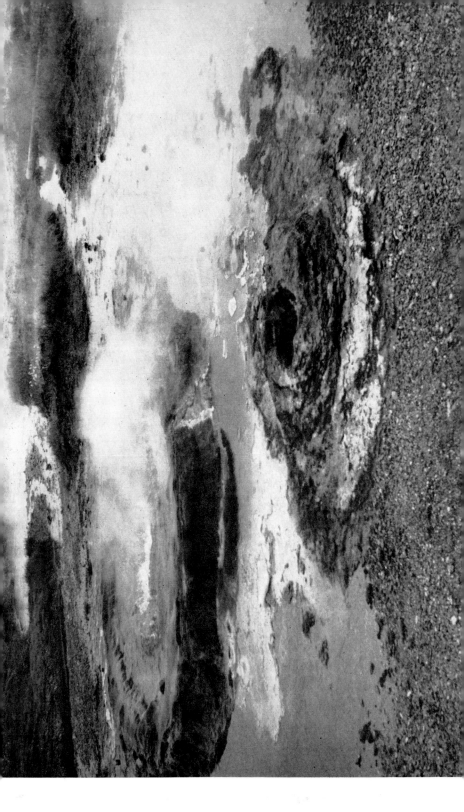

facts. The tide was at half ebb, running perhaps eight knots southwards as it ripped through the Sound, so that *Polar Star* as she approached the narrows was making twenty knots or more. it was not really dark; there was a little light from the afterglow, and the sea, apart from the tide-swell, was calm. We were heading for *Polar Star*'s moorings five miles to the south of us, and it looked as though we should make record time.

A little before we reached the narrows Alan MacDiarmaid, who lived at Glenelg (he had now left our employment, but was helping us out), suggested that there was no point in his coming five miles south to Camusfeàrna; if he could telephone to his wife from the call box by the ferry slipway at Kylerhea she would come with her car and pick him up at the mainland side of the ferry. There is no telephone there, so that the manoeuvre involved putting him ashore on the Skye side, waiting out in the channel while he telephoned, picking him up again, taking him across to the Glenelg side, and putting him off there. With the fast running ebb tide this was certainly an ambitious programme, but Jimmy Watt was at the wheel, and Jimmy could do just about anything with *Polar Star* short of making her fly; he had the sort of expertise that one associates with a lifetime's experience rather than that of a few short seasons.

The first part of the operation went with almost miraculous precision. Jimmy handled *Polar Star* as if it had been broad daylight and no tide running, but after Alan had scrambled aboard again on the Skye side Jimmy let out a long breath and said, 'Well, I hope I don't have to do that again very often.' He regained mid-channel under power and then let the tide take the boat south before boring up slowly against it to the mainland jetty. I said something congratulatory, and added that as the next part of the programme would be worse still I would rather shoulder the responsibility myself. I took the wheel when we were about two cables south of the mainland jetty. Beside me on the port side deck was one of our employees, on the starboard side deck was Jimmy—both could see more than I could through the wheelhouse glass.

It seemed darker now that I had the wheel myself. Both engines were at about a quarter throttle, nosing up into the tide, parallel with the shore and making perhaps four knots. After a minute or so Jimmy called out to me, 'For God's sake keep her off—give her more revs on the starboard engine—you don't know how much starboard leeway you're making with this tide.' Had I heeded him all would have been well, but the voice in my other ear said, 'You're all right as you go, just keep her as she goes, you're in clear water now.' So I held course. I seem to remember some violent oath from Jimmy just before we struck. I couldn't listen to two people at once, and I had chosen to listen to the wrong one; perhaps he was tired, for it had certainly been a long and weary day, and it was dark enough to make the distance to shore very difficult to judge.

So for the second time in four years I felt the sickening jolt of keel on rock, an almost physical sickness, a nausea of shame at the realization of my crass blunder and all its far-reaching consequences. We had been going so slowly, and the force of the tide against us was so great, that I thought she might drive back off the rock with both engines full astern, but I was reckoning without the fact that the faster the tide was running the faster the rock was baring. I remember small details. I remember that when I realized that she wouldn't move I tried to find a packet of cigarettes that had slipped from the wheelhouse counter and fallen by my feet, and that it took long seconds to retrieve the packet and light a cigarette. I remember Jimmy jumping down into the wheelhouse through the side hatch and saying, 'It wasn't your fault, Gavin—just let me get you a stiff whisky and then leave it all to us.' He knew exactly how I was feeling, but I couldn't respond; just as when I was a child I could never produce the appropriate response to any situation. So I looked away from him out of the port window to the dark Skye hills against the cold afterglow and said numbly, 'I don't want a drink. Please get the dinghy launched and fetch help quickly. It was my fault because I didn't listen to you.'

Because our helper's wife was already on her way with his car, rescue was not very long in coming. In the meantime I was alone on board, and I tried to assess the situation. The ship was aground forrard of amidships, canting her bows upwards, but still on an even keel. She was making no water, and I believed that she could be hauled off by the stern. I prepared a stern rope and a heaving line, and waited.

I suppose it wasn't more than twenty minutes or half an hour before the rescue boat arrived, but it seemed much longer. She passed across *Polar Star*'s bows, her motors making such a racket that I could barely hear her skipper bawling, 'Heave me a bow line!' I had no bow line ready, because to pull her by the bows could only settle her more firmly on the rock upon which she was aground. I had no megaphone; I bawled and yelled and signalled that I was going to heave a stern line. Faint above the noise of the engines I caught the skipper's voice, 'I can't hear you for our engines. Tide's ebbing fast and we can't hang about. Heave me a bow line —and quick!' Some of our party were back aboard *Polar Star* by now; in a mood of absolute despair I called upon them to witness that I thought the proposal disastrous and that if anyone was going to heave a bow line it would not be me. I dissociated myself; I went and sat in the stern cockpit and stared down into the pallid fast-running sea that I was beginning to hate even more than I feared it.

The tow line from the bows dragged *Polar Star* a few feet higher on to the rock, and with such a hideous grinding sound from her keel that I knew that if she had not been damaged before she was certainly damaged now. After that there was nothing that anyone could do until the tide turned and refloated her hours later. It could not be said to be the rescuer's fault; he had no time to make an accurate assessment.

As the ebb drained the narrows she began to heel over, though because of her almost flat bottom she never reached a dangerous angle. It was very cold, and the fastenings of my duffel coat were broken at the neck. Very gradually the mountains began to take their true shapes against a pale green sky. At dead low tide a long line of glistening weedgrown rocks showed astern of us, rocks over which we must have passed with only inches to spare. The whole of the last cable length of our course had been a full thirty yards too far inshore.

I waited on board through the chilly grey dawn until at length the tide's return refloated the ship and she was towed north to a boat-building yard at Kyle of Lochalsh.

11

The Struggle

What would the world be, once bereft
Of wet and of wildness? Let them be left,
Oh let them be left, wildness and wet;
Long live the weeds and the wilderness yet.

One day early in August, only a week or two after the *Polar Star*
disaster, the local policeman called in the course of a routine check
of firearms certificates. Any visit to Camusfeàrna from the outside
world, no matter how official the visitor may be, becomes of
necessity a social occasion, for the visitor has trudged all the weary
distance down the hill from Druimfiaclach, and it would be
inhospitable not to offer some refreshment before he starts the
steep and boggy climb back to the road. So, our business done,
we had a drink together, and sat talking for a while. After half an
hour or so I was conscious of a pain in my stomach, but it was not
a very severe pain, and I expected it to pass off. But by the time the
constable had left it was steadily increasing in intensity, and it was
something completely outside my personal experience. I had had a
duodenal ulcer during the war, but it had never recurred, and it
had not felt like this. I was alone in the house now, and I began to

search with growing desperation for some antacid, but I could find nothing. It seemed the one item missing from the sizeable medicine chests I had carried with me in North Africa. I was determined to ride this out, because I was due in the very near future for a medical examination for life insurance, and if I were to call a doctor now I might as well forget the whole project. As well might a mouse determine to resist a tiger.

After an hour all possible question of surviving this storm by myself had gone. I was in such acute pain that I could hardly drag myself to the telephone. The village doctor was a new arrival and I had not yet met him; it was going to be, I thought as I dialled his number, doubled up with pain, a curious introduction. A friendly, cheerful and essentially competent voice answered me, and I said (with difficulty) a rehearsed speech, 'Doctor Dunlop? You don't know me, but I'm in your practice—my name is Gavin Maxwell, and I live at Camusfeàrna, on the shore below Druimfiaclach.' 'Yes,' he said, 'I know just where you are—what can I do for you?'

I remember how long it seemed to take me to answer; I remember the litter of papers on the desk before me, which were all out of focus, because I am far-sighted, and during the past half hour I had somewhere lost my spectacles; I remember that through the window I could see against a blue sky a single raven circling high above the field, his guttural croaks timed to a rhythmic side-somersault. The pain seemed too great to speak.

The doctor's voice came again, calm but somehow unprofessional, as though we were old friends: 'Take your time, but try and tell me what's wrong.'

I said, 'I don't know for certain, but I think I've perforated a duodenal ulcer. I've had nothing to eat for eighteen hours, so perhaps there's no peritonitis—but I'm not thinking very clearly.'

'I'll be with you just as quick as I can. Lie down and try not to move until I get there.' He spoke as though he had no other patient, no other responsibilities nor worries of his own; as though the five mile drive and the long walk down the hill did not exist.

When he arrived he gave me morphia and said that he would return in four hours' time. This was my first meeting with Doctor Tony Dunlop, a young man, married and with small children, who had practised medicine in challenging countries such as West

Africa, and had finally chosen, as had Gavin Brown, a remote country practice where his exceptional personality and understanding of individual patients gave full scope for his powers. This was a man of wide and varied interests and broad learning, and I wished even then that our first meeting had been in more fortunate circumstances.

He returned at seven o'clock in the evening, and by then I was almost incapable of speech. The pain had become so acute that I was no longer a truly rational human being; the most I could summon up was 'Doctor, I would like to know whether this is likely to prove fatal, because if it is there are things I must do first— signing documents and so on.' He answered, 'No, I don't think so —at least I hope not, and I think I'm right. We've got to get you to hospital quickly. I'm going to give you some more morphia now, but that's the last I can give you, because the doctors in Inverness couldn't make a fair diagnosis if the symptoms were obliterated by pain-killers. Your staff has come home now, and they're constructing a stretcher. You'll go up the hill in your Land Rover on this stretcher, and at the village you'll be transferred to my car, whose seats fold back to make a bed. We've got eighty miles to go, and I've telephoned for an ambulance to meet us halfway, or whenever we happen to meet on the road—if you're lucky you'll be in hospital by midnight.'

So I was carried out on a home-made stretcher and driven—a journey I shall never forget—up the jolting Jeep track to Druim-fiaclach, empty and desolate then. At the village I was transferred as discreetly as possible from the Land Rover to the doctor's car. It was a long drive through the night; either the pain or the morphia or the combination of the two made me garrulous; for I remember talking a lot. I remember that the doctor drove very fast and with great skill. We met the ambulance some few miles west of Invermoriston. I asked for more morphia for the last leg of the journey but was gently and firmly refused. I arrived in hospital at Inverness at one in the morning.

Some thirty-six hours later the surgeon, a man of high reputation in his profession and great personal charm, showed me the X-ray plates. 'This,' he said, 'is an acute exacerbation of an ulcer probably of long standing. I want to put the alternatives clearly before you. The first, which is what I recommend, is for you to remain here and for me to operate after a short time, a partial gastrectomy which I will explain to you. The second choice is for you to remain here under treatment for about two months, without surgery. As you've explained to me that your life is very heavily committed until November, there is of course a third possible course of action, and that is for you, being fully aware of all the risks involved, to go home after a day or two's rest here, and to return and let me operate in November. If you choose this last course I should like to ask for your assurance that you really will come back in November.'

It seemed to me that this was the only possible thing to do, and I said so, though I cringed before the idea of further abdominal surgery.

It was only a few hours after this conversation, and while I was still in hospital that I received a telephone call from London. There had been a Board Meeting of the Company which had been formed to manage my affairs, a meeting which I had been due to attend. The caller, a co-director, was bleakly informative. It had come to light that owing to faulty internal accounting the Company's finances were far from what we had imagined. The assets covered the liabilities, but little more, and at this meeting it was demonstrated that the maintenance of Camusfeàrna cottage and its otters was costing £7,000 a year. A new director, a retired business man, recommended the immediate sale of all the Company's assets, including the two lighthouses, and even—owing to a misconception of what was whose—some of my own.

This policy seemed to me to lack finesse; and, moreover, to be abandoning the battle before a blow had been struck, because the enemy's strength had been found to be almost equal to our own. For example, neither of the lighthouses, upon which we had lavished so much money, were mortgaged, and we had succeeded in letting them to holiday parties for as much as £65 a week each. (This sum may sound excessive, but it usually amounted to less than £10 a head each, with the use of boats and engines and a private island.) These were the things uppermost in my mind; though no doubt at a lower level of consciousness lay the realization that the loss of the lighthouses would mean the end of my cherished Eider project, and at that time it seemed to me that my life held nothing to replace it.

So I replied that I was not in agreement; that I would return to Camusfeàrna the next day, and temporarily assume the function of Managing Director, in an effort to restore financial stability. The mouse and the tiger again.

When I came back and told the local doctor of my decision he said, 'Well, it's a novel treatment for a duodenal ulcer, certainly, but I've had ulcers myself and I found they did best on a diet of hot curries and plenty of alcohol, which is hardly the conventional treatment. I wish you good luck.'

It was in a spirit of challenge that I re-entered Camusfeàrna on 4 August—a double challenge, mental and physical. I was determined both to solve the Company's finances while at the same time finishing my book *Lords of the Atlas* on schedule, and to regain the state of physical health and activity that I had possessed before the Land Rover accident. It was an ambitious programme, and one with obviously conflicting time-factors.

My first action as Managing Director was to try to raise mortgages on the lighthouses. Everyone with whom I spoke assured me that this would be easy, but it was not. Time and time again negotiations seemed to be almost complete when they fell through, and there were so many intermediaries that I could never satisfy myself as to which link in the chain had broken. The heart of the matter seemed to be that the houses, however solid and magnificently built, were on islands, and this, despite their desirability as holiday homes, was a major deterrent to any prospective mortgagee. Meanwhile I found that, bad though the position discovered at the Board Meeting had been, there was worse to come, for the list of creditors had been far from complete. More and more bills, of which the directors had then been ignorant, began to pour into Camusfeàrna, but even with this new avalanche the assets still held the balance on paper. I closed entirely the small office in London, which, however incredibly, had been revealed as responsible for an annual debit of £3,000. This gigantically disproportionate debit was transformed, by letting the premises for a few pounds a week, into a minor source of income. Having done this, and in order to gain time, I did an extremely foolish thing; I devoted the whole of my mother's legacy to the payment of pressing Company creditors. I was in fact a minority shareholder in the Company, and this was the very first capital I had owned since the demise of the Island of Soay Shark Fisheries eighteen years earlier. Ever since then I had been a hand-to-mouth earner, first as a portrait painter and then as a writer, unable to budget because there had been no fixed income. But now, because the Company was registered in my own name rather than in the decent obscurity and anonymity of some word unconnected with me, I felt that I had no alternative but to use my own money to pay its debts. I have since been told this action demonstrated a lack of rudimentary business sense, but I can only repeat that I felt, and still feel, that I had no choice. The result, however, was to add personal poverty to Company difficulties; nor did the Company creditors appear to appreciate that I had acted from a sense of moral responsibility. For the greater part of them money was all that counted, and where it came from was immaterial. I know for a fact that many believed my personal resources to be almost inexhaustible, and that my failure to pay every Company creditor immediately was wilful parsimony on my part. Thus, anyway, I lost the last capital that I am ever likely to possess, and the fault was nobody's but my own.

In fact I came perilously close to the position of a friend, who had overlooked a tradesman's account during his absence from home and left there only a young French girl in charge of his seven-year-old daughter. To them appeared three villainous-looking characters who spoke, if their leader's written word is to be believed, in no tongue known to man. Of his two sinister henchmen who lurked skulking and muttering at his heels, one was a squat hunchback with a black patch over his left eye, and the other was thin as a piece of string and club-footed. The French girl viewed this scowling, vulpine trio with considerable alarm, as, after having performed some vocal cabalistic ritual before the door, they began to skirmish through the house, uttering the while loud cries that one must imagine to have been in unison. The Sheriff himself afterwards wrote of the incident in a racy little anecdote couched in his inimitable style, under the title of *Schedule of Poinding*. While reading it one would do well to remember the limited linguistic abilities of the young French girl.

I, Messenger at Arms, by virtue of an Extract Decree from the Sheriff Court Books containing Warrant to Poind thereon, dayed the —th day of — and Extracted the—th day of — both in the year Nineteen Hundred and Sixty —, together also with an Execution of Charge given thereupon, duly expired, upon the —th day of — Nineteen hundred and Sixty — years, PASSED, with the valuators and witnesses afternamed and designed [*alas, the slim volume was not illustrated*] to the premises occupied or possessed by X, and then and there, after my crying three several OYEZES, making open proclamation and publicly reading the said Extract Decree and Warrant to Poind thereon, and Execution of Charge and demanding payment of the principal sum due, interest and expenses, and no payment having been made or offered—in her Majesty's name and authority and in the Name and Authority of the Sheriff of said Sheriffdom, I apprehended and poinded upon the goods, gears and effects aftermentioned belonging to the said X [*unfortunately he poinded copiously upon goods that were not X's property, causing their owner no end of hard scrubbing*]. For valuing the same I adduced A and B [*his fearful henchmen*] as valuators; who, having accepted of the said office, and taken the oath *de fideli administratione* administered by me to them, particularly examined the goods, gear and effects aftermentioned and both WITH ONE VOICE valued the same at the respective sums following, VIZ:
[*Here follows a list, including some valuable antique furniture valued at £1.*]
Thereafter I made three several offers back of the said goods, gear and effects so poinded upon to the said X or to any person who would in his name pay the said debt and expenses or the value at which the said goods, gear and effects were valued; but no person appearing for that effect [*poor Giselle had by now taken refuge in the bathroom*] or to claim the said goods, gear and effects, I, by virtue aforesaid and of my office *adjudged, decerned* and *declared* the said poinding to be completed with the usual solemnities of law, and the said goods, gear and effects to be the property of the said pursuer, and I ordained the said poinded goods, gear, and effects to be left in the hands of the said X where the same were so poinded—there to remain till a warrant of the said Sheriff be obtained for their sale, and I make certification to the said X and to all others to whom it effeirs, that if any person or persons shall unlawfully intromit with or carry off the said poinded goods, gear, and effects, they shall be liable to be imprisoned until they restore the effects, or pay

double the appraised values, in terms of the statutes made anent poindings. All this I do before and in the presence of the said valuators, who were also witness to the premises.

And so, no doubt, with muttered medieval imprecations and coarse bursts of legal laughter, this outrageous poinding party shambled away down the drive, reminiscing of mighty Poindings and unlawful intromissions of bygone days.

SHERIFF'S OFFICER: 'Remember the time I poinded right in the middle of the Duchess of Cromarty's white bear-skin rug? Ho-ho!'

FIRST VALUATOR: 'Yes, that was a good one right enough, by my virtue! You hadn't had a poind for a long time!'

SHERIFF'S OFFICER: 'I had so—that very morning, after breakfast.'

FIRST VALUATOR: 'Well I do decern! It's you that's powerful in the Poinding! And taking so little of the solids too!'

2ND VALUATOR: 'And the time you sneezed three times in the middle of the OYEZES and we all had to start again? Those cries were hardly several, by my Virtue!'

SHERIFF'S OFFICER: 'That does not effeir you. What anent the lamentable occasion when you were out of time with the One Voice? The whole word 'shillings' came out of you into a dead silence after we'd spoken it. And me using the residenter's swagger stick as a conductor's baton too.'

2ND VALUATOR: 'I had poinded upon that swagger stick with the solemnity of law. By my virtue, I believe your use of it as aforementioned constituted unlawful intromission!'

SHERIFF'S OFFICER: 'If it did it was well worth it—the best unlawful intromission I've ever had! Ha-ha! But you should not have poinded on my swagger stick—not with solemnity anyway. You always poind best just when you feel like it—just like hunger and eating. I have had twenty years of poinding, and I know where the greatest satisfaction is—like in the middle of the Duchess of Cromarty's white rug.'

2ND VALUATOR *scowls and utters a fearful oath, which may be rendered as* 'de fideli administratione officii'.

1ST VALUATOR: 'I want to poind!'

SHERIFF'S OFFICER: 'Not here, not in the open. There's a house only a quarter of a mile down the road, and I do believe they've got some Persian rugs there.'

Their voices grow faint; Giselle and the little girl emerge trembling from the bathroom.

LITTLE GIRL: 'They've gone!'

FRENCH GIRL: 'Oui, ils sont partis—mais regarde, ma petite— il y a de la merde partout! Je ne comprends pas—c'est à cause de quoi? Et qu'est que veut dire ce mot OYEZ? Ils sont des foux peut-être? Mais M. le Patron—qu'est qu'il dira à son retour?—Je crois que je serai congédiée!'

Distant chorus of Poinders' voices singing in the dark to the tune of *Deutschland Über Alles*:

> 'Poinding, poinding, by my virtue;
> 'Let our voices All Be One
> 'Anent the OYEZ and Pursuer
> 'We do adjudge, declare, decerne.'

During this time I was also conducting a spirited running battle with the solicitors who had acted for me as author in the Alliata libel action. Their bill appeared to me to be excessive; I repeatedly asked for, but did not get, a detailed itemisation of the account. Nor was I initially aware of the courses open to me: to have this bill examined either by the Law Society (which could certify its reasonableness or otherwise) or by the Court which would 'tax' it (vet it and possibly reduce it). This battle did not end until more than a year and a half later and after I had employed another firm of solicitors to act against them. We had the bill 'taxed' by the Court and this resulted in its being reduced by nearly one third. This may be worth placing on record. Most people, like myself, have little idea of the law's costs and their possible reduction.

At Camusfeàrna itself I began studying its economy, and realized that the questions of transport and communication lay at the heart of all our problems. To buy in bulk and to store in bulk was the only possible solution. Food, whether for humans or otters, was costing us many times its face value because of the necessity to buy hurriedly and in small quantities, often from great distances. I have used the simile earlier; it would apparently cost little to live in an Antarctic weather station—but, living there, the moment one tried to establish daily or even weekly contact with the outside world the cost of living would be greater than that at any five-star hotel. Because practically every telephone call necessary to my function as Managing Director of a Company in distress was a trunk call, and often a protracted one, and because some of our temporary employees would often hold interminable conversations with their girl friends hundreds of miles distant, the telephone bill itself became a major problem, and one which I could do little to solve; if the employees were denied the right to use the telephone they would leave, and if they left I should not have time to write.

But on the transport and supply side there was an obvious remedy and I began by buying deep freezes that could contain enough food both for animals and humans for months at a time. This, though it represented an almost final drain upon my private resources, did temporarily solve a major problem.

It is perhaps worth mentioning, for any improbable others who might somehow find themselves in the same situation that, though at Camusfeàrna we were surrounded by natural food of all kinds— shellfish ranging through cockles and mussels to oysters; fish of many species; edible fungi and much else—the average adolescent will not eat any food to which he has not been brought up. The situation is almost parallel to that obtaining in primitive Muslim cultures, in which, for reasons long forgotten, some birds, beasts and fishes are 'unclean', while others, so alike as to be almost indistinguishable, are lawful food. I remember being sent out in the marshes of Southern Iraq to shoot for the pot because we had nothing to eat; the majority of birds that passed my way were of a species of wader called Godwit, and I shot as many as I could. When I returned with my bag it was sharply and vocally divided into clean and unclean; there were two species, the Bar-tailed Godwit and the Black-tailed Godwit, and one (I forget which) was not clean food. The extremely unpalatable Pigmy Cormorants and African Darters, were, on the other hand, clean, and I was re-proached for not having killed them.

Time and time again I tried to explain to some new temporary employee at Camusfeàrna that when he had been new born he had liked only his mother's milk and subsequently what food she served him after he was weaned; that to survive in the world one had to adapt oneself to new foods that were habitual to the people among whom one was living, but always to no avail. Food had to be 'as mother made it' (usually, it turned out, from tins) and its provision at Camusfeàrna was extremely expensive. Gastronomically, the adventurous spirit attributed to the British was completely lacking; we were surrounded by free food that no one would eat, but which would have been very costly in more sophisticated society. (I remember a Greek sailor on my brother's yacht being offered a little *vol au vent* of caviare and being asked what he thought of it. He replied that the pastry was excellent, but he didn't like the 'black stuff in the middle'.)

All this struggle was paper and telephone work; the physical target I had set myself, some sort of rejuvenescence—and above all the exhilaration of contact with the elements and the natural world, that had formed so great a part of my life—was steadily receding, for there just did not seem to be time for physical exercise. I was losing the battle on both fronts, although like Queen Victoria I was not interested in the possibility of defeat; I believed that it simply did not exist.

I had my minor trivial triumphs in the economic field. Because our mail was not delivered to Camusfeàrna but to a wooden box on the roadside at Druimfiaclach, two and a half miles away from us by jeep track, the daily collection of letters was costing us a small fortune in petrol and mechanical deterioration—a mild word to use of, say, broken axles and half-shafts. I applied to the Post Office for subsidy, and was refused. I, in turn, refused to take no for an answer, and at the end of an impassioned correspondence I was awarded £100 annually for collection of mail for Camusfeàrna and for the old croft across the field. With this and many other economies effected in the whole management of the establishment I had no real doubt that I could make the place viable once more.

But I felt the absolute necessity of occasionally getting far away from that desk at which I sat for something like twelve hours every day, trying to give six to the writing of a book and six to Company management, eating snack meals and ending each day too tired to talk. Though the sporting tradition and the bloodthirstiness of my youth had largely deserted me (why is fishing so widely considered a respectable blood-sport and shooting in any form so despicable? —I suspect here an identification with weapons used against man, and that if man-hooking was part of warfare there would be an equal outcry against the patient angler) I accepted in October an invitation to stalk at a distant deer forest. This had been one of my major hobbies in the past, and I felt that—if I were still physically capable of the tremendous effort involved—it might prove to be the tonic I so badly needed.

It was. The days that I spent on the hill, in worse weather conditions than it is easy to visualize, gave to me a feeling of complete and utter release, of a unity with nature that I had long lacked at Camusfeàrna.

One afternoon especially, though it was bloodless enough to satisfy the most squeamish, is fresh in my memory as I write.

From where I stood on the hilltop, with the wet wind tearing in great gusts at my face and sodden clothing, I could see no further than a radius of twenty yards into the surrounding mist. The abyss below me to my left, a two thousand foot fall of scree and rock-face and straggling heather, was filled with moving grey-white cloud; here on the bare summit of the huge ridge, where all that grew underfoot was lichen and mosses amid granite chips, small ragged clouds, darker than the mist that covered all the hilltop, came streaming up out of the great blanketed gulf; they sailed by swiftly and low overhead and were gone into the dimness that covered all. The only sound was the rushing of the wind as it broke and scattered the drops of ever-falling rain.

Suddenly, from far away, from the hidden hill-face beyond the gulf, borne thin and clear on the wind, wild and elemental, came the sound that during all the many years I have spent among the Red deer of Scotland, in their aloof tempestuous territory of rock and mist, has never lost its fascination for me—the voice of the stag in rut. It begins low and throaty like a bull's roar, then hollows out to a higher, dying cadence, that seems to hold at the same time challenge, despair and frustration. I stirred to that desolate music as I stirred to the whip of wind and rain, to the ice-cold cling of my drenched clothing, to the hard ache of long unused muscles that had climbed from the infinitely distant floor of the glen below. With the water running down my neck and spine all the way to water-logged shoes, with the cold so bitter that I was conscious of my own shivering, I felt an actual buoyancy, an uplift of spirit. This was my world, the cradle of my species, shared with the wild creatures; it was the only world I wanted, and I felt that I had no place at a writing desk.

In these primeval situations man the hunter reacts to unexpected sound as does man the hunted—instantaneously. Suddenly, from no more than fifty yards away, from just inside the encircling mist, came the same wild voice, magnified by my loss of vision to a nearness, an immediacy, that set my heart hammering and my eyes straining; the instant drop to a prone position was atavistic. (There is, I have always found, something revitalizing, re-energizing, in this contact between hands and body and the small growth of the mountain earth.) Wind and cloud whined past my face, but borne on them now was the strange, elusive, pungent smell, musky and sour-sweet, of the rutting stag.

In the edge of the mist shapes without apparent context formed and re-formed. A tuft of heather, only yards away, assumed the aspect of a far-off wooded crest; a whitened, weather-worn double heather-stem took on the shape of the distant antlers of an archetypal stag.

I began to crawl forward, wet belly to wet heather that changed after a few yards to soft black peat, relic of vegetation rotted a million years ago, and the dark paste was thickly packed beneath my finger nails. The smell of the stag grew stronger.

With tremendous impact now his voice came again, so near to me that it was I who was afraid, returning in that moment to the dim red dawn of our race when man was both hunter and hunted. In exactly the same instant I saw his horns before me, indistinct but twenty times the size of the impostor heather stems, and from the corner of my right eye I saw simultaneously the ears of a hind, blurred by the mist, but so near to me that I could have touched them with a fishing rod. I was right in among the deer, and the wet, stinging wind was whipping at my left cheek, so that my scent must have missed the hind's nostrils by inches rather than by feet, but she was still unaware of my presence. The cloud which lay on the hilltop began to thicken and whiten, and the stag's horns became intermittently invisible, but when he roared again the sound seemed even nearer than before. I slipped the leather foresight protector from my rifle, and lay with my chin pressed to the ground, the wet woodwork clammy in my palms and my teeth beginning to chatter.

The small, tattered black clouds still raced by low overhead, forming a ceiling, so that one felt as if in a small fog-filled room, crowded with invisible inhabitants. Then, driven by the wind, an eagle swept low out of the speeding clouds, so low that as he saw me the rasp of air between the great pinion feathers of his wings as he sheered off was audible even above the din of the gale and the rain. He tilted upwards and away from me and was at once lost in the clouds. But the violent sweep of those vast wings as they banked not ten feet above me must have set up some momentary shift in the direction of wind current, for the hind was suddenly towering dimly over me. She was not more than fifteen feet away, but she looked as though seen through frosted glass. She gave one grunting, exhaling bark, and faded quickly into the murk.

With the deer gone, I was left upon the clouded hilltop with the light going, soaked and with the almost horizontal rain cutting to my ribs, and five miles to walk home in the dusk, but I was content. Here, perhaps, I was beyond the range of the rowan tree.

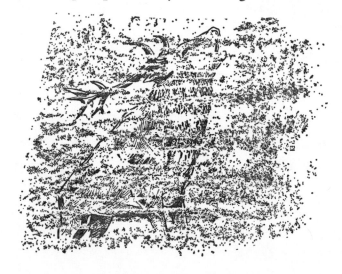

12

Hounds and Hares

I went back to the paper war at Camusfeàrna, and in November I returned to hospital at Inverness for the abdominal operation I dreaded so much. I left Camusfeàrna with a reasonably calm mind, for my literary commitments were fulfilled, the lighthouse mortgages now seemed certain, and the deep freezes were full of food for dogs and humans and fish for otters.

I was back at Camusfeàrna within forty-eight hours. The X-rays had shown the ulcer to be completely healed, and the surgeon said he could find no excuse whatsoever for operating. At that moment I felt that the tide had turned on both battle fronts, and that victory was in sight.

Although paper work had now become my daily routine, I had one more venture that autumn into the outdoor world that meant so much to me. For three years I had owned a vast Deerhound called Dirk (the replacement of a predecessor by the same name, who had met a tragic death by drinking petrol) and in September I bought for him a mate, a bitch called Hazel. Both were, by Deerhound standards, past their prime, for they are a short-lived race—past their prime, that is to say, either for coursing or for breeding, and by purists the former is considered the criterion. However, when I bought Hazel I was invited to join that select body the Deerhound Club, and to bring both hounds to the annual coursing meeting in the central Highlands.

I accepted, and entered Dirk and Hazel; not that either of them could be expected to put up much of a performance, Dirk because he was completely inexperienced, and Hazel because as a bitch who had already borne several litters of puppies she was seemingly already too old for speed. But I was, apart from anything else, intensely curious to see for myself this sport, about whose unthinkable brutality I had received so many circulars from anti-blood-sport bodies and individuals. Hares, I had been told, were literally torn slowly in half, screaming the while, by the coursing couple of hounds that overtook them. Hares do scream when in pain, and that voice is horrifying like the wailing of a distressed human infant, producing in all but the most hardened and impervious observer a feeling of identification that is nauseating. I had heard it often, not only in the man-made situations of the shooting party, but from hares taken by foxes and eagles, whose predatory instincts could patently not be banned without still further bloodletting by man. No hare can ever die of old age—and very rarely indeed does any other non-predator do so—so that the killing of a hare by a man-controlled dog rather than by fox or eagle (or by the wolf exterminated in Scotland by man) seemed to me nearer to the ecological normal than the undoubted horrors of the battery farm and the fat-stock slaughterhouse. The predators, on the other hand, do quite often die what for some curious reason we call 'natural' deaths—that is death from old age or disease—as opposed to violent and painful death at the hands of some species other than man.

(This word 'natural', as applied to human life and death and all that lies between our beginnings and our ends, carries a really stunning distortion of fact. For centuries we have described as 'unnatural' ways of living and dying common even to our closest cousins, who must surely be the referees as to what is natural. Now that new prophets such as Konrad Lorenz and Leonard Williams are among us we may perhaps hope that in another hundred years or so these words will be used more accurately; if, that is to say, the human species has not by then died a communal and highly unnatural death.)

If these 'natural' deaths (and both categories must surely be accepted as natural to anyone who deplores man's intervention on the scene) are for some reason less regrettable than the normal bloody deaths of the non-predators, then it appeared to me that the anti-blood sport societies should confine their energies to the carnivores; who, without man's pursuit, might die of malnutrition and exposure. Most of all I felt this in the case of otter-hunting, the only blood sport (other than bull-fighting) in which the animal has virtually no chance of survival—because, unlike fox-hunting, the whole 'field' of human followers is actively combined with the hounds to make impossible the escape of a harmless predator that is actually beneficial to man. The fact that otters do somehow survive in otter hunting territories, in however decreasing numbers, is a tribute to their exceptional mental abilities, which sometimes prove superior (if the animal is adult) to those of a large group of humans and hounds trained in their pursuit.

The quarry at this coursing meeting was the Blue or Mountain hare, which turns white in winter, and before describing those days I ought perhaps to say at the outset that though I saw some thirty or forty hares killed I did not see one that did not die instantly—'chopped' by the hound's jaws so that its neck was broken, and not once did I hear a hare utter a sound. This is in marked contrast to a hare taken by fox or eagle, and the fact merits some consideration by those who condemn the sport as I have seen it.

This was a mixed meeting for Deerhounds and Salukis, and the large and comfortable hotel where the members stayed was considerably fuller of dogs than of humans. In the morning the long procession of cars drove some miles to an old farm house high on bare moorland. It was bitterly cold weather; snow lay everywhere in patches, and from a dull sky it blew in, fine and powdery, on a keen east wind. Under the orders of the red-coated judge (I am not certain whether the convention of calling red 'pink' extends beyond fox-hunting circles) the party spread out in a long line across the moor, each owner leading his or her hound or hounds. Jimmy Watt led Hazel and I led Dirk. Some thirty yards ahead of the line walked the slipper, attired as the judge, his two selected dogs on a special coupled leash that could be slipped at the pull of a finger. The judge had to be extremely active, for points were awarded to each hound not only for his pure speed and stamina, but for his contribution to the kill by co-operation with his partner; thus in the case of a long course over broken ground the judge must keep hounds and hare in view, and with the aid of binoculars be in a position to observe the details of the kill and the part each hound has played.

The first two hounds in the slips were Salukis, their delicate, slim, silk-soft grace and feathery coats somehow making them appear far too gentle to kill even a mouse. Both were experienced; though they came from different kennels they adapted their movements to each other on the coupling leash, and though they strained lightly upon it they were not dragging their handler behind them.

The first hare, pure white, started from a patch of snow-free heather some twenty yards ahead of them. I was surprised that the hounds were not immediately slipped, for I had never seen Salukis in action, and I was totally unprepared for their perform-ance. The slipper allowed the hare a full sixty yards' start before he unleashed the now wildly straining hounds. The speed of their take-off was breath-taking, unimaginable; it did not seem possible that any living creature could possess that ferocious acceleration. A fine spray of powdered snow rose in the wake of their flying forms as, running neck and neck at unguessable speed, they relent-lessly overhauled the fleeing hare. He had been running straight, *ventre à terre*, but when after a quarter of a mile the hounds were no more than twenty yards behind him he changed tactics and began to dodge and to twist. It was here that the extraordinary team-work of the two hounds became apparent; neither rushed in to the kill, each headed the hare as it turned until the moment came when one hound had the perfect opportunity. Then there was one swift chop of those long and deceptively slender jaws, and the hare was dead. It was a striking display of speed, skill and precision, and the Salukis had certainly killed more cleanly than would the hare's natural enemies.

The next pair in the slips were Deerhounds. We were on higher and harder ground now, near to the crest of a long rounded ridge where the snow lay thinly among scattered stumps of burned heather. This time the hare started nearly eighty yards ahead, and the hounds were slipped on the instant. If the Salukis' take-off had been amazing, that of the Deerhounds was positively awe-inspiring. Their great backs arched, their mighty thigh muscles thrusting, their long necks straining forward, they came racing diagonally across my front at something like fifty miles an hour, and the thunder of their flying feet hitting the hard ground was like the sound of furiously galloping horses. Their speed seemed to me even greater than that of the Salukis, and to have a quality of irresistible impetus, like the sweeping downward rush of a stooping eagle.

It was only when they began to close on the hare that I realized how the Deerhounds were handicapped by comparison with the Salukis. This couple were as clever a combination as their predecessors, and manoeuvred the zig-zagging hare with the same perfection of timing, but their great height was against them. Time and time again the hare would have been within jaws' range of one or the other, but in the split second that it took to reach down a yard and more the hare had tacked again. That hare escaped, as did many others, both from Salukis and Deerhounds, sometimes simply by outrunning the hounds, sometimes by tactics, and sometimes by slipping into a hole or a hillside crevice.

When Hazel's turn came she astonished me as much as she did her previous owners, who were present. She showed an astounding turn of speed for a middle-aged matron; on her first course she outran her younger partner, and, with complete disregard for team spirit, killed the hare single-handed. During the two days she was slipped four times and killed three hares, but only once did she make the least attempt to co-operate with the other hound, and on her final slipping, seeing the hare running up a steep slope, she gave up after three hundred yards and came walking quietly back with a reproachful expression on her face. She clearly felt that too much was being demanded from a woman of her age, more especially under the prevailing weather conditions. The bitter, biting east wind never ceased, and bore upon it flurries of fine fluttering snow. Hazel wanted to be stretched out, as was her wont, on a sofa before a log fire; her killer instinct, like my own, had diminished with age, though she had remained an exhibitionist, and had satisfactorily demonstrated that she was still worthy of admiration in the physical field.

At length it was Dirk's turn. I had been prepared for failure, but not for farce. He was coupled with another, younger, Deerhound, and from the first moment he seemed unable to co-ordinate his movements with those of the hound to which he was linked. When the hare was started and the couple slipped, Dirk simply did not see the quarry. His partner shot off in pursuit, and he seemed mildly puzzled by this; he followed for a few yards and then turned back and began to prance and gambol in an aimless, amiable way up and down the waiting line. He appeared particularly fascinated by the female humans who were being literally dragged helter-skelter across the moor by uncontrollable couples of his own species who had sighted the hare and would answer to no word of command. Overt laughter from all sides prompted me to apologize to the judge, who replied, 'Well, if he has no other function he is at least the perfect court jester.'

The second time, he was coupled with a very beautiful blonde Saluki bitch. He was clearly anxious to make closer acquaintance with her than their parallel position in the slips permitted. When the hare was started she was far faster off the mark than he, and, being left behind in the first twenty yards, he suddenly seemed to have no further doubts as to what this sport was about. It was quite clearly a competitive sport—to see whether a Deerhound dog could catch an attractive Saluki bitch and reap his reward. At first he never even saw the hare, and when he did he ignored it; it had nothing to do with him—the bitch was his business. He had the heels of her, and after a couple of hundred yards they were nose to tail—his nose, that is to say, remaining jammed under her tail, while both were racing at forty or fifty miles an hour. The bitch completely ignored this intimate and inappropriate contact, and contrived to kill the hare on her own, despite these whirlwind attentions from her unwanted partner. When she returned, trotting quietly with the dead hare in her jaws, Dirk came prancing back beside her, patently proud of her prowess, but in human eyes in deep disgrace mitigated only by his powerful potential for comedy.

After this second farce, I apologized again to the judge, who said, 'If he's ever going to course at all he'll have to learn now. He's got the strength and the speed, but he thinks it's just a bitch hunt. From now on you have my permission to slip him at any hare in reasonable range, no matter what other hounds are officially in the slips. That's the only way he can learn what he's supposed to do.'

The long line began to move again, wheeling across a vast boggy flat where the snow clustered thick in the heather tufts, and the inch-deep water crackled and crunched underfoot as the ice splintered among the sphagnum moss. Far away from me hares were started and killed by other hounds, too far away for me to slip Dirk and risk a further farce. Low in the wind, beating their way against the finely falling snow, came a herd of Whooper Swans, dazzlingly white against the deep blue-grey sky, the golden bugles of their voices lingering long on the bitter air. Grouse whirred up from the heather, cackling as they lifted and let themselves be swept away on the wind in a great curving arc, but as yet there was no hare at which I dared slip Dirk. My foot was periodically painful, and I began to wish that this were all over, and like Hazel, that I could return to some cheerful fireside away from the chilling cold and miserable physical discomfort of this bleak and wintery moorland.

Then, as we left the frozen flat bog and began to ascend a slope, I saw before me a patch of long heather, sharply and darkly distinct from the bare snow-dusted ground surrounding it, and I was instantly certain that it held a hare. I readjusted the rope through Dirk's collar and prepared it for instant release. The hare started twenty yards ahead, pure white against the background of dark heather, and for the first time Dirk really saw it and knew what was required of him; it was my fault that I snarled the rope and delayed his pursuit. He took off like a meteor while the hare was still in sight, mounting an horizon slope, and it was seven long minutes before we saw him again. The line stood still, awaiting word from the judge, and when at last they reappeared, the hare leading and Dirk a panting thirty yards behind, both were heading straight back for the line of hounds. Both hare and hound were exhausted, and any fresh hound unleashed could have killed in seconds, but the judge called to me to take in my hound and the hare went free as he deserved. He passed through the line of straining predators, crossed a deep peat-bog ditch, and was finally lost to sight in a flurry of snowstorm. But Dirk's reputation was restored; he had pursued a long course without flagging, and he lost the name of Court Jester.

The day after the meeting was over the snow began to fall in earnest, big white flakes drifting down from a still and silent sky, and we crept slowly back towards Camusfeàrna, the Land Rover rescuing en route, with her winch, a number of cars that had become helpless in a pale frozen white world.

It was not until after our return that I realized that the mort-gaging of the lighthouses had become a mirage, and that only a miracle could now save Camusfeàrna from closure.

13

So Far from Home

That was the autumn of 1965; the final, decisive blow came early in the New Year of 1966. Jimmy Watt, who had been in charge of the whole changing household and its ever-increasing ramifications for eight long years, decided, not unreasonably, that he must now leave us and make some life for himself elsewhere. Having made this difficult decision he was generous enough to give five months' notice, and was thus prepared to remain in charge of Camusfeàrna and its tiny but complex empire until May 1966.

This was the death-knell of the old Camusfeàrna. Nobody but Jimmy, with his long experience of all our practical problems, and his unique ability to tackle them with a supreme and well-justified self-confidence—problems ranging through household supplies from distant towns to maintenance of buildings and of boats of all types and sizes, vehicles of many sorts, the management of otters, dogs and humans—could have kept the place alive. I recognized his own absolute necessity, as a young man of exceptional talent, to form a creative life of his own; but I recognized, too, that I had allowed him to become irreplaceable. (I remembered, too late, an incident long ago during the war. I had been pleading with my Commanding Officer to retain a specialist assistant who had received posting orders to another establishment. My Commanding Officer appeared to give the matter serious thought and kindly consideration. He doodled on his blotter for a minute or so, and then said, 'You mean he's literally indispensable to you in your branch of our work?' I fell instantly into the trap, and said, 'Yes, Sir, just that.' He replied, 'Then he must certainly go. We can't afford to allow anyone to become indispensable in S.O.E.' But, I protested, I was in the present circumstances myself indispensable, and had personally trained my assistant. 'Then we must certainly take immediate steps to see that all your knowledge is committed to paper. I shall inform H.Q. and ask for a typist and two trainees. I appreciate that this will mean extra work for you, but I have no alternative.') Unfortunately I had failed to learn that lesson, that now returned after so many years to put an unequivocal end to all my plans and projects. It would mean finding zoo homes for the otters, and the final closure of the place as it had been, for the house could not stand without its corner-stone.

When I had assimilated the facts I visualized this weary task as being difficult but not impossible; I thought in my innocence that the right homes could somehow be found for all the animals; and that, however painful after eighteen years, I could transfer my loyalties and my interests from Camusfeàrna to somewhere else, perhaps to Kyleakin Lighthouse island, and make for myself a new life, with the Eider experiment as a temporary focus of interest. Much of my zest, however, had gone with the knowledge that the Camusfeàrna epoch was over.

With research still necessary to complete details of *Lords of the Atlas*, I left Scotland for North Africa in February 1966. Two employees, under the nominal supervision of Jimmy Watt, were to prepare the Kyleakin island for the Eider experiment; the creation of fresh water pools, flat beaches made from concrete, nesting boxes on the Icelandic plan, and the erection of flag-poles and bunting. Both employees left before my return and with their work incomplete, so the Eider experiment was never attempted. The magic that had once glossed the world of Camusfeàrna had been wearing thin for a long time; now only the base metal of mistakes showed through, bare and ugly.

When I left Camusfeàrna in February 1966 there were, as I have said, still three employees—Jimmy, and the two temporary assistants working at Kyleakin. During my absence in Morocco the three were joined at Camusfeàrna by a young lady who had previously typed some of my manuscripts, and who now wanted temporary asylum in Scotland from personal problems. She came there in the spring of 1966, while I was abroad, with her seven-year-old daughter and an unimaginable host of wholly unexpected livestock (donkeys; ponies; miniature poodles and Great Danes; cats and geese; and a curious and enchanting breed of dogs which was the result of crossing the great woolly Old English Sheepdog with the slim, silky, slender and shy Shetland Sheepdog) and the casual copulations of this curious community resulted in a spectacular population explosion. At one moment there were, to say nothing of other species, twenty-six dogs. Camusfeàrna became an Animal Farm, where the four-legged ruled with an exigent and destructive dictatorship; the house had entered upon a new and more visible phase of its decline.

At first I learned of all this at second hand, because when I came back to England in May I could not face an immediate return to my home and all that it now entailed. I remained in London and continued my fruitless and increasingly febrile attempts to mortgage the lighthouses. At length I abandoned the idea and put them both up for sale as furnished houses. It seemed that fortune could never come my way again; every piece of news from day to day was of delay, disaster, or death. In the course of forty-eight hours, I remember, I learned of the death of my Pyrenean Mountain Dog at Camusfeàrna and of a white Barb stallion I had bought in Morocco. The dog died because he had been left out all night, tied by a chain to a running line on the field; it was a wild night, and in his efforts to find shelter the dog strangled himself while trying to cross a wire fence. The superb white stallion, who could dance and rear at command, and who loved human beings for themselves, died of neglect and ill-treatment in a squalid *foundouk* in Marrakech, while in charge of an Arab whom I had trusted implicitly. He died perhaps the worst death an animal can die, and I do not want now to recall the details of an event that made me physically sick. (I was sent, by an English observer, not only a detailed description but coloured photographs.)

Financial survival now called for full but orderly retreat, and I began to sell our small possessions. I sold the cine-camera (which had cost us almost a thousand pounds) with which we had visualized making a series of documentary films in the Highlands and Islands, for little more than a third of what we had paid for it. This seemed a particular symbol, the first outward acknowledgment of the epoch's end. The only project left was to close Camusfeàrna as decently as possible.

I delayed my return to Scotland as long as I possibly could, and it was not until August that I went back to Camusfeàrna and tried to make sick-hearted preparations for the transfer of the otters to a zoo. Jimmy had gone, and there was no employee left at Camusfeàrna; only the young lady and her daughter and her incredible animal ménage.

Richard Frere, who had accomplished the conversion of the lighthouse cottages, had taken over the management both of the Company and of my own personal affairs when Jimmy had left in May—because, he said, he liked challenges, and he could scarcely have found a greater one than this. He foresaw clearly the part he would have to play, that of the commander of a desperate rearguard action against insolvency until we could find buyers for Isle Ornsay and Kyleakin. He entered upon the task with the same spirit of enthusiasm that he would have embarked upon the climbing of some cliff previously considered unscalable, and with no illusions as to its difficulties and hardships.

Camusfeàrna seemed a sad place then and one already greatly changed, but in that sunny late September of 1966 I had one last memorable day in *Polar Star*, which I had decided should be moved the following year to Loch Ness to serve the tourist trade. We had had a week of gales and hurricanes which were about the worst I can remember in all the Camusfeàrna years. Anything that could blow away did so, and my worst fear was that the wooden paling enclosing the otters would fall before the tempest and liberate the otters among the great milling miscellany of undisciplined livestock to which Camusfeàrna was now playing temporary host. The fences held, however, and when the storm subsided it went, as so often, into a flat calm and a cloudless blue sky. Alan MacDiarmaid had returned to our employment for a fortnight, since I was by now the only male at Camusfeàrna, and we had various odd jobs to do at Kyleakin Lighthouse and Kyle of Lochalsh.

When we left the moorings in the morning I was immediately aware that something was amiss. Both engines started evenly, but the starboard motor appeared to have no transmission to its propeller. On opening the throttle the revolutions rose on the counter, but there was no increase in speed. From inside the boat we were able to establish that the hydraulic transmission from the engine was in order, and we assumed that there must be a dislocation at the propeller shaft. We started north on one engine.

It wasn't until we tied up alongside the pier at Kyle of Lochalsh that we found out that the starboard propeller wasn't there at all; somehow the tremendous punishment the boat had taken during the prolonged storm, the perpetual pitching on the high waves at her moorings, had found a weakness in the work of whoever had fitted that propeller, and it now lay in several fathoms of water below the mooring buoy. (Immediately after our return we began a search for the costly rubber skin-diving suit that we kept at Camusfearnà against such emergencies. But it was no longer there; it had disappeared, together with much else, and despite lengthy police investigations it was never traced.)

So, in the afternoon, we returned from Kyle on one engine. This gave us eleven or twelve knots; enough, anyway to confront the north-running flood tide in the narrows of Kylerhea. We came down past Glenelg, and a mile or two north of *Polar Star*'s moorings, close in under the huge cliffs, we saw mackerel 'rushing' at the surface. This happens when their great shoals have pushed up their prey, the fry of their own and other species—called in this part of the world 'soil'—to the absolute limit, so that the pursuit is taking place almost above water. The effect to the onlooker is that of an intermittent moving flurry of white spray, often iridescent, and to those who depend upon fish for food, it holds an irresistible and intrinsic excitement.

This was the first evidence we had had that the mackerel were still in the area; they arrive in June or early July and leave, with the tourists, in early or late September, according to weather conditions. Apart from salmon heads and tails, and leaving aside a staple diet of eels, mackerel were the favourite food of the otters, and since the mackerel were still there, and I had invested in deep freezes, I had obviously to make the most of this opportunity.

We had two 'darrow' lines aboard (thirty fathoms of line, with a tail of twenty hooks on cat-gut, baited with dyed hens' feathers) and we set to work to take what mackerel we might from that shoal that was possibly the last of the season—so that the deep freezes would be full for the winter.

The results of that twenty minutes' fishing were little short of fantastic. There were moments when we lost the shoal, but always we found it again after a slow quartering of the ground, and time and time again we hauled in a wildly gyrating darrow holding between ten and nineteen (this was Alan's, and, I think, a Camus-feàrna record) flipping, flapping, fish whose coloured bars of lapis lazuli blue and emerald green took me back to my childhood in Galloway, where we trolled for these same fish with a single bait and a day's catch of thirty was worthy of note. Now we were sometimes taking in thirty mackerel in one minute, and by the time we were finished and had finally lost the shoal we had more than a hundredweight of fish.

We started off on our one engine for the mile-distant moorings of *Polar Star*. About halfway we found a Fulmar Petrel in our path on the still sea, and he seemed unable to rise. He paddled awkwardly away from *Polar Star*'s course, but seemed incapable of taking wing. I said to Alan that we ought to rescue this derelict, and he set off in pursuit of it in an inflatable rubber dinghy while I stood off with *Polar Star*. It was, by any standards, a comic performance; no matter how closely the rubber dinghy could approach the Fulmar, the bird could turn quicker than the boat and I could hear Alan's rich flow of invective across the few hundred yards of smooth sea that separated us. But in this situation, as in all others, Alan would not accept defeat, and after a quarter of an hour he was back on board *Polar Star* with the helpless but protesting Fulmar. Protest, with Fulmars, is direct and unequivocal —they shoot out from their mouths a liquid so nauseating and noxious in smell as to deter all but the most hardened ornithologist or would-be helper. While I was tying the bird's legs and wings he ejected a liberal dose of this hideous substance both over me and over the seat cushions of *Polar Star*'s cabin, but at length I had him secured in a cardboard box, and we headed home for our moorings.

We had more than a hundredweight of fish on board, and no very obvious means of carrying them to Camusfeàrna, a distance of half a mile by dinghy and half a mile on foot. I had a canvas yachting smock, and apart from my trousers that was all. We knotted the sleeves and the neck, slithered the great mass of fish inside this brimming receptacle and set off for Camusfeàrna, Alan carrying the fish on his heavily bowed shoulders, and I hugging tenderly to my breast the cardboard box containing the Fulmar.

We were less than fifty yards from the house, passing over the sand dunes, when Alan said, 'Well, this certainly is an odd day—just look at that!' Almost at our feet, shuffling helplessly among the rank Bent grass of the dunes, was a Manx Shearwater, the enormous scimitar wings appropriate to the long glide and wave-swoop of the Albatross family to which both the Shearwater and the Fulmar belonged used now as a means of terrestrial locomotion. 'Blown ashore,' said Alan, 'and they can't take off except either from water or a height. Better take him in too, until we can let them both go in decent condition.'

So we arrived, that evening at Camusfeàrna, with a Fulmar in a cardboard box, and a Manx Shearwater held in greaseproof paper (for the contact of human hand can remove the 'water-proofness' of a seabird's plumage, so that it remains sodden after the bath it so ardently yearns for).

We put them both in the bathroom, the Shearwater in the shower compartment, and the Fulmar at liberty. It was a very messy performance, the Fulmar excreting, it seemed, far more than it ingested, and to the human nurses it was a painful one too. To start with, neither bird would eat of its own freewill; both were force fed, while one person held the beak open the other crammed in food and forced it down into the unwilling crop. The diet I had selected for each was different; I gave the Fulmar fish and fish-liver and great quantities of bacon fat (remembering from the past how they had swarmed round sharks' and whales' livers and any fatty substance available) and the Shearwater I fed upon mussels, fish liver, and the black proteinous heads of limpets. We avoided all direct contact between their plumage and human hands, but despite this they refused to become waterproof. (A situation of

shock or trauma is often responsible for this condition.) The Fulmar
—awkward, *gauche*, clumsy, and entirely without fear—would
bathe with relish, stamping about in the water and making ritual-
istic gestures towards total submersion, but emerged completely
sodden and draggled. The Shearwater had forcibly to be bathed,
appearing to loathe the water and everything to do with it; but
they shared one characteristic in common—their twice-daily
feeding was extremely painful. As the human fingers withdrew
from the bird's crop, the hooked, parrot-bill tips of their beaks
would snap to with an entirely unexpected force, more than enough
to draw blood, before one could snatch one's hand away, and at
the end of the first week my right hand was covered with innumerable scars.

Since these two ocean-living birds were rarely if ever seen by the
zoo-frequenting public, I suggested to a Scottish zoo that they
should now take over from us until the birds were fit for liberation.
The reply was that they might be prepared to take the Fulmar for
a time, but not the Shearwater, as they were impossible to keep
alive in captivity. At length we found an R.S.P.C.A. official who
was prepared to try; by that time we were apparently the only
people to have kept a Shearwater in good and increasing health
for more than three weeks. In our case, too, both birds had to be
defended from all the other predatory livestock at Camusfeàrna,
and they added their own problems to a household that had
become nothing less than an ill-ordered menagerie. We drove the
birds 200 miles to the R.S.P.C.A. in Aberdeen.

Seaweed in the bathroom, banked up so that the Fulmar's breast
could rest against it as he preferred, great sploshy, white, slimy
bird-droppings between oneself and the bath, scattered fragments
of fish liver underfoot, the stamping clumsy gait of the Fulmar
whenever he felt like moving; these are my recollections of the
two birds whose triumphal release by the R.S.P.C.A. a few weeks
later was perhaps a vindication of all we had suffered on their
behalf.

The animal situation, with the added presence of these birds in
the bathroom, was really extraordinary. There were so many
creatures that one just couldn't move. Any opened door was an
automatic invitation to a vast and vocal avalanche of dogs, of all

sizes and shapes, but with patently conflicting desires. The fantastic fertility of the household was crystallized for me by the discovery one day, previously unknown to anyone, of a litter of weaned kittens living in the loft above the lobby.

With the necessity to make immediate and practical plans for the few animals that were my own, I circularized a short list of zoos with the following letter, every word I wrote rending me, for this was the overt end of Camusfeàrna.

Dear X

I am writing to you because it seems likely that this autumn I shall have to find a home for my two otters Edal and Teko, and I should like to donate them to a zoo which would keep them in the style to which they are accustomed.

I suppose that, since the lioness Elsa's death, Edal (of *Ring of Bright Water*) is probably the most famous living individual animal, and she would no doubt be a considerable draw to any zoo that owned her. Teko, also, has a very considerable fan public. Edal is *Aonyx Capensis* from Nigeria: Teko, from Sierra Leone, would appear to be of some unrecognized sub-species. They are not mated, and have to be kept separately.

I am naturally anxious to secure ideal conditions for them. This means, basically, what they have now—indoor quarters heated with overhead infra-red lamps, and extensive and varied water-works outside. They are not happy with only static water, and require some system of fountains, waterfalls, etc. to keep them content, besides deep water to dive in. As these things are not easy for everyone to provide, I am writing now to a short list of zoos to find out who would be keen to try.

Teko is fed mainly on fish and a few eels, though he is almost omnivorous; Edal will not eat sea fish other than mackerel, and is fed mainly on live eels. Though Teko is now the more playful of the two, they will both play for hours with any suitable object presented to them.

I should be most grateful for your first reactions to the idea, so that I may narrow the field.'

The response to this circular was enthusiastic, and in August 1966 I chose a zoo whose Council, I understood, had undertaken to provide completely suitable accommodation for the two otters Edal and Teko. This was to include a fountain in each pool, and numerous other amenities that would safeguard both the public and the otters. It seemed to me then that, even if this solution was distressing, I had solved the problem of how to close Camusfeàrna and ensure the welfare of the animals. These two things were by now my only targets, and I wanted to do them efficiently and cleanly.

At first the zoo asked for the otters at the end of September; then, owing to labour difficulties, the date was postponed until mid-October. I left Camusfeàrna, and went to live within an hour's drive of the zoo. In October the date was again postponed for a month, for the same reasons. It was December before I realized that the project had finally broken down. I visited the zoo for the fourth time, greeted unexpectedly by a hoard of reporters and television cameras, and found that preparations for the accommodation of one otter only were just—but only just—under way. There were representatives of many newspapers; one had already prepared his piece, and it read, 'Recognize this picture? Is it?—yes, it *is*, the hero of Gavin Maxwell's *Ring of Bright Water*, MIJBIL—Maxwell's otter, in Latin *Lutrogale perspicillata maxwelli*, now presented to X Zoo.' I was not in good humour, and remarked acidly that there would be little point in presenting to a zoo an animal already dead nine years. I had never been a reporter, I said, but I imagined that, like most other professions, its success presupposed a reasonable amount of homework; in this case at least a cursory perusal of what I had written about my otters. He said, 'Very sorry—I've only read one of your books, *A Reed Shaken by the Wind*, but the wife and kids have made it their family bible. I don't know about any otter after Mijbil, and I got the *Ring of Bright Water* stuff on the telephone from London.'

Even leaving aside the Press—who, to give credit where it is due, have usually been kind—it was a haywire morning. A zoo committee, I was now informed, had cancelled the expenditure necessary to construct even one fountain. I was also made aware for the first time that our original understanding that Edal would be 'deposited' for six months and then donated if she had settled into contentment in this new environment, was not acceptable to the zoo, who would now only take her as a direct and immediate donation, despite the entirely inadequate accommodation provided. Originally this was not a decision of the Council but an untimely inspiration on the part of an official. It represented, anyway, a dead-lock, and for me a peculiarly unpleasant one; I had screwed myself up to the point of parting with Edal after years of mutual esteem, and now I had to unwind on the instant like a broken watch spring.

I did not feel that I had any choice other than to cancel all our arrangements, and to postpone the question of the otters' future home for a further year. Only my absolute faith in Richard Frere's ability to fight a financial rearguard action made this possible. The young lady, who, with her daughter and her uncountable animals, was in tumultuous occupation of Camusfeàrna, consented to tend the otters until some satisfactory and permanent alternative had been achieved; they were thus still at Camusfeàrna when I came back in August 1967.

After all this I wrote a letter to the zoo:

Dear X,

Thank you for your letter of December 15th which has been forwarded to me by Mr R. B. Frere.

I believe that we notified you of our decision not to send Edal to your Zoo by telegram on the evening before you wrote, and I think that I should explain the principal factors that influenced me in making that decision.

(1) It was agreed between Dr Z, as representing the Zoo, and myself on 30th August 1966 that Edal should be 'deposited' for the first six months, and then donated if the animal had settled satisfactorily. On 11th December, when the premises were still not completed, Mr Y refused to take her on this basis.

(2) Also on the 30th August, and again during my visit to the zoo, it was agreed between Dr Z and myself that the shallow end of the pool should contain a fountain, and Dr Z passed on the instructions in my presence. On 11th December I was informed that this fountain had been cancelled by some committee without any reference to myself. I would point out that the 11th December was long after the proposed date for moving the animal.

(3) Dr Z originally asked for Edal to be moved by the end of September. This was later changed, owing to delay in construction at the Zoo, first to end of October and then to end of November. I visited the zoo, by previous arrangement, on 23rd November but was told by Dr Z that it was not worthwhile looking at the otter enclosure as there was nothing to see.

(4) Owing to forecast weather conditions I attached great importance to a travelling box that would enable the animal to be fed and watered should the transport vehicle become, for example, snowbound—To the end of constructing such a box, the city architect's assistant travelled to Camusfeàrna to obtain the necessary measurements for construction of a box suitable both for capture and for transport. Before Dr Z left for Germany he informed me that the box had been constructed and dispatched and was now awaiting Mr Frere at Inverness station. He and I made several journeys to Inverness, but the box was not traceable. On 11th December I was informed by the city architect's assistant that no box had ever been constructed and that he had no clear idea as to why he had visited Camusfeàrna.

(5) Meanwhile, an 'emergency' box had been despatched by Mr Y, with internal measurements of 1' 9" by 1' 9", with a depth of 1' 7" and with a sliding lid and no means of securing it. Mr Watt, who had travelled from Perth especially to effect the move, pronounced the box to be not only thoroughly unsuitable but also dangerous. Despite the considerations set out under (4) above, Mr Y suggested using the box and nailing down the lid. Mr Watt refused, and returned to Perth.

(6) On 11th December I visited the zoo with a view to establishing the state of readiness or unreadiness. I arrived at 10.45 a.m., having previously asked Mr Y to ensure that we had the full morning for discussion. Despite this, I was required to meet reporters within ten minutes of arrival. I then learned for the first time of Mr Y's refusal to accept Edal on the agreed terms of six months deposit before donation, and of cancellation of the agreed fountain. The pool had no water and the fences could not be completed even during the following week. Despite these facts, I had been urged to transport Edal on the previous day (10th December).

(7) Various individuals at the Zoo attributed these circumstances to an almost total lack of liaison between responsible members of the staff; a conclusion which from all the above facts is inescapable.

(8) Mr Y stressed that to him Edal was 'just another otter'—an attitude that can be reassuring neither to her owner nor to the Council which has given so much publicity to her acquisition. Her only real value to the Zoo is, surely, her fame; and, as I explained, I have received a great number of letters from the public censuring my decision to send her to any Zoo, no matter how ideal. I am sure that you would agree that to date no member of the public would have found reason to lift that censure in the light of the course of events that I have set out.

May I ask that this letter be shown to all members of the Council as a clarification of the position? I am sending a separate copy to Dr Z.

Yours sincerely,
Gavin Maxwell

To this I received a three-line reply undertaking to pass on to the committee the information in my letter.

14

Return of Mossy and Monday

The otters were to remain at Camusfeàrna until some true solution
had been found; it was on this unhappy but temporarily reassuring
note that I left what little remained of the old Camusfeàrna in
December 1966. So far I have written this factual narrative
thousands of miles from the centre of its subject; living alone and
abroad in a town previously unknown to me I have tried to
reassemble in sequence the happenings that led to the disintegration
of the Camusfeàrna myth, and, at the same time, to my determination to return to there at least for a last summer; to restore for
a little while the situation as it once had been.

In late April of 1967, far from the focus of my story, I received
two telegrams from Camusfeàrna. The first read 'Monday came
home with the dogs today let me know what to do'; and the
second, two days later, 'Feeding female indoors pink spots nose

injured by trap feeding male under lobby Alan [Alan MacDiarmaid, a previous employee and friend who had looked after Tibby] does not recognize stop confinement unnecessary writing.'

She wrote, three times, but changes of address and postal uncertainties to a distant country made her narrative tantalizingly fragmentary; the first of her letters, describing the miraculous return after four years of two of our liberated indigenous otters, did not reach me.

So it was with a sense of unreality that I read the second, as one might read an isolated serial of a detective story whose beginning one has missed.

I often see them over at the islands and in the river estuary. The strange thing about them is that they are so active by day, return to the house at night to eat and to sleep. How wonderful it is to see them swimming and playing naturally in the sea and dashing around with each other quite free. Monday is always the leader. One good thing is that I think she would be far too clever to be caught in a trap for a second time. . . . I have persuaded the owner of the trap at the lochan by Druimfiaclach to have it removed; which is as well, because the otters often go fishing in that loch. Her leg is quite healed now—only a small lump on the bone where it was broken. They have been like phantom otters for the last two weeks. I had a guest staying, and they only came to the bathroom at night for the fish. But after the guest left Monday came back to sleep, and on Sunday morning I got up very early and found her still sleeping in the shower compartment of the bathroom, on her back like Edal does. AND her belly was moving—I thought she was pregnant before, but now I am certain. I don't think she will have her cubs in the shower now, because there have been so many people about, and also I don't think that the male (which we think is Mossy) would go in there to her, but I am hoping she will have them under the coatroom floor, where they spend a lot of time, but I do not know if they are using that box. [Four years before, we had cut a hatch in the coatroom floor and constructed below it a box for their benefit.] I dare not lift the hatch to see, in case they feel that I am invading their privacy.

Monday eats as much fish as she wants in the bathroom, and then drags the rest out to Mossy. He is a bit of a glutton; he didn't feed her when her leg was broken by the trap and she couldn't fend for herself. Now she makes sure of her share; she eats hers first, taking no notice of us watching, and then drags the remains of a fish almost as big as herself across the linoleum, out of the door and then through the hole under it that leads to her quarters below the floor. . . .

Besides the tantalizing speculations as to what the first and missing letter might have contained (beyond the lines quoted above there were hints that Druimfiaclach was no longer untenanted, and that there had been a further and even more spectacular population explosion among dogs and donkeys at Camusfeàrna), I read this letter with mixed feelings, because about halfway through it I began to realize that the implications were far-reaching and contrary to the policy that I had formed with difficulty—the policy of spending one last summer at Camusfeàrna and then closing it completely, with the two original otters Edal and Teko as well provided for by a public institution as I was able to contrive. Now I was faced with the possibility that the returned and wounded wanderer, Monday, had come back to Camusfeàrna, still unafraid of man, with the intention of giving birth to her cubs in what had once been her home and shelter before she was even weaned—a home which I had intended to vacate with all its animals and leave to the wild winds of heaven. If a further race of domesticated otters, unafraid of their worst enemy, were to be reared there, I could not shed this aftermath of a past responsibility and leave them to be slaughtered for their skins as they assuredly would be. It seemed that Camusfeàrna would not let me go.

In response to a telegram, a substitute for the missing letter arrived.

The female otter arrived on the afternoon of Tuesday, April 18. The coat room door to the field was open, and also the connecting door from the coatroom to the living room. Two of my dogs were coming and going, and the otter just walked in with them. I hurriedly fetched two omelettes which I had already cooked for Edal and Teko, and shut the doors. Then I sent you a cable to find out what you wanted done. [I had replied, 'Please encourage and feed but make no attempt confine.'] I enticed her into the bathroom with a fish, and made her a bed in the shower compartment. She took up residence in this bed, and drank water from a bowl I held out to her. She was quite tame and unafraid;

she allowed me to touch her, and I managed to put some chloromycetin cream on a large pus-discharging swelling on her right foreleg.

Later that evening when I was outside I saw another otter's head looking out from under the coatroom doorway. I went in and checked, but the female was still asleep in the shower compartment in the bathroom. The second otter couldn't be tempted to come into the house but he (it was a male) was tame enough to take food from the hand. Now that there were two I at first thought I should open the bathroom door and let the female out, but on second thoughts I felt that her leg might require more attention, and I saw that her mate would not leave the house while she was inside. When I got your cable I did let her out, but she just ate her fish as usual and then went back to sleep. She seemed completely unconcerned about her mate. She would go to the bathroom door and look out and then push it shut before retiring to bed—from which I had the impression that she had used it before.

[She had indeed; it is a sliding door, and during my efforts to confine her four years earlier she had learned its difficult mechanism by heart.]

It was difficult to get her to swim in the bath. All other enticements having failed, I got her to get her teeth firmly into a fish and just lifted her in by it. She immediately found herself facing the big mirror above the bath, and was fascinated by the otter she saw reflected there. She moved from side to side and chattered her teeth with annoyance when the other otter she saw did the same thing; then she started patting the glass with her hands. She seemed to have very definite ideas about how an otter hotel should be run. When she messed on the floor she would keep on tapping at the edge of it until, looking up at me and chattering her teeth, she persuaded me to clean it up.

When she is well fed and contented she lies on her back and nibbles and sucks her 'bib', the loose skin on her throat, like Edal does and which you photographed so successfully in your previous books about the otters at Camusfeàrna. Then she goes to sleep on her back, with her legs in the air. Whatever has happened, she seems to consider herself a member of the household by right.

Having a bath has been very difficult, because she has a habit of nipping one's toes; not, I think, from aggression but from mischief—so I go into the bathroom only in Wellington boots. Having undressed down to these, one removes one boot and puts that foot in the bath. Have you ever tried balancing on one leg in a bathful of hot water trying to get an unco-operative boot off the other foot? It's an experience only equalled by trying to get out of the bath afterwards.

It was not until she had been in the bathroom for four days that she seemed to wake up to her surroundings and began a tour of inspection. By this time she had put on a lot of weight, and she was much stronger and remarkably agile. She started by climbing up and throwing everything off the shelves, trying everything with her teeth and then scrutinizing it before disdainfully discarding it. Her face when she bit into a cake of soap is something I shall always remember.

Her *tour de force* was her assault on the mirror-fronted cupboard above the washhand basin. Having got on to the basin, she paused for quite a long time to examine the new otter face confronting her, apparently comparing it with the other otter face she had seen in the mirror above the bath. Then, finding that it smelt of nothing ottery, she opened the cupboard door. She held on to one of the shelves with her left hand, and used her right to throw out all the contents on to the floor. She wore the expression of a small child, who, strapped into a pram, throws out all its toys to see what effect it will have.

Nothing would make her leave the bathroom, and she seemed frightened of going out, so I cut a hole in the wall [plaster board and wood] so that she could come and go without fear of being shut out. For the next two weeks, that is up till now, she and her mate have been away all of each day, returning at night—she to the bathroom and he to his quarters under the floor.

It was some time before I found out how she had come to be wounded. I had suspected that she had been caught in a trap, but I didn't know anything definite until I was having a cup of coffee with the new people at Druimfiaclach. The lady of the house told me about an otter that her son had trapped. He had set a trap at the edge of the lochan below the house, and one day they saw something moving in it. Her son went down to investigate, and found that it was an otter. As soon as he opened the trap, instead of trying to run away she flew at him, and he fought her off with a stick. She returned to the attack, and again he defended himself with the stick. Then she made off, but turned round several times, as if trying to make up her mind whether to have another go at him. All this was five days before she arrived at Camusfeàrna, and she must have been unable to fend for herself all that time, because the trapper said that when he saw her she was in good condition, but she was very thin when she got here. How lucky that she remembered where to go in time of trouble, and that I was here to look after her.

It was, as nearly as I can calculate, just four years since either Monday or Mossy had visited Camusfeàrna house or come within sighting distance of it—for that brief appearance at the waterfall in the summer of 1964 had clearly been contrary to Monday's intentions—but the description contained in this letter left me in no possible doubt that these were the same two otters that I described in detail in *The Rocks Remain*. Mossy, with his stupid, timorous, egotistical nature; Monday with her miraculous powers of climbing and her apparent comprehension of all basic mechanical principles. In the very last sentence of that book I had written, 'If I ever again write of Camusfeàrna, I hope that I shall not have to write of the death of Monday, her whole dynamic personality wiped out as a result of the inner emptiness that is the desire to kill.' I have not, at least, had to do that. Injured and unable to fend for herself she had remembered and returned; she must have recalled that besides the free fish and the affection there had been prolonged and forcible confinement to fight against, but in seeking the sanctuary of Camusfeàrna in her present distress she had perhaps remembered also how constantly and contemptuously she had outwitted us, and felt confident of doing so again should the necessity arise.

So far away from Camusfeàrna, the last paragraph of the letter gave me a deep nostalgia for what I had once known. 'Camusfeàrna is more beautiful than ever now; there are great banks of primroses, bluebells, violets, and a great profusion of wild flowers everywhere.'

But the letter had a P.S. 'A poltergeist has come here; yesterday it broke two windows; one while I was sitting on the corner of the sofa you yourself normally occupy, and one in the kitchen while I was washing up.'

Watchman, what of the rowan tree?

15

Many Maladies

I came back to England on 18 June 1967, having engaged by correspondence only and without interview a temporary employee to help me at Camusfeàrna during my final summer there with the otters. This was Andrew Scot, a boy who had written to us periodically over the past five years, but whom I had never met, and who was now leaving school at the age of 17. Meanwhile I had to wait in London while the young lady who had been occupying Camusfeàrna arranged to move with her small daughter and her innumerable livestock (which now included two female donkeys said to be in foal—or is it in hinney?—to her pony which had been erroneously believed to be a gelding) to a house near to the village.

I began immediately to attack the problem of a final home for the otters, for the experiences of the previous year, and the final collapse of arrangements with the chosen zoo, had taught me that time could not, in this respect, be treated as expendable. I thought that Camusfeàrna as a household must be closed before the onset of winter, and negotiations must be begun at once.

I had given many hours of thought to this while I was still abroad, and I had returned with the outline of a plan. I did not now believe any zoo to be the answer; the great majority suffer from space restriction, and even with the sum of money voted by that Council it would be difficult anywhere to secure what I would regard as ideal conditions. So I ruled out all zoos, and I had simultaneously to dismiss the possibility of a private home, for the necessary type of eccentric millionaire just did not exist.

This seemed to leave me with one possibility only—someone who would invest money in giving the animals perfect living conditions because they would earn him high dividends which would be immediately calculable—unlike a zoo, in which it is of necessity difficult to assess the earning value of any particular animal exhibited.

Lord Bath's lions at Longleat . . . the Duke of Bedford's great park at Woburn—but what had Woburn in the animal line that could really compete with Longleat's lions? I doubted whether the Longleat lions would have been so great a draw had not the public become lion-conscious through the story of Joy Adamson's lioness Elsa and after all, Edal had come near to outselling Elsa, and Edal was still alive whereas Elsa was dead. True there were very great rarities at Woburn—European Bison and almost the whole world's population of the otherwise extinct Père David's Deer, but these were not individually famous animals with a fan public of thousands as were Edal and Teko.

So I came home with the half-formed plan of approaching Woburn, a plan strongly reinforced by two happenings during my first few days in England. The first was being told of a cartoon in a daily paper showing two vans arriving at Woburn, one labelled 'lions' and the other 'Christians', with the caption 'Anything Bath can do Bedford can do better'. The second was the discovery that an acquaintance, Michael Alexander, held certain concessions, specifically to do with animals, at Woburn, and that there was at least a chance of these concessions being extended.

Michael was enthusiastic, and he drove me down to Woburn little more than a week after I had returned from abroad. He led me through Pet's Corner, where an improbable miscellany of animals both wild and domestic—but all sublimely ignoring the public who threaded their way between them—were brooded over by a benign and motionless vulture perched majestically upon the wooden railings of a small central enclosure. Three glorious macaws, free and untrammelled, flew from tree to tree above us or around us, the fantastic splendour of their plumage lit by a bright afternoon sun. We passed through Pets' Corner and out beyond it to an undeveloped site that Michael had visualized as a possible home for the otters. The moment I saw it I knew that here, if it was obtainable, could be the otters' paradise. We were looking out over a small lake, heavily overgrown with waterlilies, a roundish but not quite round lake perhaps 65 yards one way by 50 the other. The water, I was told, was some twelve feet deep in the middle, shelving to five feet at the edges. There was plainly a water system of inlet and outlet somewhere, for among the waterlilies near to us I caught sight of a Golden Orfe, and further out there were some small fish jumping, too far away for identification. We were standing in a colonnade of wooden pillars and arches, decorated in the Chinese manner, that stretched round almost half the lake's circumference, an ornamental covered passage-way separated from the lake by a few feet of grass bank. The official name of this spectacular 'folly' was the Chinese Dairy, built in spacious days of long ago, as a separate jewel in the Bedford coronet; and just behind us where we stood a large room opened off the colonnade. Here was the perfect situation in which even the most cautious business man would surely feel justified in a lavish outlay, because the otters would be an isolated exhibit which the public would pay individually to see. It was only unfortunate that the incompatibility of Edal and Teko presented its own problem, for the lake would have to be divided in two.

We planned artificial islands and fountains, the position of the heated sleeping quarters; in fact, though this was no more than a reconnaissance, we covered almost every detail. It remained for Michael to acquire concessions over this part of the estate that was not at the moment earning any significant money.

Having reached the stage at which there was little left to discuss, Michael took me on one of his safari trips through the great park. This vast and magnificently unspoilt piece of countryside, 3,000 acres enclosed by no less than thirteen miles of high brick wall, contained ten species of deer, living in a completely wild state in beautiful surroundings—to say nothing of both European and American Bison, wallabies, llamas, alpacas, guanacos, breeding pairs of the ostrich-like rhea, and sarus cranes. The running of safari trips in huge four-wheel drive vehicles, so that the public could see all these splendours at close quarters, much as they might do in an African game reserve, had been Michael's earliest venture at Woburn, and met with a richly-deserved popularity. I felt as though I were slipping back into an earlier century, a century before the beginning of industrialization, when much of England must have been like this, great sweeps of grassland with noble oaks and herds of grazing deer. Robin Hood and his green-clad men would have seemed no more out of place here than the deer themselves. Apart from the fascination of the animals, many allowing the safari car to approach within a few yards of them, it was the lack of any carving up of this great piece of land that held its own exhilaration—that and its silence; and I could well understand how even those with no intrinsic interest in animals could find in a half-hour's safari tour a magic world in complete contrast to the waste land of brick and stone and mechanical noise in which so many are condemned to live. On my return from the safari through that green parkland of quiet and peaceful animals, I felt that even though this was basically a commercial enterprise it was also a deeply-needed public service.

Meanwhile I had begun to produce a succession of curious and alarming physical disorders. Not long after my return from North Africa I sat down at my desk one morning to make some telephone calls. When the first number answered I was astonished to find that, with no premonitory symptoms, I had literally no voice at all; I could not even whisper. The next day I felt thoroughly ill, with headache and sickness and digestive troubles. I began to treat myself with antibiotics, but when after five days Ledermycin had proved ineffective I sent for the doctor. While he was examining me I noticed that he spent a great deal of time over my left lung, and when he had finished he said, 'I've no doubt that a change of antibiotic will soon clear up the general condition, but there are some crepitations from the base of your left lung and I think you have an early pneumonia. I should like an X-ray report as soon as possible.'

I replied, 'Well, I suppose I'm a classic for lung cancer; I'm the right age, and I smoke eighty cigarettes a day.'

He said, 'I'd like to make an appointment with the chest clinic by telephone now.' He did so, but he could not obtain one until Friday, and it would be the following Tuesday before he would know the results. I asked him what was the worst that the X-ray could reveal, and he answered, 'Well, just what you said yourself.' Pressed upon the probability of this finding he would say neither that it was unlikely nor likely, but when I asked him whether he would tell me the absolute truth after the results were in his hands, he replied, 'Yes—you are one of my patients with whom I should feel that to be the right course of action.'

The time between Wednesday and Friday passed very slowly indeed, and during those two days I became absolutely convinced in myself that the findings would be positive. I was, as I had said to the doctor, a classic case for the disease, and now that the idea was in my mind I recognized that I had many of the textbook symptoms. Millions of people have been through this time of suspense and for very much longer periods than I, but I have never seen any subjective account of it, so it is perhaps worth recording my own reactions. Primarily, I felt it impossible to see or to talk to anyone who was not or had not been a cancer patient—this seemed a private, shut-off world that would be bewildering and frightening to anyone who had not shared it. To a few people whom it might affect I told the bare facts, but I did not feel able to discuss them. Because of this feeling of being outside and shut off from the normal world I cancelled all engagements until after the following Tuesday, when I should know the details and the prognosis. Unexpectedly, a complete resignation, one which I suppose might well have proved temporary, came very early on; I was concerned less with the fact that I had cancer (as I had convinced myself beyond all reasonable doubt) than with the alterations to plan and programme that this would involve; how Camusfeàrna would be run until the otters were moved to Woburn; who would move them; the general ordering of my affairs. Fear and despair would, I suppose, have come later, but during those forty-eight hours I felt neither.

At half past one on Friday afternoon I presented myself at the Chest Clinic, and after the X-ray photographs had been taken I was on the point of leaving when the radiologist said, 'Normally speaking you would have to wait for the findings until next week, when you would receive them from your own doctor. But that would keep you in suspense for another four days, so if you would care to wait for a while we may be able to tell you something today. That is if you would prefer it.'

33 The author and Edal

34 and 35 *Opposite:* Teko. *Above:* Teko feeding from a plate

38 The Chinese Dairy Lake at Woburn

39 'Literally hundreds of man hours had by now gone
into the Woburn model . . .'

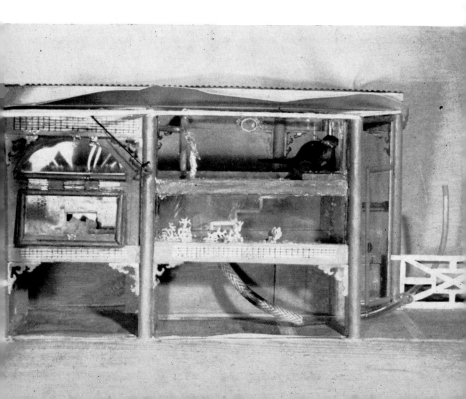

40 'Like long-lost, intimate friends who have suddenly
rediscovered each other'—Andrew Scot and Teko

I said that I would certainly prefer it and that I was very grateful indeed, which was an understatement. I sat in the waiting room reading back numbers of *Punch*; most of them contained political jokes whose significance was unintelligible to me, for I had been unable to follow home news during my six months in North Africa. There was a 'No Smoking' sign; I very much wanted a cigarette, arguing to myself that if I had cancer of the lung one more could not make any difference, and if I had not the same applied. But to walk even as far as the door to the street might mean that I missed the news when it came, and I sat on. As I considered my position I realized that only in the case of a negative result would the Clinic be likely to tell me anything; if it were positive, it seemed to me, they would somehow arrange matters so that the news was broken to me by my own doctor. In this case, therefore, no news would be bad news. At the end of half an hour nothing had happened. There were three other patients in the room; looking at them I tried to determine from their demeanours whether they too were waiting for news all-important to them, but their faces told me nothing. I hoped that mine was as impassive.

After a little more than three-quarters of an hour a nurse came in and looked questioningly round. 'Mr Maxwell?' I stood up and she beckoned me into the corridor.

'Doctor said to tell you that your X-ray plates are perfectly satisfactory.'

There was a Delphic quality to this utterance, and I was desperate for certainty.

'Does he mean,' I said carefully, trying very hard to keep my voice to a casual tone, 'that the quality of the plates is satisfactory, or that my condition is satisfactory?'

She beamed at me from behind heavy horn-rimmed spectacles. 'He means that he can find no trace of any pathological condition. In other words, there's nothing wrong with you.'

I resisted the temptation to hug her or to do a jig where I stood. I thanked her, and walked out into the summer sunshine and the streets busy with people into whose world I seemed suddenly to have re-entered.

Reprieve from life sentence, or perhaps from death sentence, was followed almost immediately by a short term upon another charge. Although I was as yet unaware of it, I had not returned from North Africa alone.

I had brought home with me an extremely rare disease not previously recorded from Morocco, where I had been living. It made a neat and compensatory double with my discovery there of a colony of Spoonbills, not known to breed anywhere in North Africa, for they had disappeared from Algeria many years ago. This ornithologically important event took place at the absolute height of the Middle Eastern war; Arab newspapers tended to be uncommunicative on world affairs during this period, and my find was published—complete with a drawing of the bird—on the front page of the local journal. It was, after all, just what was expected of Englishmen in world crises. A letter asking the Governor of the Province for immediate protection of the rarity was dispatched over the names of more than half a dozen prominent signatories. The translation of colloquial French into literal dictionary English is perhaps too well-worn a theme of comedy for me to add to it more than two sentences from this letter: 'They [scientific bodies] will not miss the opportunity to seize the government of His Majesty King Hassan II with a demand for integral protection of this bird and its site of nidification. Unfortunately it is menaced by troops of goats who nourish themselves upon the samphire and are responsible for the destruction of many eggs by their footwork.'

I thought I had paid a reasonable fee for this scientific discovery by incurring a very painful snake-bite on the marshes where the Spoonbills bred, but in fact this turned out to be no more than a payment on account, for I had imported into England yet another living organism not recorded from Morocco—an extremely unpleasant intestinal protozoa by the name of *Coccidia isospora belli*. The last word ('of war') refers to an epidemic of the then unknown disease among troops at Gallipoli during the First World War; as if to justify its christening, it reappeared among German troops in Tunisia and Algeria during the Second World War. There was no known cure; it was said to be self-limiting, and to run a course of six to seven weeks. The symptoms are violent and exhausting diarrhoea, nausea, vomiting, and more or less acute abdominal pain. At times I suffered from all these at the same moment, and the combined effect is devastating; at the end of a fortnight I had lost more than a stone and a half in weight, and I began to feel so weak that I could hardly drag myself across the room.

It was in this condition, disguised as well as I was able, that I visited Woburn again, made detailed drawings of otter quarters decorated in the Chinese manner to blend harmoniously with the motif of the Chinese Dairy, and finally received approval in principle for the whole project.

Meanwhile drug after drug had been tried upon the thriving colony of *Coccidiae* that had taken up residence in my intestines. The first antibiotics they appeared to regard as so much free champagne; they became gayer and merrier and even more uninhibited. Then we had a short-lived moment of hope; after five days' treatment their numbers were reported as greatly reduced and to appear so sickly as to suggest severe hangover. Only three days later, however, on 16 July, they were found to be back in full strength, and indeed the symptoms left no doubt on this point. Since there was no known cure, and the disease was so rare that subjects for experiment were not easy to come by, my doctor tried drug after drug—but all to no effect. By 28 July I decided that in these circumstances I would be as well in Scotland as in London, the more especially as on 15 July (my birthday) we had at last sold Isle Ornsay and there would be matters concerning it to be discussed on the spot.

I still could not go to Camusfeàrna, for the young lady and her great animal brood were still in occupation, and there was no clear date on which the house would be available to me. Already the last summer that I had planned to spend at Camusfeàrna was dwindling alarmingly.

I went instead to stay near Inverness with Richard Frere, who by the sale of Isle Ornsay had brought almost to a close his long and gallant rearguard action. I arrived at his home on 1 August, and by 4 August I had developed an acute and violent pain in my right lung. I could take only the shallowest of breaths, and to laugh or cough was agony. I had known in the past the sensations caused both by broken ribs and by pleurisy; this was like both, but as I knew I had no broken ribs I assumed it to be pleurisy. On 8 August I received the expected request to visit Isle Ornsay and discuss the inventory in person with the new owner, and because I felt that I could not now risk any possibilty of a delay in the final conclusion of sale, I motored across Scotland doped with the maximum amount of pain killers that could be trusted not to kill me as well.

Camusfeàrna was vacant by then, occupied only by Andrew Scot, who was looking after the otters and my two Deerhounds Dirk and Hazel and the remnant of the great migrant hoard that the young lady had as yet been unable to transport to her new residence—one white Roman gander, one timid but vociferous cat, two donkeys, and six poodles.

So I came back to my home at last, but the next day I was spitting blood profusely, and the day after that I was in a glass cubicle of a T.B. hospital, and Camusfeàrna was all the world away. It seemed that I had escaped cancer only to contract tuberculosis.

When, twenty-four hours later, I learned—utterly by chance—that I had not got T.B. but a blood clot in the left lung, possibly attributable to a parting shot from my *Coccidiae*, I signed my own discharge, and returned to the long-suffering hospitality of Richard and Joan Frere. I had to remain within range of some hospital for blood tests every three days, so it was not until the very end of August that I finally reached Camusfeàrna. By then the living relics of other occupancy had been reduced to one gander, one cat, and four poodles.

I had not reached my target on time or as planned, but I had reached it.

16

Return to Camusfeàrna

Coming back to Camusfeàrna after so long I was conscious of two impressions, though by their very nature one was very much quicker to register than the second.

It did not take long for me to realize that in the nineteen years of my occupancy I had never seen the house and its surrounds in such a state of damage and dereliction. An unusually wild and wet winter had combined with the presence of the host of livestock to leave hardly a single sheet of plaster boarding intact in the rooms we had built on to the old pine-panelled cottage, and even there the woodwork was in places deeply scarred by the marks of petulant paws. The plaster boarding was studded with actual holes, as though it had been under shell fire; only the claw and tooth marks surrounding these apertures showed that, by some curious feat of engineering difficult to comprehend, they too could be ascribed only to the drilling of determined dogs. The bathroom ceiling had collapsed under the weight of a cache of poodles temporarily stored in the loft above it; there were ten broken window panes and twelve broken window catches; not only the keys to all three outside doors were missing, but even those of the bathroom and the lavatory. Carpets and rugs had been so fouled that they had to be burnt; it was as though some omnivorous locust swarm had passed through the house on a mission of destruction.

Outside, the situation was little better. The sea winds had whipped the white walls to a dirty grey, grown over in places with a powdery green fungus; the white post-and-rail fence in front of the house was broken in a score of places, and all along the dunes between the house and the sea lay rubbish dumps of rusty cans and bottles, exposed, perhaps, by the wind's lifting of the sand that had originally covered our deep-dug pits. It had been a long time, too, since Camusfeàrna had housed a lusty male capable of digging one of those great graves for the unburnable detritus of the tinned food era. Worse, much worse, was a horror to which I am even more susceptible than most people—a remembered nausea going back over the long years to the Soay Shark Fishery and the day we discovered that sixteen tons of salted shark flesh had turned rotten in the closed brine tank. Here at Camusfeàrna someone had switched off the electric current to the largest of our deep freezes, and the fish inside were putrescent. In a final analysis I know now that it would take a finer olfactory sense than mine to distinguish between sixteen tons of rotten shark flesh and eight hundredweights of rotten haddock.

A visible touch of squalor was added by the presence and activities, both excremental and by 'footwork', of some forty head of heavy black cattle, great gravid creatures who trampled every soft piece of ground into a squelchy mire of dung and mud. They forced the flimsy gates protecting our tiny enclave and munched the few remaining gladioli that persisted among the weeds of once orderly flower beds below the windows; they leaned or scratched themselves upon everything that could—and did—give way beneath their weight; they, or something equally heavy, had broken the timbers of the bridge that spanned the burn; they escaped into the surrounding forestry ground, so that Andrew Scot spent the great part of his time rounding them up and ejecting them. Camusfeàrna was in a mess, and the prevailing images were of mud, rust, and decay.

So pervasive were these depressing pigments that it was some days before I began to see that there were others, completely conflicting with this scene, that could form quite another picture. By engaging, at a distance of thousands of miles, a temporary assistant whom I had neither interviewed nor even met, I had somehow stumbled upon perhaps the one person who could confront the whole situation not only without dismay but with confidence and even relish. Andrew Scot, whose letters over five years had been filed under the heading of 'juvenile fan' (they had not differed greatly in content from others whose authors I now know would have proved patently unsuitable) began to take shape as the ideal rescuer of Camusfeàrna in its sickness. The wild weather and the wet and the wind; the living conditions that had by now returned to the primitive; the absence of cinemas and social life; the enormously hard and often unpleasant work that every day involved; the daily weary plod up the steep hill path to Druimfiaclach, often ankle deep in mud and water, to collect our mail and heavy stores ordered from the village shop; the search for firewood along the desolate and chilling beaches in driving rain —these things were meat and drink to him, and never once did he complain or suggest that he might be happier elsewhere. To him everything seemed easy.

Nor was this all. Despite his detailed knowledge of the terrible injuries that both Edal and Teko had inflicted upon people in the past, and the obvious risk to himself, his aim and desire was to be able to handle them, to take them for walks, to be on terms with them that would not be those of a zoo-keeper in charge of dangerous animals. This knowledge came to me by a then not unexpected, but still disconcerting question: 'When do I start taking the otters out for walks?' I replied, 'Never, as far as I'm concerned—I'm the only person they've never threatened and has no fear of them. I'm not going to expose anyone else to what might be terrible injury.'

But he wouldn't take no for an answer; in fact he fought to achieve a situation of grave potential danger. He won his parents' permission, and the only remaining obstacle was my own. In the end I too had to give it.

It was eight months since I had had any personal contact with either Edal or Teko, and I myself was far from certain of my reception. I began with Teko; because, as I described very early in this book, I had a strange and reassuring momentary reunion with him in November 1966. So after the first few days at Camusfeàrna, days devoted to reorganizing my forces after the multiple mishaps of the past weeks, I went out one blustery but sunny morning to re-establish contact with Teko.

He was not visible in his enclosure, so I knew that he must be asleep in his house. I opened the gate and called him, and an answering, welcoming chirrup came from the darkness beyond his half-closed door. I waited and called again, and after a minute or so he walked out a little uncertainly into the unconfined world that he had not seen for more than four years. The right hand side of his face was swollen and his right eye completely closed; he looked a sick animal, unhealthily fat, and plainly suffering from an exacerbation of one of the tooth socket infections that had periodically bedevilled the lives of both these West African otters. He appeared bewildered and lost, but as he came nearer and caught my smell he began talking again—the little joyful, affectionate cries that I had not heard for so long. I bent down and put out my hands to him, and a moment later he was nuzzling my face with his wet nose and bristly whiskers, pushing his little monkey fingers into my ears and nose, and redoubling his cries of love and joy. I responded to him emotionally; what, I thought, had I done to deserve this warmth of continuing trust and devotion. I had confined him for four years; I had deprived him of the human society to which as a baby he had been conditioned by no will of his own; I had even at one point determined to send him to a zoo and into the possibly unloving care of strangers. I had betrayed him, and because our common language was so limited I had not even been able to explain to him the reasons for which I had done all these things.

This, our first walk together for so long, was a sad and guilt-ridden half hour. Teko, clearly in pain with something akin to acute toothache as we know it, was confused and bewildered by the half-remembered outside world, and would hardly stray from my feet. Every few yards he would stop me to seek fresh reassurance, fresh loving conversation; he would not swim nor take delight in any of his old haunts, whether still, placid pools to explore or the stimulus of white water in cataract. At that moment it was me he needed and me only, and all else was subordinate. When I took him home to his house his only concern was that I should not leave him alone again. What torture the human species inflict upon their 'pets'.

In any other community it might seem strange to call upon a distinguished doctor to advise upon the condition and treatment of an animal, but this would be to ignore the personality of Dr Dunlop. Our local (fifty miles by road and sea-ferry) vet, Donald MacLennan, who had tended the otters with such miraculous skill for eight years, was on holiday, and so it was the doctor whom I consulted. He made a characteristically quick and accurate decision as to the antibiotic to be used, and in five days Teko was once more a healthy and active otter with an interest in all around him.

Thus my second walk with him was very different from the first. True, he stayed closer to me than he had once been used to do, but he remembered his old haunts and he made for them; he chased fish and porpoised in the calm reaches of the river, emerging every few minutes to stand up against me and apparently thank me with squeaks of pleasure, depositing a heavy skin-load of water on my already soaking trousers.

It was only when I brought him back to the house that difficulties began. It was a conflict of wills, and one that took me more than an hour to resolve. Teko simply would not re-enter his enclosure. He was tired, having taken more exercise than he had done for four years, and it was plain that he wanted nothing more than to curl up in his blankets under the infra-red lamp, but he would not voluntarily become a captive again. Time and time again he would come to the gate in the wooden paling and put his face in, talking all the time in low whimpering tones either to himself or to me, but nothing I could do would persuade him to come far enough in for the gate to be closed behind him. Gone were the days of harnesses and of leads; nothing could succeed but cajolery, and cajole I did, using every ruse I knew. Every time that I called to him he answered, with a small variation on his usual welcoming note, a variation I had not heard before, and which registered as plainly as articulate speech both protest and reproof. Just outside the gate he rolled and rubbed himself in the grass, movements that had always been a prelude to sleep, while I called and called, and Andrew Scot, sitting as sentinel on the steep hillside above us, was driven almost demented by devouring hordes of midges. Some change of tactics was clearly a necessity; I stopped calling, went into his house and sat down on his bed below the heating lamp. After a few minutes the initiative had significantly changed; now it was he who was calling to me with increasing urgency, and I would not answer. His voice changed to the note, between a whistle and a squeak, with which an otter cub calls for parents whom it cannot find. It came nearer and nearer, and it held an audible and anxious question mark. I remained obstinately silent, and suddenly his face looked round the door. Instead of retreating again now that he had established my whereabouts, as I had half feared, he came bouncing across the floor, chattering with pleasure, and climbed up beside me, going through all his rituals of love and affection as though it were months since he had seen me. I fell in with his mood, and gave the full repertoire of reassurance that he had known in the distant days when he was a cub; blowing into his fur as though it were a woollen glove on a white winter's day; taking the tips of his little monkey fingers between my lips; responding to his nose against my mouth by an exchange of saliva. All very well, I thought, as his heavy, shiny body squirmed and wriggled all over me, but how was I to get myself out without employing some trick that would destroy his confidence in me. But I had completely misjudged the situation; he was like a child who, scarcely stifling its yawns, protests that it is far too early to go to bed, but who will when tucked up by a parent figure fall instantly asleep. Teko was in bed, he had received his equivalent of being tucked up and kissed goodnight, and I doubt whether I could have called him out again had I tried. My cautious, stealthy attempt to leave unnoticed was wholly unnecessary; he was occupied only with the question of finding the most comfortable position for sleep, and he had found it before ever I closed the gate behind me.

I had achieved at least part of what I had dreamed of on that wild autumn evening the year before; I had restored at least a measure of freedom and contentment to this creature that had once been a companion at Camusfeàrna, and neither he nor I were captives any longer. From that day on, as I took him up to the waterfall or out to the island beaches of white sand, watching him swim and dive in the glass-clear water of the ebb tide, some of the colour of the Camusfeàrna landscape began to come back for me.

Within a week of this total reunion with Teko I began to realize that my own image of Camusfeàrna could not be truly re-created without a similar restoration of my relationship with Edal. I did not know whether this was possible, but I was prepared to risk much to find out. For five and a half years no human being had touched her, for five and a half years she had not seen beyond the confines of her small enclosure. No one understood what had caused the explosions of rage and violence that had periodically punctuated her record of affection and good humour. Yet the facts were there; she had inflicted terrible injuries, and had at last, early in 1962, broken even Jimmy Watt's nerve, by chasing him into the rafters of his own room and holding him there, screaming her rage at every attempt he made to move. From then on the history of Camusfeàrna with all its vicissitudes and its multiple occupants, had left me no opportunity to try to re-establish contact with her myself; and if I am to be honest I must confess that I think that when Jimmy became afraid of her I did too, because I knew that in all other things but this one Jimmy feared so little. But I knew, too, that she had never given me, personally, any cause to fear her, and I knew clearly that I could not respect myself or see Camus-feàrna whole again if I did not try to do for her what I had succeeded in doing for Teko. Both had, by the human killing of their parents when they were infants, been conditioned to unnatural dependence upon humans and their company, and both had been deprived of it because when they became adult they had behaved like wild animals instead of like well brought up Pekingese dogs. If their behaviour had been bewildering to us, ours must have been even more so to them; they had both received life sentences for actions, which by the very hysteria that characterized them, were probably unremembered.

I thought about all this, and I saw that if I postponed from day to day any positive action towards restoring her old status the project would become part of the pervading decline, the atmos-phere of business unfinished and abandoned, that had stained the whole Camusfeàrna picture over the past five years. So on Sunday 10 September I determined to take her out the next day.

The decision may have been compulsive, but I think the prepara-tions and safeguards showed an adequate degree of foresight. It would have been irresponsible, in view of her history, to risk her meeting strangers on the beaches, so we arranged that Andrew should sit on the hillside in a position to command visually both approaches to the Camusfeàrna bay and warn any unexpected visitors that there was a potentially dangerous animal loose on the beaches. He was to follow my progress with binoculars, and in the event of my receiving any gross injury he was to regain the house and telephone to the doctor at the village five miles away. For my own safety I laid out dressings, including surgical needle and thread, on the bathroom table. As an afterthought I added a hypodermic syringe and cocaine solution. As an emergency measure, that proved so mercifully unnecessary, I equipped myself with an item which I cannot understand why we never thought of before—a pot of pepper. Any attacking animal of Edal's size could, I thought, be rendered completely helpless by this means.

There were three ways to take Edal from her quarters into the outside world. One, which was out of the question because of the amount of objects that could be destroyed by an interested and inquisitive otter, was through the long prefabricated room that had been Jimmy's, and which led into the lobby. The second led directly into the lobby itself, and thence to the open air. The third was a new gate in the wooden paling, leading out on to the sand dunes, which Alan MacDiarmaid had made a few days before— while I was bringing myself to the boil, as it were, about the liberation of Edal.

When Andrew was positioned and the moment came to open this gate and call her out I remembered what Malcolm and Paula Macdonald had said to me when Edal first came to Camusfeàrna eight long, wild years before: 'Let her come to you; don't force yourself on her. Just ignore her, and she'll make friends with you.'

So I opened the gate to the dunes and called her as I had used to long ago—'Whee-ee! Ee-eedal! Whee-ee!' There was a pattering of paws in the tunnel that protected her sleeping quarters from the wind, and suddenly she was there beside me—but much more interested in the mechanism of the gate than in me. She felt all around the hinges with her hands, went inside again to investigate them from another angle, and then suddenly set off on a tour of inspection of the premises of the house. Everything was new to her, everything had to be investigated with the thoroughness and attention to detail of an insurance company's detective. After only a few yards she arrived at the broken down jeep standing at the end of the work shed. She went underneath it and remained there for a long time, feeling everything with her fingers as if she were about to prepare a report on the condition of the vehicle. It must have been five minutes before she emerged, emitting one of her refined and lady-like sneezes (often *actually* stifled by the hand), and climbed up into the driver's seat. She fumbled with switches, descended to the floor to insert her fingers round the shafts of the brake and clutch pedals, and suddenly appeared standing on the driver's seat, her hands on the steering wheel, peering over the bonnet as if to test visibility. She left the car with an expression that suggested the words, 'Make a note to censure whoever was in charge of that one', and went on to an upturned dinghy that had suffered damage to several planks during a winter storm. She disappeared underneath it and was out of sight for several minutes; only an occasional probing finger appeared to be testing damaged woodwork. At last she emerged, climbed up, and made her way along the keel ridge, using both fingers and face to assess the situation. Satisfied anew that someone had blundered, she left the dinghy and began to follow me toward the sea, but suddenly she turned back. The work shed itself, which she had never even seen, demanded a full survey.

Besides a litter of tools and mechanical equipment, the shed at that moment contained the two Deerhounds, Dirk and Hazel. They were awaiting transfer to their new home in Perthshire (for despite my determination to restore the otters to partial liberty I was at Camusfeàrna essentially to close it down as a house which required staff) and for this occasion they had been shut in. The key to the shed, like all other keys, had disappeared, and so we had, as part of our preparations, jammed the door shut with a diagonal piece of angle iron, bolstered at its ground end by two heavy stones.
Edal was obviously fascinated by this situation. Over months and years she had become accustomed to the smell of the Deerhounds, and here they were shut up in a way that was a challenge to her ingenuity. She started to work on the piece of angle iron; she pulled at it with her hands, and finding that it would not yield

she rolled over on to her back and tried to yank it downward. Discovering that this did not pay off, she walked round the construction several times and then deliberately set to work on the stones that jammed it in position. By this time I was becoming alarmed, because I could not visualize with anything but dismay what might happen if she set the Deerhounds free. I walked away towards the sea, and, mercifully, she followed as I called.

Between her and the tide stood the massive form of *Polar Star* on her wheeled cradle, and this also demanded a lengthy and detailed appraisal—axles, wheels, everything that could be investigated to the full by an otter bent on factual knowledge. When we left *Polar Star* for the exposed sands of the ebb tide she came with me, but in a physical sense she ignored me; she was about her own business, and she did not acknowledge that this included me. In the shallows of the sand-ribs where the sea was no more than perhaps three feet deep she chased dabs and caught one; she was plainly happy, and I no longer felt afraid of her; nor, I think, did she in any way mistrust me.

But to take both otters out (they could never, as I have explained, be allowed to meet) brought us back to a situation that had its origin in 1959, when Terry Nutkins had been engaged as assistant otter keeper to Jimmy Watt. Obviously I could not exercise both animals and at the same time do my own work of writing. Andrew remained insistent upon complete contact; granted this absolute aim on his part and his parents' permission to try, there was no logical alternative for either of us.

It was, in brief, that if Andrew could achieve his goal of a trusting relationship with both animals he should not regard his present position as merely that of a temporary assistant in the closing down of Camusfeàrna, but should accompany the otters to Woburn and remain in charge of them there, responsible directly to myself. This project, which he regarded with an enthusiasm second only to the unfortunately impracticable notion of remaining with the otters at Camusfeàrna for ever, took a great weight from my mind. It meant that they might be tended by someone in whom I had already learned to place much confidence, someone who knew them, understood them and was fond of them, someone who might handle them in ill health when a stranger might be helpless.

It meant, too, that the human contact re-established after so desperately long an interval need not be broken—and to this I attached great importance, for I believed that the present splendid condition of both animals was due at least in part to a psychological rejuvenescence.

Andrew himself was already taking a much deeper interest in the future of the otters than he himself realized. During my convalescence with Richard and Joan Frere I had begun a scale model of the complex new otter premises at Woburn, and when I had finally arrived at Camusfeàrna I had brought this with me and worked on it daily. Literally hundreds of man hours had by now gone into the model, in an effort to combine four almost irreconcilable principles—the Chinese decorative motif, so that the appearance of the Dairy Lake should not suffer; the wellbeing and comfort of the animals in the space at disposal; the convenience of their keeper, so that every part should be accessible for cleaning without the necessity to crawl on all-fours; and, finally, the ability of the public to view, so that the large capital outlay for this ambitious scheme should not be lost to that inveterate optimist Michael Alexander.

All these problems had by now been resolved as nearly as they might be, but from a welter of different proposals put forward both by Michael's side and my own we had not yet reached agreement on how to divide the lake in such a way as to keep Edal and Teko safely apart. Diagrams and drawings, samples of material, involved mathematical calculations and costings littered my table, but the whole subject was still in dispute by mid-September. On the 17th I went to bed a little before midnight, having spent the whole evening reviewing the various plans. I sleep very lightly, and was awoken by the creak of a stairboard outside my door. The

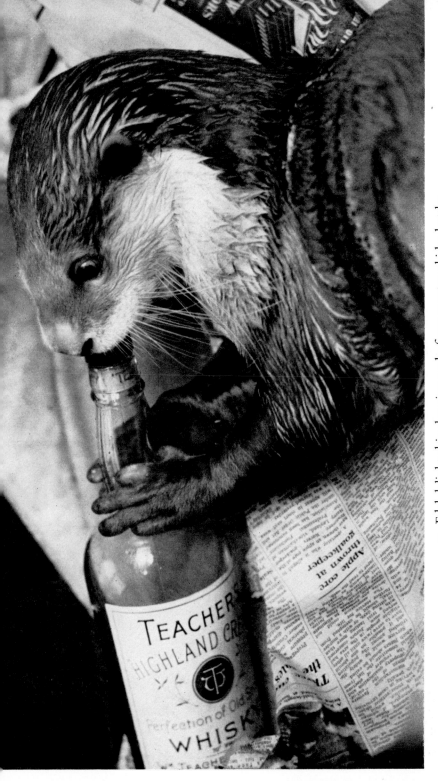

41 Edal delighted in drawing corks from empty whisky bottles

42 and 43
Freedom after years
of prison: *Above:*
Edal on her first walk

Left and opposite:
Andrew and Teko

44 Andrew and Teko
in the snow

45 The author and Edal

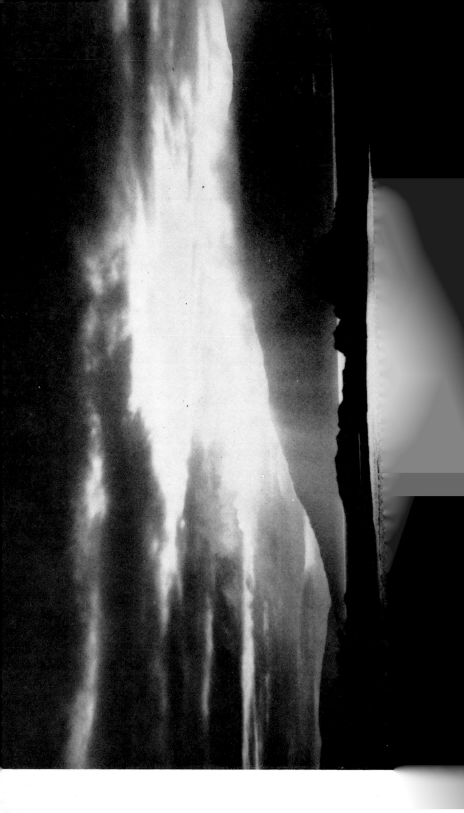

next second I heard the door handle turn, and Andrew's voice said, 'Are you awake? Had you gone to sleep already?' I glanced at the luminous hands of my watch; it was 3.25 a.m. I said, 'No, I'm awake—is there something wrong?' There was a pause before Andrew replied, 'Well, do you think Edal's all right?'

I switched on the light. Andrew was standing there in his dressing gown and bare feet. I asked, 'What do you think is wrong with her?'

'It's her pool—the new one. I don't think it's safe. You see, she's standing on it.'

Outside, the rain was battering at the window, as it had been when I went to sleep, as it had been for days. I looked carefully at Andrew. His hair was dry, and very tousled, as though not long from a pillow; his dressing gown was dry, and his feet were dry. I felt more or less certain that he was fast asleep. I said, 'Tell me about this pool.'

'Well, it's this new round fibre glass pool—at least something like fibre glass but it's transparent. I don't think it's safe, because it's three foot six high, and by standing on it as she is now she can climb through to Teko and kill him.'

Edal had three pools, all were years old, and all were sunk; it was clear now that Andrew was sleepwalking, and I didn't feel at all sure how to act, because it was a state of which I had no experience at all. I took a chance on a question from which he might wake himself up. 'Was it very wet out there?' He appeared to think for a moment, and then said, 'Out where?'

'Out at her pool—it's raining so hard.'

'But I haven't been out,' Then, suddenly, 'Good heavens, I'm not *asleep* am I?'

'Well, half asleep, and certainly very sleepy. You go back to bed and if there's any trouble with Edal I promise I'll deal with it. Goodnight.'

'Goodnight,' he said cheerfully, and disappeared.

The extraordinary thing about this incident, hazily remembered by him in the morning, was that within a few hours of waking he outlined a new scheme for dividing the lake, the visible portion above water to be three foot six inches high and composed of a semi-transparent material resembling fibre glass in texture. There must, he pointed out, be no foothold for the otters at water-level, for if there were, Edal, anyway, would be able to reach to the top of the glass and climb over to Teko. Andrew's subconscious was, if a little inarticulate while at work, evidently most industrious.

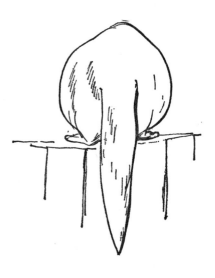

17
Peace before Nightfall

That same morning Andrew put to me again the question whose reply was causing me continued conflict—'When do I start taking Teko out?' The issue could no more be postponed than my own self-demanded question about Edal, and I realized that this time I must make a firm decision, however difficult it might be. I could no longer make excuses on the grounds of the hazards inherent in the presence of other livestock; the five poodles had gone at last; the huge white Roman gander had followed a few days later, sitting grotesquely but majestically on the passenger's seat of the Land Rover in a sack tied at his neck; and finally we had at last succeeded in catching—not without many scratches, a querulous and highly vocal cat, elusive as a will o' the wisp, that haunted the premises long after the rest of the menagerie was remembered only by the mighty havoc it had wrought on the house and surroundings.

This was a Monday, and there were genuine reasons for postponing the experiment for several days. On the other hand Andrew, though not dreading the day with the same cold fear as I, was plainly mustering all his nervous energy for an ordeal of suspense. I decided to fix the day as Saturday, and then to spring the request upon him at five minutes' notice on Thursday, so that he should have no time to lose his confidence during a possibly sleepless night on Friday.

Meanwhile I rehearsed him carefully in the behaviour best calculated to produce a calm attitude in Teko's mind. Throughout the world of animals and birds, and of human infants, it had long been apparent to me that repetitive, sing-song sounds represent an attitude of amiability and thus of reassurance; conversely, a single note, especially if harsh in tone, invariably means alarm or challenge. This I am convinced, is the unconscious motive underlying human 'baby talk', which tends to a distortion of words, rendering them rhythmic, lending them a cadence, a rise and fall, that has its counterpart throughout much of the animal kingdom. As a single instance one may contrast the contented chattering of jackdaws with the harsh, drawn-out alarm note announcing the presence of danger.

For these reasons, and not only because the otters had become conditioned to it before ever they came to me, I had always been accustomed to speak to them in a sing-song baby language, an iambic rhythm, to which they had responded with calm and affection. (When, in the autumn of 1966, I had been on the point of sending them to a zoo, it had been an acute embarrassment to me to make a lengthy tape recording of these humanly ridiculous sounds for the benefit of their future keepers—who would, in all likelihood, never have used them. Fortunately, since the otters did not go to the zoo, the compact little spool of potential ridicule remained safely in my possession.)

Andrew had none of the inhibitions that might be expected towards chanting my silly words and phrases, even though I advised him to do this continuously throughout his walks with Teko; in this as in all other matters he displayed a wisdom and sanity far beyond his years, qualities that might well have saved Camusfeàrna had he arrived upon the scene long before he did, for he seemed born for the life.

On Thursday morning, as he finished the washing up, I remarked that it was a fine, sunny day, and asked whether he would like to take Teko out at once. He looked only slightly startled, and replied at once, 'Certainly I'd like to.'

He did not like being equipped with the pot of pepper, but I insisted. Now that it had come to the moment he was to all appearances completely confident, and it was I who had to exert all my reserves of self control to conceal my agitation.

The window situation at Camusfeàrna—what in educational documents perused with R. F. Mackenzie, Headmaster of Braehead School, I have so often seen with wonderment referred to as 'fenestration'—is as inadequate for all round observation as educational authorities tend to find it for health reasons in every building genuinely suitable as a base for an exploratory outdoor life. Camusfeàrna was built with its back to the prevailing south-westerly winds, a lesson learnt from its predecessor some seventy yards across the field, whose occupants were driven to escape from a tempest-driven sea by a single tiny window on the sheltered, landward, side of the house. I had added only two windows to the original cottage of Camusfeàrna as I had found it, portholes from H.M.S. *Vanguard* when she was broken up at a Clydeside shipyard. Both were upstairs; one looked north-east directly over Teko's enclosure, the other south-west to Camusfeàrna bay and the long reach of sea beyond it to the far islands of Eigg and Muick. Thus there was no single window from which I could follow the progress of the first experimental contact between a possibly dangerous animal and a courageous boy. I would have to begin by sticking my head out of the north-easterly porthole, set far back in the thickness of the house wall, and then move from room to room as the two progressed, as I hoped they would, towards the sea.

Andrew showed no sign of nervousness as, carrying a plate of Teko's favourite delicacy, tinned pilchards, he went to Teko's closed gate and called to him in a fair imitation of my own chanting language. With my head through the porthole and my shoulders jammed into the alcove that gave access to it, I watched as Teko lingered in his house and made no response. Andrew was wearing my clothes so that he should smell of security (a dubious policy, this, and one that might have led to the animal treating the human as an impostor to be punished) and at length Teko caught the scent and emerged. He appeared confused to find that it was not I who awaited him; he refused the pilchards and returned to his house. His gate to the outside world was still closed, and knowing for an absolute certainty that sooner or later Andrew was going to open it I was conscious of a steadily mounting nervous tension. After a minute or so Teko came back to the gate, and while Andrew was opening it Teko grabbed the edge with his hands and emerged with force; he was talking, but in a language I understood imperfectly, a muted variation upon his 'wow-wow-wow' that could mean moderate anger, satisfaction in possession of interesting food (and presumably defence of it), or what I can only describe as aggressive affection. Then he rolled on his back, which in all the mustellines can be either a gesture of defence preceding violence or one of submission to dominance in a hierarchy; I simply did not know which of the two this was, and I began literally to sweat. Then I saw Andrew bend down and put a finger in one of Teko's paws, as one does to a baby whose grasp is still unsure; I saw the little monkey fingers close upon it, and suddenly I knew that all was well, that even if a complete and intimate accord might be postponed for a little the basis for it was already there.

As Andrew walked away toward the sea with Teko at his heel, a sea lying light and bare, milky below a pale sky, the dark rocks and seaweed shining in the low glint of an autumn sun, time once again shut up like an old, well-oiled telescope, and I was watching Jimmy or Terry setting out with one or other otter for their routine morning walk so many years before. Life, in the sense that I understood life, had returned to the house and its occupants.

I moved from room to room, trying to keep the two in sight as—after an exploration of unfamiliar objects less minute and conscientious than Edal's—Teko accompanied Andrew over the dunes and down to the estuary of the little river. At length I lost sight of them, and went out on to the dunes, so that I could follow and if necessary direct their progress along the beach. After an hour they were back within a hundred yards of the house, and to spare Andrew the weary business of re-confining an animal that had so amply demonstrated his intransigent attitude on this point, I went into his house and acted as a vocal bait to which Teko responded immediately.

The suspense was over, and I felt certain now that Teko would not harm Andrew; though, judging by the aloof way the animal had ignored the human except in the role of some sort of official guide to the terrain, I thought it might be a long time before they established any closer contact between each other. I thought Teko's affections were fixed on me, but I flattered myself. It was only four days later, at the end of their third walk, that the almost unbelievable happened. It was a grey day, with gusts of wet wind blowing in off the sea, and almost continuous small rain. Andrew and Teko had been away for some two hours or more when from

my writing desk I noticed them across the field, Andrew calling unavailingly to Teko, who was pottering about the first steep slope of the jeep track and occasionally disappearing into the bushes at its side, where a little hidden stream flowed down deep between sheer sides. It was raining harder now, and I went to fetch an anorak before going out to lure Teko home. When I had put it on I looked out of the window to see Andrew and Teko rolling and romping together on the soaking grass of the field, and Teko's voice of greeting and pleasure came to me even through the closed window. Flat on his back Andrew lay in the drenched grass while Teko clambered over his chest and nuzzled his face and ears with ecstatic squeaks of delight; I saw Andrew blow into his fur as I did myself, and Teko nuzzling under his jacket; I saw Andrew's expression of deep delight, and I was full of wonder. The two were like long-lost, intimate friends who have suddenly rediscovered

each other; and I wondered how much and by what means Andrew's desire for this *rapport* had communicated itself to the animal. How very small is our knowledge.

The relationship never looked back, though it was a further week before Andrew was able to re-house Teko unaided. The following day he was determined to try it himself, but after the pair had lapped the house in patient procession more than thirty times, sometimes the one leading and sometimes the other, all in the pouring rain, I felt it only humane to come to the rescue.

It was only a few days after this that I myself achieved a full restoration of my old relationship with Edal. It was one of those rare autumn days when there was no breath of wind, and the sun shone upon the gold and russet and red of turning leaf on the steep hillside above the house. The tide was far, far out, and the still, cerulean sea broke only with a tiny white lather of foam upon the sculptured sands; the hues were so delicate, so finely contrasted, as to give the whole scene an air almost of fragility, as if at any moment it might burst like a soap bubble and leave the onlooker in a colourless vacuum.

I took Edal out to the island beaches and the white coral sands; she herself was in some way elated by the sunshine and the stillness, and she scampered about with a greater display of speed and enthusiasm than I had yet seen. When we had crossed the island bar and came to the bay called Traigh a Ghuirabain, I saw that the tide was lower than I ever remembered seeing it; the great stems and rubbery brown leaves of umbrella weed stood naked and glistening on the beach of sand and scattered stone, and further out still they showed ranked above the flat water like the canopied fronds of some primeval forest. I found some big clams exposed near to the shrunken tide's edge, and I began to wade out in search of more. The water was so clear that even when it was above my knees I could see every minute detail of the bottom; the multi-coloured fan shells and mussels; the mother-of-pearl top-shells; the chalk-white hieroglyphics, like some forgotten alphabet, left by the serpulid tube-worms upon shell and stone alike; the fine tracery in crimson and white of little fern-like weeds. I was absorbed in looking at these things beneath the surface, and had momentarily forgotten Edal, who, when I had last seen her, had been porpoising at high speed some hundred yards away. Now I felt a sudden nudge at my leg from behind, and turned to find her touching me, 'corkscrewing'; revolving at enormous speed, that is to say, like a chicken-spit gone demented. I remembered suddenly how she had been used to do this when she was small; an expression, it seemed, of immense delight in her surroundings, something more than a feeling of well-being; almost, it seemed, one of ecstasy. I remembered another thing long forgotten, how I would take her by the tail and swoosh her round in circles by it until a human would have become giddy, and how she would respond with a vacuous expression of happiness and contentment.

Now, if ever, was the moment to restore these little rituals of *rapport*; I took her by the tail and began to swing her round by it faster and faster, and she let herself go limp as I did so, her face wearing that same long forgotten look of fulfilment. When I let her go she went shooting away in the clear water, and as I watched her I wondered which had restored most to the other. To me the sky and the sea and the mountains looked brighter, more real, the shallow sea's floor more brilliant than before, for an enduring mist of guilt had been lifted from them all. I was content now to let the future resolve itself, for I knew that I could no longer break the trust of animal friendship.

As we went home Edal paused upon a mound of heather and grass and began to roll and polish herself upon its surface. I sat down a few yards away from her, determined not to destroy this recovered confidence by intrusion, and lit a cigarette. During the past few years I suppose I had experienced these sights and sounds before—Ben Sgriol with its first cap of lace-like snow against a pale blue autumn sky, the distant roaring of stags upon the slopes of the Skye shore, the rowan berries scarlet, and the river running ice-cold into the calm Camusfeàrna bay, fringed everywhere by the fallen leaves of autumn; but they had meant little to me—the impact had been sensory only, for I had been no longer part of them, and in an ecological sense I had already become an outsider. Now I reached out towards this once familiar world, as out of nothing Andrew and Teko had reached out to each other, and I felt at one with all that my senses could perceive. High above me, wheeling in taut arcs, two buzzards mewed like kittens, and a single wild goose flew northwards over the Sound—a Pinkfoot, calling continuously, lost, as I had been lost for so long.

Foot by foot Edal squirmed nearer to me, now wriggling upon her back, now ostentatiously polishing her chest and throat. Her fur had a sheen that I had not seen for years, and her eyes were bright, in place of the dull, existent look to which I had become long accustomed. Down the slope she pushed herself, for the most part upon her back, with arms and monkey fingers waving, until at last her nose was in contact with my thigh. I still did not know how much liberty I could take with her on land, but then and there the feeling of unity, of shared pleasure and joy, took absolute control. I treated her as I had when she was a cub, in the days when everything was taken for granted and antipathy was out of the question; I took her by the shoulders and pulled her to me and stroked her and blew into her fur and rolled her over and tickled her toes and whiskers, and she responded as Teko had done, with little snuffles of affection and squirming movements to make closer contact. When we started home Edal and Teko had between them given back to me the land in which I lived, the vision that I had lost. Only the winter and the deadly dates of all our departures made a barrier between me and my own realities, but it was at most a partial barrier, for I knew by then that both the planning of the best and the expectancy of the worst are dreams without future substance. Something intermediate, without recognizable form or voluntary purpose, takes the place of both, washing away both tears and aspirations alike, leaving only acceptance, and the wait for some truer test. In moments of peace such as I experienced that day with Edal there exists some unritual reunion with the rest of creation without which the lives of many are trivial. 'Extinct' applies as much to an essential mental attitude as to the vanished creatures of the earth such as the Dodo. We can no longer await some scientific revelation to avoid the destruction of our species in this context; the evidence is all there, the writing on the wall. The way back cannot be the same for all of us, but for those like myself it means a descent of the rungs until we stand again amid the other creatures of the earth and share to some small extent their vision of it, even though this may be labelled Wordsworthian romanticism.

Epilogue

Exactly one year, to a day, after the breakdown of our negotiations with the zoo in December 1966, I received a telephone call from Woburn to say that it had proved impossible to adapt the Chinese Dairy Lake for our requirements. The Comptroller offered alternative sites, and I travelled south in Arctic conditions to view the white and frozen ponds that were available. None was, to my mind, suitable; and furthermore our otter quarters had been constructed to stand under the cover of a colonnade.

The future was uncertain but the present contented; Teko was restored to the old puppy-like situation in which he would spend hours playing in the living room, chasing a torch beam with his tail and romping with his human playmates. Edal was once more a friend of whom we were unafraid, and I felt that we had truly reached our goal.

In the small hours of 20 January fire swept through Camusfeàrna, gutting the house and destroying everything that was within it. No human life was lost, and Teko was saved, but Edal died with the house, and she is buried at the foot of the rowan tree. On the rock above her are cut the words 'Edal, the otter of Ring of Bright Water, 1958–1968. Whatever joy she gave to you, give back to nature.'

Tonight at the last sentence of a dream I stand in thought before the Camusfeàrna door. Someone someday perhaps may build again upon that site, but there is much that cannot ever be rebuilt.

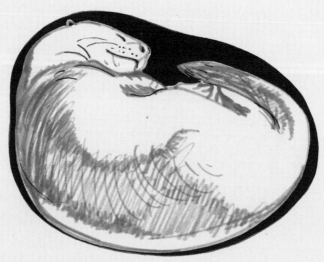